REGIME CHANGE

REGIME CHANGE

Toward a Postliberal Future

PATRICK J. DENEEN

FORUM

FORUM

First published in Great Britain by Forum, an imprint of Swift Press 2023

First published in the United States of America by Penguin Random House 2023

1 3 5 7 9 8 6 4 2

Book design by Ellen Cipriano
Offset by Tetragon, London
Printed and bound in Great Britain by CPI Group (UK) Ltd, Croydon, CRO 4YY

A CIP catalogue record for this book is available from the British Library

ISBN: 9781800753297
eISBN: 9781800753303

MIX
Paper | Supporting
responsible forestry
FSC® C171272
FSC
www.fsc.org

To my parents,

Richard and Irene,

und für meine Schwiegereltern,

Rudolf und Doris—

in gratitude and with love

CONTENTS

INTRODUCTION

No sensible reader of the news could look at America and think it is flourishing.

Massive economic inequality and the breakdown of family formation have eroded the foundations of society. Once-beautiful cities and towns around the nation have succumbed to an ugly blight. Cratering rates of childbirth, rising numbers of "deaths of despair," widespread addictions to pharmaceuticals and electronic distractions testify to the prevalence of a dull ennui and psychic despair. The older generation has betrayed the younger by saddling it with unconscionable levels of debt.

Warnings about both oligarchy and mob rule appear daily on the front pages of newspapers throughout the country, as well as throughout the West. A growing chorus of voices reflects on the likelihood and even desirability of civil war, while others openly call for the imposition of raw power by one class to suppress the political ambitions of its opponent class. Unsurprisingly, the louder the calls for tyranny, the more likely the eruption of a civil war; and the more likely a civil war moves from cold to hot, the more likely it is ultimately resolved through one or another form of tyranny.

What we are witnessing in America is a regime that is exhausted. Liberalism has not only failed, as I argued in my last book, but its dual embrace of economic and social "progress" has generated a particularly virulent form of that ancient divide that pits "the few" against "the many."

How to reconcile "the few" and "the many" is one of the oldest questions of the Western philosophical tradition. The answer devised by authors as various as Aristotle, Cicero, Polybius, Aquinas, Machiavelli, and Alexis de Tocqueville was the idea of the "mixed regime": a mixing of the two classes. By this telling, the aim was a kind of balance and equilibrium between the two classes, and the good political order was one that achieved a kind of stability and continuity over a long period of time and secured the "common good," the widespread prospect for human flourishing regardless of one's class status.

The classical solution was rejected by the architects of liberalism, who believed that this seemingly permanent political divide could be solved by advances in a "new science of politics." Rather than seeking a "mixed regime," instead it was believed that a regime governed by a new commitment could overcome the divide: *the priority of progress.* The first liberals—"classical liberals"—believed especially that economic progress through an ever-freer and more expansive market could fuel a transformative social and political order in which growing prosperity would always outstrip economic discontents. Far from seeking stability, balance, and order, the aim was the unceasing instability of an economy that has fittingly been described as a constant process of "creative destruction." It was held as an article of faith that the inequality and resulting discontents generated by the new capitalist economic system would be compensated by a "rising tide" of prosperity.

Later liberals—"progressives"—decried the resulting economic inequality, but retained the belief that progress would eventually give rise to the reconciliation of the classes. While they called for greater economic equality, they also demanded dynamism in the social order in order to displace not now the remnants of the old aristocracy, but the instinctual conservatism of the commoners. This imperative has been especially pursued through transformations wrought in the social sphere, and has in recent years culminated in the sexual revolution and its attendant effort to displace "traditional" forms of marriage, family, and sexual identity based in nature, replaced instead by a social and technological project that would liberate humans from mere nature. Progressive liberalism has held that through the overcoming of all forms of parochial and traditional belief and practice, ancient divisions and limits could be overcome and instead be replaced by a universalized empathy. With the advance of progress, the old divisions—once based in class, but increasingly defined in the terms of sexual identity—would wither away and give rise to the birth of a new humanity.

Both liberal parties—"classical" and "progressive"—believed that *progress* was the means of overcoming the ancient division between the classes and instead how political peace might be realized; but both recognized and feared that such progress would, in each instance, be thwarted by the common people who would most immediately find the fruits of that progress not to be beneficial, but destabilizing, disorienting, and an affront to their beliefs, practices, and even dignity. The faith that political peace could best and only be achieved through progress required that effective control of the political order be reserved to liberal elites on both the *right* and the *left* who would secure the blessings of progress, whether economic or social.

While the two sides of liberalism opposed each other over *means*, at a deeper level they effectively combined to ensure the prevention of a dedicated "people's party" that would oppose progressivism in *both* the economic and social domains. The liberal fear of the *demos* resulted in a political order that was, at its foundations, dedicated to the rule of more progressive elites over the threatening *demos*, and, throughout American history, has been impressively effective at preventing the rise of a genuine populist party. The ideal of "mixed regime," or "mixed constitution" (as I will label it in these pages), was replaced by the creation of a new and entrenched progress-oriented liberal elite, one that today

increasingly views the *demos* as a threat to its project—whether economically or socially.

During the brief Pax Americana of the post–Cold War world, the
liberal West had grown accustomed to a political divide between right
and left liberals, a contentious yet manageable political division in which
each side of liberalism would be advanced successively in the economic
and social spheres through the oscillation of electoral victories. This
brief *interregnum* of "neo-libertarianism"—in both its "conservative"
and "progressive" forms—has been shattered by the reappearance of
that oldest political division—the division between the "few" and the
"many." Whether "classical" or "progressive" liberals, their inherent fear
and mistrust of the *demos* was and remains expressed in a shared panic
over the rise of *populism*. Strenuous efforts are today exerted to prevent
a political realignment that would result in a people's party opposed
to the liberal progressive project. On the notional "right" of the liberal spectrum, extremely well-funded efforts ceaselessly attack the "au-
thoritarianism," anti-expert ignorance, and economic "socialism" of
populism; on the progressive liberal "left," relentless efforts paint every
conservative opposition to social and sexual progressivism as racist,
bigoted, and fascist. The two liberal oppositions have coalesced in the
form of "Woke Capitalism," the perfect wedding of the "progressivist"
economic right and social left, a combination that aims to produce a
populace that is satisfied with diversion, consumption, and hedonism,
and, above all, does not disturb the blessings of progress. And, if that
doesn't work, there remains the use of levers of political and corporate
power to suppress populist threats.

Yet these efforts are proving inadequate because *the consequences
of unfettered progress are no longer acceptable to the demos*. The populist backlash around the world is simultaneously against liberalism in
both its "right" and "left" forms. It rejects the economic "neoliberalism"
of the post–Cold War American imperium, demanding political and
economic boundaries, protection of national industries, a robust social

safety net, greater worker protections, and a more muscular prevention and even dismantling of monopolistic concentrations of economic power. Equally, it pushes back against the social liberalism of progressives, opposing the self-loathing embedded in contemporary approaches to national history, combatting the sexualization of children, seeking limits on pornography, rejecting the privatization of religious belief, and even has achieved an overturning in the legal domain of the libertarianism at the heart of America's half-century abortion regime.

In other words, the liberal "solution" now generates a worsening of the very divide that it claimed to be able to solve through the application of "progress." While ruling elites strive to double down on an acceleration of economic and social libertarianism, the accumulating negative consequences of the resulting policies have led to the rise of populist commoners opposing both sides of liberalism. "The many" are achieving "class consciousness"—not as Marxists, but as left-economic and social-conservative populists. If the liberal "solution," in fact, only worsens the political problem it claims to have solved, then a new approach is demanded.

With the dimming of the bright light of liberalism and its seeming historical inevitability now relegated to the dustbin of bad theories of history, both the need and the prospect for liberalism's true and natural opponent arises: a movement that begins with, and is defined by, a rejection of the ideological pursuit of progress along with the baleful political, economic, social, and psychological costs of that pursuit. This project is one both of *recovery* and *reinvention*, plumbing our own tradition for resources capable of addressing our current political impasse, but now articulated in contemporary terms that would be at once novel as well as recognizable to such thinkers as Aristotle, Aquinas, and Tocqueville.

What is needed—and what most ordinary people instinctively seek—is stability, order, continuity, and a sense of gratitude for the past and obligation toward the future. What they want, without knowing the right word for it, is a conservatism that conserves: a form of liberty no longer abstracted from our places and people, but embedded within duties and mutual obligations; formative institutions in which all can and are expected to participate as shared "social utilities"; an elite that respects and supports the basic commitments and condition of the populace; and a populace that in turn renders its ruling class responsive and responsible to protection of the common good. What is needed, in short, is regime change—the peaceful but vigorous overthrow of a corrupt and corrupting liberal ruling class and the creation of a postliberal order in which existing political forms can remain in place, as long as a fundamentally different ethos informs those institutions and the personnel who populate key offices and positions. While superficially the same political order, the replacement of rule by a progressive elite by a regime ordered to the common good through a "mixed constitution" will constitute a genuine *regime change*.

While the "postliberal order" will cut across current political parties, its current best hope is a "new right." This label obscures as much as it assists, since a great deal of the economic program of the "new right" takes its cues from the older social democratic tradition of the left. However, today's left has largely abandoned the central commitment accorded to the working class, viewing its socially conservative tendencies as a deeper threat to progress. It has become clear that the right is more willing to "move left" economically than the left is to "move right" on social issues. This tendency is more than merely accidental, but represents a *return* of conservatism to its original form—a consolidated opposition to liberalism. Any advance of economic equality will be accompanied by a greater effort to foster and support those institutions from which deep forms of solidarity emerge: family, community, church, and nation.

The emergence of a "postliberal" new right is, in effect, a rediscovery of early-modern forms of conservatism, and echoes conservatism's earliest thinkers, who warned of the dangers emerging from an ideology of progress. These thinkers, in turn, reached back to the ancients to learn anew lessons about the "mixed constitution." While ancients such as Aristotle, Polybius, and Aquinas had no word for "conservatism," they offered its original articulation: a political and social order of balance, stability, and longevity that achieves the common good through forms of political, social, and economic "mixing." This revival of a core teaching from the very origins of Western political thought might properly be labeled "conservative" if we understand that any undertaking to "conserve" must first more radically overthrow the liberal ideology of progress. For our purposes, I will give this alternative a label that combines its ancient and modern labels: "common-good conservatism."

This book is an effort to offer not just another critique of liberalism, but a positive and hopeful vision of a postliberal future. In the chapters that follow, I will trace the way liberalism has not only failed, but generated a particularly virulent form of the ancient divide that pits the "few" against the "many." I will argue that the answer lies not in the renewed application of liberal "solutions"—whether "right" or "left" liberal—but in a rediscovery and updating of the ancient tradition of the "mixed constitution," and I will show how a common-good conservatism, which seeks to implement a "mixed constitution," rejects the ideology of progress, repudiates a political order that is premised on elite restraint of the anti-progressive instincts of the people, and is informed by the "wisdom of the many," is the way forward. Finally, I will suggest practical ways of "mixing" the elite and the populace.

Today's elites must be forced to abandon their self-serving efforts in the face of overwhelming evidence that the social, economic, and political course they have pursued for the past fifty years has deeply harmed the prospects for flourishing among the working classes.

This change will not occur simply by a mythic revolutionary uprising of the many against the few. Rather, it will require some number of "class traitors" to act on behalf of the broad working class, articulating the actual motives and effects of widespread elite actions. Even if relatively small, an elite cadre skilled at directing and elevating popular resentments, combined with the political power of the many, can bolster populist political prospects as a working governmental and institutional force. In turn, a new elite can be formed, or the old elite reformed, to adopt a wider understanding of what constitutes their own good—a good that is indivisible and common—and to steer America to a state of flourishing.

PART I

OUR COLD
CIVIL WAR

1

The End of Liberalism

L iberalism has generated its own undoing. As a philosophy and practical political project, one of its main aims was to overthrow the old aristocracy, in which one's social station and political position was secured by birthright. No matter how much one strived—or how dissolute one became—one's social and political rank could not be changed. This immutability was true not only in regard to one's political position, but as a consequence that much of one's identity was the consequence of birth. Liberalism proposed to overthrow this *ancien régime* and put in its place an order in which people, through their striving, ability, and hard work, could create an identity and future based upon the sum of their own choices.

Several hundred years into this experiment, we have witnessed firsthand the rise of a new ruling class, a "meritocracy" that has thrived under the conditions established and advanced by liberalism. Liberalism is today in crisis, not just because of the bad behavior of the new elite, but because its rise has corresponded with the attrition of institutions that benefited the lower classes while restraining the ambitious who wished to escape its restraints. The weakening of the family, neighborhood, church and religious community, and other associations has resulted in the degradation of the social and economic conditions of "the many," even as "the few" have garnered a monopoly both on economic and social advantages.

In the advanced liberal democracies across the world, working-class voters have risen up to reject the leaders who have regarded those who have been "left behind" with disdain and contempt. In response, liberalism has unmasked itself, revealing itself as an ideology that will force those who oppose it into submission, and advancing an increasingly "illiberal" liberalism. Efforts to limit the political power of the culturally dispossessed and economically disadvantaged—frequently by accusing majorities of being "antidemocratic"—increasingly reveal liberalism not to be a mutually shared comprehensive system that always allows self-determination, but rather a particular partisan set of commitments. The once unassailed public philosophy has been delegitimized.

As liberalism has careened toward its inevitable failure, politics across the Western world have been scrambled, no longer dividing between left and right liberals. Rather partisans who criticize the "people" (often composed of left and right liberals) and partisans who criticize the "elites" (today, most powerfully on the right, but also present on the left—for instance, Bernie Sanders and his criticisms of corporate elites) oppose each other. More than standing in opposition, they are in a vicious cycle as each side declines in virtue and strives for the destruction of the other, a cycle that will continue as long as liberalism remains the regnant regime.

To understand how the rise of liberalism resulted in this vicious cycle, it is necessary to understand how liberalism's conception of liberty created both a new ruling class and degraded the lives of the masses.

A premodern conception of liberty—expressed in the pages of Plato, Aristotle, the Bible, and the confluence of the philosophical schools of Athens and the biblical theological tradition in Jerusalem—was premised upon the ideal of self-rule, self-discipline, and self-government. The institutions of family, religion, and government raised guardrails on the otherwise natural appetites and desires that, when succumbed to, resulted in what this tradition regarded as a condition of servitude or slavery. The person who surrendered to the appetites was not only a slave, but also had the soul of a tyrant—a gluttony for power that would allow the enslaved tyrant to commit any act, any crime, any awful deed. All of the citizenry, including the powerful, needed to be habituated to the virtue that accorded with freedom, and the guardrails helped with that education for liberty.

By contrast, liberalism's architects proposed a vision of freedom as liberation from limitations imposed by birthright. To realize this liberation it was necessary not only to overthrow rule by inheritance but the older social forms that had taught and reinforced the cultivation of virtue. The realization of a new liberty required the dismantling of older institutions that had cultivated the classical ideal of liberty.

What had previously been considered as "guardrails" came instead to be regarded as oppressions and unjust limitations upon individual liberty. As a result, the advance of liberal liberty has meant the gradual, and then accelerating, weakening, redefining, or overthrowing of many formative institutions and practices of human life, whether family, the community, a vast array of associations, schools and universities, architecture, the arts, and even the churches. In their place, a flattened world arose: the wide-open spaces of liberal freedom, a vast and widening playground for the project of self-creation.

Today, liberalism's dismantling of guardrails is often described as a heroic story of progress in which past injustices were overcome, ushering in an age of enlightenment, justice, liberty, and equality. Oppressed people were liberated from the unjust constraints of a dark age. Anyone questioning the narrative is accused of defending privilege and nostalgically craving to reinstitute the injustices of a benighted past.

This narrative is a classic example of "Whig history," a self-congratulatory story told by the ruling class about its inevitable and beneficent ascent. The story told by liberals—like all "Whig history"—

is self-serving to their cause, even at the cost of getting the history wrong and ignoring lessons of the past about "limiting" institutions that actually served freedom.

Consider, for instance, arguments made by one of liberalism's heroes, John Stuart Mill. In his classic text *On Liberty*, Mill denounced the constraining role of tradition in favor of an open, liberal society that advantages those who seek to disrupt these kinds of formative institutions. In Mill's parlance, custom was a "despot" over the lives of those who wished to instead engage in "experiments in living." While it's doubtless the case that custom appears to be a "despot" to those who seek to disrupt and overthrow long-standing traditions and customs of society, *from another perspective*, custom and the associated array of institutions that support and perpetuate ongoing cultural practices exist not merely to prevent the liberty of self-inventions, but to protect ordinary people from the potential rapaciousness of the ambitious. Viewed in such a light, these informal but pervasive cultural forms not only prevent efforts of a revolutionary character from reordering society around the imperative of individual liberty, but they protect the stability and order that most benefits ordinary people, people who are not well served by instability, generational discontinuity, institutionalized disorder—in short, what Mill calls "progress."

Mill's contemporary across the English Channel, Alexis de Tocqueville, precisely in this light understood the threats of liberation from ambient culture. Observing the likely rise of a more "revolutionary" class in a liberalizing America, Tocqueville wrote admiringly especially of the constraining power of religion.

> But revolutionaries in America are obliged to profess openly a certain respect for the morality and equity of Christianity, which does not permit them to violate its laws easily when they are opposed to the execution of their designs. . . . Up to now, no one has been encountered in the United States who dared

to advance the maxim that everything is permitted in the interest of society. An impious maxim—one that seems to have been invented in a century of freedom to legitimate all the tyrants to come.[1]

Understood in light of Tocqueville's argument, the "guardrails" that limited those of a revolutionary temperament—limits that might be understood as a *benign* form of "tyranny of the majority"—can be properly understood as deeply democratic. They are democratic first because they are the creation of countless generations of forebears who contributed to their creation, won through hard experience, and assembled and bolstered them through institutions in order to protect the prospects of life flourishing *no matter the economic or social position of the person*. Those likely to defend a preeminent role of cultural institutions implicitly recognize that there is inevitable inequality in the world, in any number of forms—whether the ongoing presence of arbitrary social differences, or their replacement by natural inequalities due to differences of talent and self-direction—and, rather than falsely claiming that all inequalities can ultimately and someday be overcome, instead insist that the governing cultural forms and norms are the best means of securing the prospects for flourishing *especially of the weaker and disadvantaged*. They were democratic, secondly, because the accumulation of customs and practices embedded in social structures acted as a break especially upon those of distinct ambition and even tyrannical impulse, those who would benefit especially from conditions of instability and disorder. It was for this reason that G. K. Chesterton stated his belief that "tradition is only democracy extended through time. . . . Tradition may be defined as an extension of the franchise. Tradition means giving votes to the most obscure of all classes, our ancestors. It is the democracy of the dead."[2]

Contra Mill, long-standing cultural institutions and practices should be given the benefit of the doubt, precisely because they largely

develop from the "bottom up" in order to achieve two simultaneous
ends: foster conditions of flourishing for ordinary people, while restraining the tyrannical impulses of the powerful to be free of the mod-
erating and sustaining strictures of custom, tradition, and culture.
Tocqueville stressed that the obeisance of those who are potentially
revolutionaries may only be "ostensible"—that they may harbor unstated
desires to break free of all restraints—but even grudging acknowledgment of cultural norms, won through social pressure from below, can
be sufficient as a form of restraint. For such cultural forms to exercise
widespread influence, the customs and norms must be widely shared
and generally embraced by the populace.

In effect, those who ascend to positions of power, influence, and
wealth are "controlled" and limited by such forms—not merely by passage of positive law or separation of powers, but by the governance of
the "democracy of the dead."

Today, the essence of elite formation consists of two main objects,
irrespective of major or course of study: first, taking part in the disas-
sembling of traditional guardrails through a self-serving redefinition
of those remnants as systems of oppression; and second, learning the
skills to navigate a world without any guardrails. College—especially at
selective institutions—is a place and time in which one experiments in
a safe atmosphere where guardrails have been removed, but safety nets
have been installed. One learns how to engage in "safe sex," recreational
alcohol and drug use, transgressive identities, cultural self-loathing,
how to ostensibly flaunt traditional institutions without bucking the
system—all preparatory to a life lived in a few global cities in which the
"culture" comes to mean expensive and exclusive consumption goods,
and not the shaping environment that governs the ambitious and settled alike. Those outside these institutions also have had the guardrails
removed—all are to be equally "free"—but without safety nets in sight.

Elite opinion thus officially condemns the older cultural institutions and forms while learning a new kind of internalization of norms that function as a kind of privatized guardrail, not unlike the secured spaces of those gated communities that many in this class will eventually join. Cultures rich with norms that applied to high and low alike had been a kind of "public utility," serving everyone in society equally, but the official messaging of elite-driven society comes to attack and dismiss many of the long-standing ideals that were encouraged by older cultural forms. Thus, for instance, media, popular culture, and the education industry come increasingly to express disapproval of the ideal of family or marriage by redescribing it as "the traditional family" or "traditional marriage." By adding the designation "traditional," disrepute and disapproval are signaled by elites of the liberal order, in which the merely "traditional" is most often associated with arbitrary impositions of the past that are irrational, oppressive, and constraining. Yet—as social scientists such as Charles Murray and W. Bradford Wilcox note—those who enjoy the benefits of advanced university education implicitly learn how to form families in an anti-culture without guardrails, depending especially on the benefits of privatized norms as well as greater wealth and opportunity.[3] Meanwhile, the demolition of the cultural norm and ideals—both through economic and social destruction—results in the growing dissolution of family formation among the less advantaged.

A third lesson follows these two: those who succeed deserve their status; those who have been left behind have only themselves to blame. As Michael Sandel has recently argued, educational "credentialism is the last acceptable prejudice."[4] In a world increasingly arranged to guarantee financial and social success for those who have been formed by the "sacred project" of modern liberalism, those who fail to rise from the curse of being rooted "somewhere" come to be viewed as deserving their fate. The only obstacle to rising comes to be seen as a moral failure of sorts, particularly perceived as the "clinging" to outmoded beliefs and practices that those of superior pedigree had the courage and discernment to overcome. Sandel concludes that "meritocrats moralize success and failure and unwittingly promote credentialism—an insidious prejudice against those who have not been to college." The system that had come into existence to replace the arbitrary rule of aristocrats, he notes, "can become a kind of tyranny."[5]

Michael Lind has aptly described this new divide as "the new class war," and notes that what I will often describe here in these pages as the division between "elite" and "working class" rests less on differentiation of *wealth* than credentials and access to a foothold and success in the managerial economy. Lind rightly notes that the working class is divided—arguably not only with the blessing, but active encouragement of the managerial elite—between "old-stock natives" and "recent immigrants and their descendants."[6] Without denying the reality or seriousness of racism as a scourge in Western nations and particularly the United States, comprehensive and effective proposals to redress historic injustices would have to include considering how the demise of formative social institutions and family life have harmed the working classes, regardless of race. Such considerations are studiously avoided as part of the progressive effort to redescribe all of Western history as structurally racist, rather than structurally liberal—and, hence, damaging to the life prospects of ordinary people regardless of their race and ethnic background. Arguments that give exclusive focus upon a racial basis of the Western political divide thus end up reinforcing the advantages of the managerial classes, forestalling recognition among a multiracial working class of common interest against the managerial class, which in turn benefits from the political impotence of this divided underclass. Yet, as recent American elections have shown, a growing awareness of this common interest is leading to the gradual development of a multiracial, multiethnic working class that has potential to become a powerful counterforce to the gentry liberals who govern it from their new medieval citadels.[7]

Beyond a Politics of Elite Hypocrisy and Populist Resentment

As the second decade of the twenty-first century began, a new political alignment and division came to define the Western (and even global) political landscape: the elites against the people, populists against the new aristocracy. And, as could be expected, their respective partisans were legion. In the wake of this international political realignment, the partisanship has taken the form of decrying the evils of the elites or the authoritarian dangers of populism. Within these respective stances are vested extensive assumptions about the nature of virtue and vice. For the critics of elites, the vices in evidence include hypocrisy of the wealthy, tendentious policy that benefits the upper classes while harming ordinary people, and virtue signaling that shrouds the typical vices of the oligarchy. For critics of "the people," behind their purported claims to defending a way of life lie the vices of racism, sexism, homophobia, Islamophobia, and assorted other bigotries. Deeply implicit in these critiques are suggestions of the associated virtues of those who critique their opponents. But rarely are such virtues actually articulated. Indeed, most of the purported virtues are simply implicit claims that their respective sides lack the vices of those they criticize.

Following the election of Trump, the passage of Brexit, and the rise of populist parties throughout Europe, scores of books have appeared either denouncing the elites or populists. Critiques of the ruling class ranged from academic studies to popular broadsides, including bestsellers such as J. D. Vance's *Hillbilly Elegy* (2016) and *Ship of Fools* by Fox News host Tucker Carlson (2018). Books such as Carlson's often pointed to the conditions described in more evenhanded scholarly books that explored the growing partisan divide between elites and "populists," such as Charles Murray's prophetic *Coming Apart* (2012), or the data collected by Timothy P. Carney in *Alienated America* (2019), both of which offered portraits of the social disintegration increasingly experienced by America's white working class that were intended to elicit equal parts sympathy for their plight and unhappiness with the elite.

Tucker Carlson's bestselling book, for instance, denounced the elites in a series of portraits, exposing their egalitarian hypocrisy, such as Chelsea Clinton's unbroken succession of educational and professional successes (Harvard, Oxford, jarringly high-paying jobs) juxtaposed with her expressed commitments to egalitarian social justice. Carlson built a sustained brief against the policies that have proved disastrous to the working class while feathering the nests of the well educated, including the TARP bailouts of 2008 and the war in Iraq. Other books in this genre decry the smugness and condescension of the "Elite" toward (in the words of Kurt Schlichter) the "Normals" who just want to lead decent lives without do-gooder interference of their betters. In his book entitled *Militant Normals*, Schlichter writes:

> What our Elite today feels is not duty to the Normals but, rather, contempt for them and a desire to break the Normals to the Elite's will. Politically, this manifests in the Elite pursuing policies that at best ignore the needs of the Normals and, at worst, seek to punish them. . . . Culturally, this takes the form of a nonstop barrage of hatred and invective aimed at everything the Normals hold sacred.[8]

Books in this genre paint a portrait of a vicious and hostile elite who joyously and wantonly engineer the destruction of the working class. They are books written for one "team": based upon denunciation of the opposition, they seek to shore up allegiance to a presumptively better team. Yet, their energy is mainly in the form of opposition and even resentment toward those claiming to be the social betters of "the Normals," and not necessarily (indeed, exceedingly rarely) to portray an admiring portrait of the virtues of ordinary people. The genre relies mainly on denouncing an enemy rather than elevating the virtuous.

A less incendiary approach simply allows correlation to suggest the possibility of causation: as the condition of well-educated urban and near-urban denizens has dramatically improved, the condition of the more rural and less educated has declined measurably and precipitously. Without implying intention or hostility as such, Charles Murray amassed a trove of data showing how those living in "HPY bubbles (Harvard, Princeton, and Yale)" were thriving while those of lower educational attainment and increasing geographical isolation in "flyover country" were suffering from a rash of divorce, out-of-wedlock children, poor health, drug and alcohol addiction, deaths of despair, and criminality.

Similarly, Tim Carney argued that the individualist ethos of the elites has served them well while severely and negatively impacting the daily lives of the "alienated," those who lacked the social capital to build the kinds of ties and bonds that allow the wealthy and well connected to flourish in a winner-take-all economy. Carney noted that "the story of how we got Trump is the story of the collapse of community, which is also the story behind our opioid plague, our labor-force dropouts, our retreat from marriage, and our growing inequality."[9]

According to journalist David Goodhart, a comparable situation existed in Great Britain leading up to the vote in favor of Brexit. Examining the growing divide in his country, Goodhart differentiated between "Anywhere" people and "Somewhere" people. While "Anywheres" have "portable 'achieved' identities, based on educational and career success which makes them generally comfortable and confident with new places and people," the "Somewheres," Goodhart argued, "have lost economically with the decline of well-paid jobs for people without qualifications and culturally, too, with the disappearance of a distinct working-class culture and the marginalization of their views in the public conversation."[10]

The decline of the working class—formerly, the mainstay of left politics—was due to its political abandonment by progressives and its subsequent neglect by the right. The election of Trump and passage of Brexit were born of a despair of being voiceless and unrepresented. The response of the mainstream of both parties was to denounce not only Trump and Brexit, but also the recidivism of those who supported both.

From the other side of the battlements, one frequently encountered denunciations of the vices of "the people." Critiques of the moral shortcomings of ordinary people emanating from the left have been popular fodder to stoke outrage among conservatives, and yet, both progressive and right-libertarian politicians continue to serve up their views of the deficiencies of those whose votes they have written off, most often in their candid and (they believe) off-the-record moments. While speaking at a fundraiser in 2008, candidate Barack Obama reflected on the reasons for growing resentments among the working class, stating "they get bitter, they cling to guns or religion or antipathy to people who aren't like them or anti-immigrant sentiment or anti-trade sentiment as a way to explain their frustrations." While his opponent during the 2008 Democratic primaries, Hillary Clinton, criticized then senator Obama for his "demeaning remarks" about "small-town America" as "elitist and out of touch," just a few years later in 2016—also during a fundraiser— she famously denounced half of Donald Trump's supporters as a "basket of deplorables"—"racist, sexist, homophobic, Islamophobic, you name it."[11] Such comments have not been limited to Democrats, as evinced by Mitt Romney's infamous claim at yet another fundraiser that "47 percent of the people . . . will vote for the president [Obama] no matter what. . . . There are 47 percent who are with him, who are dependent upon government, who believe that they are victims, who believe the government has a responsibility to care for them, who believe that they are entitled to heath care, to food, to housing, to you-name-it."[12]

These infamous statements—often regarded as having helped sink the candidacies of Romney and Clinton, and nearly fatally damaged the first run of Obama—are particularly noteworthy inasmuch as they reveal the *true* views of those who occupy uncontested elite status in American society. In each case, these were assessments of the shortcomings of the electorate that were shared in a room filled with donors and believed to be entirely "off the record." These statements were candid admissions that the very candidates seeking the votes of precisely these "swing voters" held them in genuine contempt and disapproval, in particular for a variety of moral shortcomings that suggest their backwardness, their superstitions, their bigotry, and an absence of virtuous self-reliance.

These charges against a resentful working class who largely deserve their diminished lot for failing to keep up with progress have not only been articulated by politicians in candid moments, but also appear in more popular press. Few have denounced "the people" as vociferously as the "Never Trumper" Kevin Williamson. In a 2016 essay denouncing conservative sentimentality (such as that of Vance, Carlson, or Schlichter) toward the sufferings of the white working class, Williamson (appealing to his own white, working-class background) argued that these thinkers were defending a group of complainers who largely had themselves to blame for their straitened circumstances. Williamson wrote that sympathy for such bad choices was simply "immoral" and argued that right-thinking people should cut loose the working class as negative assets: "The truth about these dysfunctional, downscale communities is that they deserve to die. Economically, they are negative assets. Morally, they are indefensible. . . . What they need isn't analgesics, literal or political. They need real opportunity, which means that they need real change, which means that they need U-Haul."[13]

Academics have expounded on the moral shortcomings of populists in less bombastic, but equally strenuous, condemnation. According to political scientist James Stimson, a professor emeritus at the University of North Carolina, the resentments of the working class are simply the consequence of their unwillingness to accept the structural changes in the modern economy and move to areas of greater economic opportunity. "[Those who are economically successful are] ambitious and confident in their abilities. Those who are fearful, conservative, in the social sense, and lack ambition stay and accept decline." Given that, Stimson said: "I don't see them as once-proud workers, now dispossessed, but rather as people of limited ambition who might have sought better opportunity elsewhere and did not. I see their social problems more as explanations of why they didn't seek out opportunity when they might have than as the result of lost employment." Stimson concluded that these people should be superseded politically by the "new class."[14]

Both the left and the right, whether popular or academic, have dominantly resorted to a *politics of friend/enemy*: the other side is so morally corrupt and so likely to institute tyranny that it must not only be defeated electorally. Rather, the other side must be outright eliminated.

Know Your Enemy

As this brief review of recent political positioning reflects, electorates are increasingly divided (at least by the social commentariat) between those who denounce "the elite" and those who condemn "the people."

What is perhaps most striking about these stances, but rarely noted, is that these respective positions are almost entirely *oppositional*. They stress the *vices* of those they perceive themselves arrayed against (either the condescending elites or the querulous masses), rather than identifying what is *superior* about their own partisans. Of course, rallying partisans around an oppositional stance is common in politics. But usually such an oppositional position is accompanied by some explicit claims about the *superiority* of one's own position and partisans, and at the very least, a set of *implicit* claims. A noteworthy feature of this newly established political divide across Western liberal democracies is an almost entire *absence* of any such explicit depictions of the superiority of one's own "team," and even, it could be argued, a lack of explicable *implicit* defenses. The current political realignment seems driven almost entirely by animosity toward the perceived shortcomings and even moral vices of the opposition.

Upon reflection, there is good reason for the general absence of extended reflection upon what recommends each "team": both, in fact, extensively lack discernible virtues. Critics of "elites" are generally accurate in their depiction of a ruling class that is increasingly out of touch, who for all their apparent difference between left and right liberals, divide between those who demonstrate cultural elitism (with disdain toward the backward recidivism of flyover people) or financial elitism (with disdain toward those who have failed to pull themselves up by their bootstraps). Yet, there is notable silence about the praiseworthy qualities of "the people" among those who denounce "elites." At times it is implied that the "Normals" are less likely to be hypocrites; that they might be the source of certain homely virtues, such as commitment to home, place, family, and nation; and that they are generally disrupted in their commitments due to the depredations of "the elites." When truth be told, however, "the people" are not generally held forth as paragons of virtue. Reams of statistics demonstrate that they are far less likely to exhibit certain kinds of virtues related to marriage, family, work, and criminality than the "elites" that they often disdain. People in the working class are far more likely to exhibit various measures of social pathology such as divorce and out-of-wedlock marriage than "the elites." They have become susceptible to the pathologies of various addictions, ranging from marijuana and opioids to video addictions and pornography. These social indicators doubtless reflect the strains of straitened economic circumstances and diminished upward mobility. People in these classes have experienced the first decrease in the average life expectancy of any American generation, a consequence of these choices now increasingly described as "deaths of despair."

Rather than seeking to correct these baleful tendencies through the benefits that might be more available to people in more rooted circumstances, particularly the prospects of strong civil society, by every measure, people in the working classes have abandoned their traditional affinity to associational life. Today, they are far less likely to be members of religious or social organizations. The sense of meaning and support that such institutions might once have offered even people with diminished economic prospects has been largely replaced by the attractions of consumption, whether in the form of prepackaged or social media, cheap imported products, or consciousness-altering and pain-diminishing controlled substances.

Their politics reflects their condition of despair and resentment. They are drawn to support demagogic political leaders who are implicated in corruption and marked by moral laxity, whose main attraction is their brusqueness, a willingness to say and do anything if it agitates or "trolls" the elites. In the main, attacks on the elites are driven by *blame* for this woeful condition and resentment for an increasing economic and social monopolization of well-being and even the trappings of virtuous behavior.

Meanwhile, those who criticize the deficiencies of "the people," for the most part, claim to be committed egalitarians who are philosophically opposed to assertions of the moral superiority of an "elite," per se. Rather than defend the "elites" qua elites, critics of populism tend to don what the French geographer Christophe Guilluy calls a "faux egalitarianism" in their modernized versions of "medieval citadels," generally congratulating themselves on their egalitarian commitments while denouncing the bigotry of the working class.[15] It is largely unthinkable for those who occupy elite status and populate ruling institutions to state explicitly the superiority of that status. The closest approximation is the implicit praise for those who have succeeded—and, more explicitly, the criticism of the "populists" whose resentments are born of their failures, such as the claims reflected in the critiques of someone like

Kevin Williamson or James Stimson. Such arguments thus claim that those who support "populist" candidates and policies have *chosen* to be losers in the modern economy. They deserve no pity, because the fault is entirely the result of their own poor choices.

These positions come close to invoking, without necessarily making explicit, the earned moral superiority of the "elites," marking a divide between those who have successfully navigated the demands of a fierce and competitive—but rewarding—meritocratic landscape, and those who have chosen to fail (or, by failing to engage in the competition, have failed to even attempt to succeed). Because a meritocratic system is in theory open to anyone of ability, self-discipline, and a work ethic, it invites a pervasive if often unstated form of self-congratulation among those who have successfully negotiated its demands, and, correspondingly, a subtle if rarely articulated stance of condemnatory judgment against those who have failed.[16] For every Williamson or Stimson willing to make such judgments explicit, there are likely countless others who have internalized such perspectives as well as the appropriate good taste not to speak them aloud. But, because of the stated egalitarianism of modern liberal democracies, while such views might be widely *thought*— and who can say for certain?—they are not often admitted aloud.

It is far more likely that those who occupy high-status positions, or who enjoy the benefits of higher educational or occupational attainments—and, hence, greater access to economic and social success in an increasingly globalized economy—will condemn various expressions of populism for *its* inherent elitism, privilege, various bigotries such as racism, sexism, homophobia, and so forth. A major attraction of "identity politics" for an ascendant elite class lies in claims to egalitarianism that bracket class considerations, and particularly, the status of the working class. A hallmark of the modern left has been to adopt egalitarian commitments concerning *identity* to the exclusion of its former commitment to class equality, leading to the precipitous decline of working-class identification with political parties and movements that once drew the support of the laboring classes. While the commitments of more highly educated and professional classes thus implicitly point to a certain moral superiority resulting from their greater commitment to ascendant forms of identity egalitarianism—what has come to be known as being "woke"—in the main, the most robust expression of "in-group" commitments arises from a shared condemnation of various bigotries, and not a robust or widespread expression of their own greater worth. Indeed, when it comes to the measures of their own social health just mentioned—marriage, health, work, and even religion— the elites tend to be silent about their worth or even denigrate the centrality of these virtuous practices in their own success. Thus, the aspects of life to which they might appeal to extol certain virtues are, in fact, widely regarded at least officially as "vices," based upon bourgeois sexist and elitist values that the upper class enjoys amid the denial of their value.

Thus, the two main parties today are more aligned by what—or, rather, *who*—they are *against* than by *what* they are *for*. As a result, mainly through this largely oppositional stance, both "sides"—both teams—regard themselves as *better* than they actually are, by virtue of standing against the characteristics they denounce and deny. The mere fact that "the people" declaim hypocrisy, elitism, self-deceptive "wokeness," and the condescension of the upper class does little to correct the manifest shortcomings that now afflict broad swaths of the working class. The assumption appears to be that if the elites were not so depraved, the people would not be suffering the many measurable social pathologies that now afflict the lower and working class. This might well be the case—to an extent at least—but such a position appears more likely to be a source of appeal for those capable of stoking resentments, without an accompanying program or prospect of their social improvement.

Similarly, members of "Team Elite" seem to hold the view that if the backward working classes would merely become sufficiently "woke," everyone could enjoy the benefits of a society based upon identitarian egalitarianism (while the distance to that egalitarian society recedes ever further from view, in fact). Further, as Williamson and Stimson suggest, if everyone could adopt the commitments and behavior of the meritocratic elite—just renting a U-Haul—then the deepest sources of economic and social inequality would dissipate. Whether through "job retraining," continuing education, or just the gumption to move out of a dying town, it has long been held by members of this class that the differences between the "ins" and "outs" can be solved by *making everyone an "in."* Such a view is plainly absurd on its face, and yet it has implicitly animated much of the thinking of the elites for at least a generation.[17]

As a result of these respective oppositional stances, each "team" is actually *worse* than it believes itself to be, building up its own purported virtues by ascribing to the opposition every imaginable vice. As in any civil war—"cold" or otherwise—each side believes it can finally impose its worldview through complete rout and defeat of its opponent—in the process, presumably, making the opponent into itself. But such a consummation is devoutly *not* to be wished for, if cessation of hostilities would entail complete triumph by a corrupt or corrupted class and the rout of its opposing corrupt or corrupted class. Each side in our shabby civil war is today thoroughly invested in building up the existential threat posed by its opponent, while relieving itself of the requisite self-reflection to address its own shortcomings.

Armistice

The divisions and parties that define today's politics are not new; rather, the divide represents the reappearance of the "normal" condition of politics that appears to be an endemic political feature of the human condition. After a relatively short period in which the divide seems to have disappeared—running along right- and left-liberal lines instead—it has reappeared, albeit without a corresponding ability to address this ancient political division aside from each side seeking the defeat and destruction of the other. A long line of thinkers from throughout the Western tradition counsel that this course is to be avoided. As ever more observers recognize the inevitable failures of the progressive project of liberalism, their ancient counsel needs again to be heeded.

The tradition of the "mixed constitution" recognized that the attributes arising from these different stations were at once the source of distinct vices as well as potential virtues that were likely endemic to each class. The vices of each class are easy to categorize, and the historical record is, more often than not, a voluminous if depressing display of those features. The "few" elites—whether for reason of wealth, position, rank, or status—are likely to become tyrannical, using their wealth or positions to oppress the "many" while claiming to be doing so in the name of the greater good. They tend toward hypocrisy and self-deception about their motivations. They monopolize the economic and social benefits of the political order for the narrow benefit of their own class, while convincing themselves that they deserve their status, and those below them are destined by fate, the gods, birth, or a lack of good birth, merit, or simple fortune to their lower station. The inherent feature of upper classes in every age is to benefit their own situation—while worsening that of the lower classes—through the advantages accorded by their position.

Certain vices were also endemic to the lower classes. Because of their lower station, they were more likely to harbor resentments toward the upper class, whether justified or not. These resentments could lead to damaging political instability—in extremity, civil war—or, more often, political support for a demagogue who stoked and inflamed resentments and engaged in personal and familial corruption with a populist shroud. Due to lower educational attainment, the lower classes could be crude and parochial, just as the upper classes could be pretentious and effete. Simplicity could easily shade into simplemindedness; a localist temperament could become indistinguishable from xenophobia; earthiness too easily became baseness. In the history of political thought, democracy was long listed as among the *worst* of all regimes, since the evidence too often suggested that ordinary people were not sufficiently capable or disposed to govern themselves or others well.

At the same time, the propensity of each class to develop distinct *vices* was counterbalanced by the identification of certain potential *virtues* that inhered in each class. Those in the upper class were more likely to attain cultivation and refined tastes. They were more likely to be the beneficiaries of liberal education, and hence *liberal* by the classical definition: people free from daily cares, and able to develop certain virtues or excellences of character that required leisure and refinement. They could come to appreciate and cultivate fine and high culture, often patrons and preservers of many of the world's most treasured objects of transcendent beauty. At their finest, they governed well for the sake of the whole polity, inspired by lessons of noblesse oblige and chivalry, a disposition that arose in recognition of the gift and privilege of their distinct positions, and the corresponding responsibilities and duties that such station entailed.

Similarly, the working classes also had a distinct set of potential virtues that were connected with their station. They were more likely to be grounded in the realities of a world of limits and natural processes, in tune with the cycle of life and rhythms of seasons, tides, sun, and stars. If upper classes could set their sights on higher culture, the working classes often developed practices that reflected life's constant realities, its joys and pains, celebrations and suffering. They have been extolled as the political embodiment of "common sense," bearers of a deposit of practices and beliefs born of close experience with reality, largely untouched by distorted visions of reality too often born of abstract theories made possible by a disconnection from limits. Because they lived in more straitened circumstances, they would develop certain virtues that came of necessity, such as frugality, inventiveness, craft, common sense, gratitude for small blessings, and, often, stoic cheerfulness even in the face of penury and suffering. They were often the bearers of everyday culture that acted as a kind of bottom-up law and education, offering guidance to each successive generation on how best to make one's way in a challenging world. While lacking high culture, this "low" culture was often the very essence of culture in its widest and deepest sense: the social loam in which human life grew, persevered, and was memorialized and renewed.

For much of the long tradition of Western political thought it was recognized that the same features of each class that might develop into virtues could all too easily instead become the respective vices native to each class. Thinkers in this tradition emphasized that the natural tendency for each class was to become the worst version of itself *unless it was checked and corrected by the other class.* At a basic level of self-preservation, to prevent the development of a vicious opposing class, each class *should* have the capacity and *did* have the incentive not only to "check" its opposite, but to *improve* and elevate it.

This tradition is long and deep, broadly understanding the necessity of a "mixed constitution" in the most comprehensive sense. The ideal of "mixed constitution" goes well beyond the familiar American mechanisms of "checks and balances," and, indeed, was arguably subverted at the time of the American founding by the narrowing of its definition—becoming instead focused largely on mechanisms that prevented certain exercises of power, rather than developing a true form of "mixing." By contrast, the ideal of a "mixed constitution" aspired to the genuine mixing of the classes, believing that deep interaction that at once both *checks* and *improves* will result in correction of each class's inherent vices while developing their potential virtues.

This tradition has been largely forgotten if not outright rejected, replaced instead by an aspiration for "progress" that sought its realization through the triumph over the class most resistant to progress. For liberals—right and left alike—the class most resistant to realization of progress was "the people," and liberalism was significantly developed as a program to place extensive restraints upon "democracy." In response, Marxist populism held that progress was obstructed by the elites—the bourgeoisie—and required their elimination to ensure the triumph of the morally superior people. A more global story of the immediate post–World War II period can be told as a contest between the ideologies of liberalism and Marxist socialism claiming that *one* enlightened class— either "elites" or "the people"—would eventually triumph over its opposite, ushering in an age of genuine progress and enlightenment. Our "cold civil war" in key respects reflects the outcome of these dominant understandings of politics, proceeding not with the aim of the improvement of the other class, but of its defeat and even destruction. A tradition that once emphasized the necessity of mutual improvement has been replaced by a politics of unconditional surrender. Rather than making each other better, our classes today engage in a politics that exacerbates their vices.

While both classes are responsible for this cycle, the ruling class bears the most responsibility, having the most resources. Unfortunately, the current ruling class is uniquely ill equipped for reform, having become one of the worst of its kind produced in history, as the next chapter will show.

2

The Power Elite

Today's elite is altogether new in the history of humanity. While in every known human society there has always been a ruling element, the nature of the contemporary elite arises from altogether new circumstances: the culminating realization of liberalism. In particular, four aspects distinguish this new ruling class from other aspirants that preceded its rise.

First, this elite is "managerial," possessing a certain set of fungible skills in preference to other forms of status demarcation, such as inherited rank, property, or wealth. It combines especially the classical liberal emphasis upon economic productivity with progressive liberal valorization of technocracy. While members of this elite prefer to combat each other along a liberal axis differentiated by greater commitment either to economic or social liberalism, as a class they are fundamentally arrayed against core values of nonaspirant nonmembers of this class—specifically, the more rooted and "managed" *demos*.

Second, because this class arose specifically in opposition to the inherited status that marked the old aristocracy, it is fiercely opposed both to the principle of hierarchy and the inheritance of status. Yet, while this elite comes into being through a different set of characteristics—managerial technocracy—its status has quickly become reified in the form of inherited hierarchy. Rather than agonize over this contradiction, the new elite engages in a form of self-serving self-deception (at best), or intentional obfuscation (at worst) respecting its status, one that is won at the cost of the prospects for flourishing among those who are not members of the managerial class. The self-deception or outright misrepresentation is achieved especially through an emphasis upon its egalitarianism through the pursuit of "identity politics," most vocally articulated at the elite institutions in which this class is formed and credentialed.

Third, especially through its invocation of "identity politics," the contemporary ruling class uses power not in a traditionally forthright manner, but through a recourse to a weaponized form of John Stuart Mill's "harm principle," in which perceived slights to identity are used as aggressive tools of control and domination. Particularly through claims of victimization by those occupying (or preparing to occupy) positions of power and influence, the ruling elite seeks to limit and even oppress or extirpate remnants of traditional belief and practice—those especially informing the worldview of the working class—while claiming that these views are those of the oppressors. Apparent "shields" such as calls for "trigger warnings" and denunciations of "unsafe" environments are actually used as weapons to exert control over the underclass. What is often taken to be a *contradiction* of the liberty of thought and ideas in liberalism is, in fact, its culmination—the end destination of the liberal "harm principle" to maintain the status of the ruling class.

Lastly, the main locus through which today's elite exercises control is not primarily through the exercise of governmental and public power, but "private" or semiprivate entities such as universities, corporations, media, and artistic centers of power such as Hollywood. Its political power is largely embedded within bureaucracies and quasi-public institutions, making it less accessible to electoral or popular control—that is, largely free of open and public constraint—and thus more easily imposed by those private and semiprivate entities. When necessary, this power is wielded against legitimate democratic governance and celebrated as a triumph for progress. Sometimes called "woke capital," it reflects the "managerial" and liberal nature of today's elite, preferring to shroud its power and status through nongovernmental forms of control. Such exercise of power is best understood as the enforcement of a distinct set of values and commitments that ultimately advantage the position and status of the ruling class, but—in keeping with liberalism's original mistrust of oppressive government—does so increasingly through the auspices of nonpublic institutions that stand outside and beyond the control of purportedly governing publics.

The Managerial Elite

The liberal political order has generated the form of elite most conforming to its core commitments of progress—placelessness, timelessness, and separation from cultural forms and practice. The form of elite produced by our political order replaced both the older landed aristocracy of the premodern era, as well as the industrial-era oligarchs whose position was largely the result of ownership of property, particularly in the extraction and deployment of natural resources. Today's elite, by contrast, may or may not own extensive material possessions. In the main, they are just as likely to be debtors as owners, and most "ownership" takes the form of abstract forms of value such as stocks, debt instruments, even notional "real estate," which is increasingly packaged as an investment vehicle. Rather, what confers their status is "ownership" of managerial skills, an attribute of particular value in a system designed to promote widespread separation of production from consumption, value from object, and classes from each other. The "elites" are not merely the wealthy, though many are; they are those who possess social status because they possess the requisite social and educational skills to navigate a world shorn of stabilizing norms—both through economic and social dislocation—and thus rendered unstable by the relentless pursuit of progressive change.[1]

Recognition of the rise of this "managerial elite" rightly rests with James Burnham, whose 1941 book, *The Managerial Revolution*, anticipated the rise of this "new class" at the cusp of its inception. Writing as the war effort in the United States was ramping up, Burnham anticipated that those involved with planning, manipulation of information and data, policy expertise, and increasingly abstract reasoning would displace the old industrial oligarchs for control of wealth, opportunity, and status. Taking their place would be those specially identified and trained to "manage" the public policy and private productive sectors: scientists and engineers; business executives and the consultant class; financiers and the investment sector. The skills involved in manipulating abstract information, designing systems, and directing policy would become the key "possession" of this new elite. These skills would constitute the source of the new elite's power, wealth, and status: "If we wish to put it that way," Burnham stipulated, "[these skills will] be the 'property' of the managers. And that will be quite enough to place them in the position of ruling class."[2]

The rising role of the state was a significant source of this transfer of power and authority: it would matter less who "owned" the materials than who controlled the overall distribution and value through the avenue of public and quasi-public policy. Burnham foresaw that there would be a "separation of ownership and control," and that the elite would increasingly see an advantage in "no direct property rights in the major instruments of production."[3] Rather, control of the state and quasi-public institutions such as media, educational institutions, the nonprofit sector, and corporate boards would become the prize of the new class. "Control over the instruments of production will be exercised by the managers through their *de facto* control of the state institutions—through the managers themselves occupying the key directing positions in the 'unlimited' state which, in managerial society, will be fused with the

political-economic apparatus."[4] Burnham anticipated a managed economy that was neither purely capitalist nor socialist, but rather what is often
today described as "crony capitalism." In such an "apparatus," well-placed
private and public actors ensure continuous advantage that might be
jeopardized either in a system that permitted genuine capitalist risk of
failure or genuine socialist risk of egalitarian redistribution.

The ascent of this new aristocracy derives from navigating a credentialing landscape in the pursuit of managerial skills. Those "skills,"
in the main, consist of the manipulation of abstract data, often financial manipulation, risk management, cost-benefit analyses, actuarial
calculations, "consultation" for efficiency maximization, and the like.
While many in this class are wealthy, and most are better off than the
nonmanagerial lower classes, many are rank-and-file elites whose credentials and managerial skills nevertheless give them access to the
bounties of elite society—much as an aristocrat lower in the birth order
might once still have enjoyed manorial life.[5] Celebrated by Richard
Florida as "the creative class" whose members share the skills and
emulate the lifestyles of the "super-creative class"—the genuine "one
percent"—it consists of a minority of upwardly mobile professionals,
in stark contrast to a more massive array of servants in the form of various service workers, whose low pay and insecure social safety net re-
places the "downstairs" servant class of the old aristocracy.[6] This new
aristocracy exercises a monopoly on social capital, congregating in select urban geographic enclaves that often absorb some of the most
charming traditional towns and villages in the United States while ex-
cising any actual traditional culture that might have distinguished those
places.[7]

Liberalism's elite class is particularly adept at reproducing itself,
intermarrying through "assortative mating"—thus ensuring a monopoly on wealth and social capital—even as they are not biologically fe-
cund. Marrying relatively late and producing generally one to two
children (and fewer with each passing year), they devote extraordinary

resources to cultivating a successor generation of comparably advan-taged elites, with as near-total success as the "artificial aristocracy" of old. While the Botox-smoothed meritocratic mask of this smart set was lifted when members of its class—including actresses Lori Loughlin and Felicity Huffman—were revealed to have bribed and cheated to ensure admission of their children to elite universities, these blatant abuses were merely a small step over the line of illegality of otherwise widely embraced manipulative activities, which include but are not lim-ited to: access to elite private schools or their public school equivalents; family-supported international "volunteer" activities; sports camps that elevate athletic prowess to gain scholarships; SAT prep courses; and precollege summer education opportunities, among other ways of gaming the system. Burnham recognized that a key feature of any elite order was its ability of self-replication, and that the conduit would be control of the main managerial institutions of new political and economic order. "Through the possession of privilege, power, and command of educational facilities, [the managerial elite] will be able to control, within limits, the personnel of the managerial recruits; and the ruling class of managers will thus achieve a certain continuity from generation to gen-eration."[8]

Members of this new class are vocally disdainful of older systems of elitism, particularly ones that were based upon hierarchical order-ing. The older aristocracy is particularly objectionable, based upon in-herited position, primogeniture that especially advantaged males. Claims about the virtues of "noblesse oblige" are dismissed as hypocritical self-delusion, shrouding deep, systemic, and pervasive inequalities behind self-flattering veils of solicitude.

Yet, for any of the justified claims in these dismissals, important differences less flattering to modern elites are frequently glossed. This new elite contrasts sharply with both the old, landed aristocracy as well as the industrial oligarchy. For all the differences between the two su-perseded elites, predecessor elites were defined by long-standing relationships to geographic locations and the lower or working classes. The landed aristocracy, in particular, was bound to place and cognizant of generational continuity. As Tocqueville described this waning aristocratic order, it tended to produce the opposite of democratic individualism.

> In aristocratic peoples, families remain in the same state for centuries, and often in the same place. That renders all generations so to speak contemporaries. A man almost always knows his ancestors and respects them; he believes he already perceives his great-grandsons and he loves them. He willingly does his duty by both, and he frequently comes to sacrifice his personal enjoyments for beings who no longer exist or who do not yet exist.

Tocqueville not only praised the aristocratic ethos for fostering a more extended sense of time and generational bonds, but for the bonds of obligation that developed between the higher and lower elements of society: "Each of them always perceives higher than himself a man whose protection is necessary to him, and below he finds another whom he can call upon for cooperation." Elites in liberal democratic ages, he anticipated, would be solicitous of the poor and dispossessed as a universal class, but would systemically arrange to avoid *particular* obligations to those less useful people: "When the duties of each individual toward the species are much clearer, devotion toward one man becomes rarer: the bond of human affections is extended and loosened."[9]

The age of the industrial oligarchs was often abysmal for the working class, but, in contrast to the contemporary arrangements, eventually gave rise to an era of both strong labor membership and mass political parties, both of which influenced oligarchs (eventually) to share wealth and ensure a degree of social stability. The ruling class was subject to territorial political governance, and the prosperity of their industries was generally aligned with the health of their cities, regions, and nation. The industrial oligarchs tended to identify strongly with national ideals—often, doubtless, with a generous dollop of hypocrisy—but intuitively understood the sentiment behind the quote "What was good for our country was good for General Motors," and as GM CEO Charles E. Wilson went on, "and vice versa."[10] Many became storied philanthropists who left a visible legacy, such as the Carnegie libraries that still dot American cities and towns. Perhaps motivated by equal parts altruism and self-defense, even begrudging contributions to the public good are today looked at with nostalgia, the prosperous post–World War II period that Michael Lind has described as marked by "democratic corporatism." Lind highlights historian Robert Griffith's description of these years: "Common to all of these activities was an attempt to fashion a new corporative economy that would avoid both the destructive disorder of unregulated capitalism and the threat to business autonomy posed by socialism." Griffith depicts especially the post–World War II Eisenhower-led nation as a "corporate commonwealth."[11]

Most members of the ruling class were not, in fact, robber barons, but the leaders of smaller American communities whose names are largely unknown to most of us except those who might have grown up in one of those towns or cities. Many of their number are often memorialized in the names of streets, theaters, schools, and town squares in civic spaces around America. Some became famous not for the most justified reasons of civic beneficence that attracted the national spotlight, but by serendipity, such as Archibald "Moonlight" Graham, the small-town doctor and, briefly, professional baseball player who became famous through the film *Field of Dreams*. While he is known today for never getting to bat (except in fictional Iowa), he was best known in Chisholm, Minnesota, for the quiet leadership and philanthropy that was so often the hallmark of small-town doctors and others in the professional class during much of the nation's history.[12]

The denunciations of the injustices committed by a previous set of elites not only are rightly intended to call attention to abuses perpetuated in previous eras upon disadvantaged people—especially today with a focus on racism—but, invisibly, to impugn what might be worthy of admiration and revision for a differently constituted elite. Because the contemporary managerial class achieves its status precisely through a detachment from place, generational connection, and its relationship to an enculturated lower and working class, it must reject these conditions as necessarily the sources of all previous injustices and inequality, while loudly expressing its commitment to equality. It must keep shrouded the ways that these separations are, in fact, the deepest sources of today's widening divide of wealth and opportunity and, ultimately, have proved destructive to the prospects of social stability and decently lived lives among the lower and working classes.

A first defining advantage of the managerial class is its studied placelessness. A key feature of the managerial meritocracy is its mobility and view of places as fungible. A vast testing and assessment regime exists to identify managerial talent in every location around the globe, extract the human raw material from whatever arbitrary location it happened to be born and raised, refine that material in elite educational institutions, and insert it into the global economy in key urban hubs that become magnets for the refined product. As the experience with COVID-19 revealed, this work can be done nearly anywhere, and often through a screen and wireless access, making the connection to any particular place tenuous and revisable. While those deemed "essential workers" increasingly resemble a class of serfs, the liberal aristocrats reside above and beyond the plague, often supportive of economic shutdowns and closures that leave them largely unaffected. Because their work actively seeks to transcend any arbitrary geographic boundaries, its denizens have become the most critical of any residual form of "nationalism" as a form of erstwhile prejudice and bigotry, rather supporting and advancing the project of globalism and borderlessness that serves as a key economic advantage to people with highly deracinated skill sets. Its political alignment with immigrants and refugees who also perforce seek mobility, while offering to the managerial elite a steady supply of low-cost servant labor, serves as a shroud of egalitarian self-congratulation and a corresponding condemnation of the working classes who oppose the undercutting of work and wages.

Second, the managerial meritocracy rests upon an assumption that the past is largely irrelevant and even a hindrance to the advancement of the abstract economy resting on manipulation of information, data, and symbolic analysis. Cultural forms and practices that are often carriers of tradition and memory must be displaced—here, placelessness is key—and, in their stead, culture is reconstituted in the form of consumer goods and experiences. Detached from broader continuities and contexts of meaning, culture is emptied of what Philip Rieff called "interdicts" and rather repackaged through commodification.[13] The managerial elite is arguably the first ruling class that actively rejects appeal to a shared well of common experience and practice, preferring a kaleidoscope of rapidly altering and temporary touchstones whose significance expires at their launch. It is a civilization whose shared culture consists of memes, a corruption not only of the word, but of the original concept "mimesis," in which the thing being mimicked is now as insubstantial as the imitation.

A final defining feature of this new elite is its near-complete disassociation of the new class from the lower and working classes. Educational and geographic separation is a marked feature of the new ruling class, with education providing both the economic means and psychic ability to navigate the high cost and relational instability of the modern urban setting. The working classes, by contrast, often rely on and prefer the thicker web of ties in their home communities, finding it difficult—even unthinkable—to pull up stakes for economic advantage elsewhere. While the ruling class often regards those who have not left their native places as backward and parochial, the lifestyles and experiences of the ruling class in various global cities are themselves remarkably parochial, selectively "multicultural" with those sharing the elite anti-culture and marked by a successful limitation of exposure to the underclass to transactions in the service, household work, childcare, and similar "servant" industries. Described by French geographer Christophe Guilluy as a ruling class enclosed within "new citadels," its denizens engage in "self-segregation" through a "uniform style of thinking and speaking." Its residents enjoy a monopoly of the benefits of globalization while draping a "fig leaf of diversity" over their privilege. They seek to portray their commitment to a "faux egalitarianism," while in fact viewing "the new ancients" living on the "periphery" as "the backward looking, the unqualified, the weak minded."[14] From their commanding heights, secured through wealth and status, their apparent openness in fact shrouds the opposite: "A society that imagines itself to be open to the world turns out actually to be just the opposite." What Guilluy describes as the sociological condition of France is today true in nearly every advanced liberal nation. We increasingly take for granted that there are simply certain parts of every Western nation that are (to use the American terminology) "red" and "blue," increasingly today denoting areas dominated by more rural or postindustrial landscapes versus "new citadels" dominated by thriving urban cores and nearby affluent suburbs preferred by managerial meritocrats.

The elite today is thus especially defined by a blithe fact that is otherwise a source of deep concern for every previous elite: a near-complete lack of serious reflection upon its relationship to the lower and working classes. This is not to say that there is a lack of stated commitment to the poor and downtrodden, which is a visible and vocal feature of the new elite. Rather, what is strikingly lacking is the presence of serious reflection as a matter of regime viability upon how to treat, reconcile, moderate, or negotiate the divide between the many and the few. The conceit among today's elite, promoted especially in its educational institutions, is that the only real answer to the division between the many and the few is effectively to make "the many" into "the few"—to equalize through the notional redistribution of *managerial status* to every human. "Diversity and inclusion" become the watchwords of an elite who believes amelioration is through largely symbolic inclusion of designated disadvantaged groups into formative managerial institutions.

The general response among contemporary elites is thus a form of emotive soft egalitarianism, expressed in the vague hopes that a better and fairer economy will raise all people to the approximate level of material comfort as the lowest-level meritocratic clerk—think, for instance, of the status of an adjunct assistant professor. A generation ago, this hope was expressed by the likes of Robert Reich, who called for the retraining and retooling of a workforce in preparation for a world in which the only marketable skill would be to become a "symbolic analyst."[15] Today, while that hope is still held by certain social democratic technocrats, this yearning is more likely to be expressed in the faith toward the benefits of a "universal basic income," supplying through redistribution of taxes a similar hoped-for effect as a redistribution of skills. How a UBI would square with a borderless and globalized world simultaneously encouraged by many of its supporters has not been especially of concern, and the likelihood of such programs functioning as globalized "welfare magnets" and causing a political backlash seems to be less worrying than the importance of being seen supporting trickledown skills or cash.[16] Both these hopes are largely aimed at assuaging the inegalitarian guilt of the upper classes, schemes that—even if effectual, which is altogether unproved and unlikely—would leave intact the systemic advantages of the managerial elite.

The "power elite" is thus especially pernicious because it is shaped to be nearly impervious to serious and sustained evaluation of how best to address this most ancient political divide. The educational program of the managerial class is today intentionally designed to ensure radical disconnection from a shared cultural inheritance that might link it to lower classes, and, in fact, relies upon the active destruction of any shared cultural understandings and practices that might be understood to be a kind of "distribution" of cultural opportunity. This education in turn encourages a deep and pervasive form of self-deception over the very nature and position of the elite, shrouding its status with the patina of egalitarianism while leading in turn to the denunciation of the insufficient enlightenment of the lower classes (except select groups whose inclusion is part of the self-deception). These two obstacles to serious reflection and redress of the divide between many and few deserve further and deeper exploration, with special focus on elite formation at the university level.

Self-Deception and Status Maintenance

At the time I was teaching at Princeton University in the late 1990s, *The New York Times* reported on the persistent campus culture centered around selective "eating clubs," the private mansion-clubs that most Princeton students join after their first year and—depending on the club to which one is accepted—can indicate one's status within and beyond the university. Commenting on the practice, Janina Montero, then Princeton's dean of student life, stated: "I think there are problems with selectivity of any kind on the college campus, because selectivity excludes people."[17] This was reported without comment by *The New York Times*, and seemed not to faze any of my colleagues at the university. Despite an admission rate that stood then, and still stands, around 5 percent, once admitted to the exclusive club of an institution like Princeton, loud and persistent denunciations of "selectivity" and "exclusion," and proclamations of one's deep commitment to egalitarianism, have the desired effect of rendering the inegalitarian basis of elite institutions completely invisible to their denizens.

We find ourselves in a curious place in the history of regimes. The elites of modern Western society have uniformly embraced the self-description of being exemplars of egalitarianism and a vocal force against elitism and privilege. Yet, their greatest animus is no longer against the aristocrats of old—since most of the vestiges of the old aristocratic order have been dismantled—but marshaled today especially against the greatest perceived source of privilege and inegalitarianism in today's world, namely, *the unwashed masses*, specifically, the rise of a populist movement in the United States, England, and throughout Europe. One can easily imagine future historians relating the extraordinary tactic of the twenty-first-century elites, no longer seeking as in times of old to justify their position by appeal to such ideals as being *"aristoi,"* "nobility," "patricians," or "dignitaries," but by claiming the mantle of egalitarian opposition to privilege, which is found especially among the masses, and by distinguishing their breathless defense of "democracy" against the authoritarian threat posed by "populism."

In this genuinely unique new form of elite governance, the powerless are denounced as oppressors and the powerful—often graduates of the most elite academies in the world—in turn commend themselves as victims. In effect, we are witnesses to an ancient battle being fought with new weapons, pitting against each other the two main parties of every political regime with claims that the other is practicing unacceptable forms of elitism, each side claiming the mantle of being oppressed by those with privilege. This form of politics in fact masks what is an age-old contestation between mass and elite in which the elite is generally advantaged by power and wealth, but either called by some among its own number, or forced by the populace, to act at least in part against its own class interests on behalf of the lower classes. The elite today, instead, veil their status—even, and especially, to themselves—through efforts to root out privilege especially in elite institutions, engaging in a stupendous effort of self-deception about the nature of their own position.

Today's elite college campuses are hotbeds of activism against inequality, especially inequality perceived to be manifested toward members of various disadvantaged identities centered on race, gender, being transgender, disability, and sexual orientation. Countless incidents have taken place on a number of our most prominent campuses with students, faculty, staff, and administrators protesting speakers or incidents of perceived bias and bigotry, from UC Berkeley to Yale to Reed College, but few incidents have been quite so remarkable as the protests that greeted the social scientist Charles Murray at Middlebury College in March of 2017. Before speaking a word, Murray was greeted with twenty minutes of unbroken denunciatory chants by dozens and possibly hundreds of students in the audience, leading to the decision to leave the room for a studio where a discussion between Murray and Middlebury political scientist Allison Stanger might take place. Students beat on the walls and windows of the studio as the two attempted to discuss Murray's ideas, and, as they left the studio, they were set upon by a large crowd that buffeted and grabbed at Murray and Stanger, leaving Stanger with a neck injury and a concussion.

More remarkable still, Murray had been invited by some Middlebury students to discuss his book *Coming Apart*, a study of various sociological measures of white Americans between 1960 and 2010. Murray's book focused on two main phenomena. First, he pointed to the ways that there has been a decisive separation of Americans into separate geographic enclaves according to wealth and class, a geographic divide that today closely tracks with educational attainment. Second, he described a different kind of separation, in which less wealthy and educated Americans are showing striking evidence of suffering from a host of social and economic disadvantages, particularly higher rates of divorce, nonmarriage, out-of-wedlock childbirth, crime, addiction, un- and underemployment, bankruptcy, disintegrating social networks, and declining religiosity and moral formation.[18]

The students who prevented Murray from speaking mostly came from, and will settle into, what Murray calls "HPY bubbles (Harvard, Princeton, and Yale)," select urban or near-urban locations of remarkable ideological, class, and social homogeneity. Middlebury College is among the most selective schools in America—accepting only 17 percent of applicants in 2017, the year of Murray's visit. Its cost for tuition, room, and board topped $64,000 in 2017, and while Middlebury touts its generous financial aid packages, like most elite schools, its main clientele is drawn from comparatively wealthy families. According to one study undertaken in the same year of Murray's calamitous visit, the median family wealth of Middlebury College students was sixth highest out of the nation's nearly 2,400 colleges and universities, at $244,300, while those coming from poor families constituted 1.3 percent of Middlebury's student body.[19] Recognizing the extreme levels of privilege in such a community, it would have seemed obvious that students so vocally committed to equality would have been interested in hearing a lecture by an author who would explore the evidence, basis, and implications of economic and class divergences in America today. Instead, they shouted down a man who was going to speak with them about just this topic—and shouted him down in the name of equality.

Of course, it wasn't the subject of Murray's lecture that was itself being protested; instead, protests were organized against what many had concluded were racist claims from his 1994 book, *The Bell Curve*. For many, their vociferous protests were based upon secondhand information about Murray's earlier argument: according to Professor Allison Stanger, some of her fellow faculty "acknowledged publicly that they had not read a thing Charles Murray has written, but still knew everything they need to know from what the Southern Poverty Law Center (SPLC) website had to say about him."[20] Rather than challenge or seek clarification by Murray, his lecture was shut down as a public act demonstrating opposition to inequality, largely based upon rumor or secondhand accusations of imputed racism. Yet, for students at a top-ranked university to protest so vehemently, preventing even a word of presentation by a speaker who had written extensively on class inequality often based upon inherited familial advantage, is revealing of an impassioned commitment to equality that appears to serve the purpose of distracting attention from their own class advantages and inherited position.

The ruling class today is arguably as blinkered about its dubious legitimacy as was the ruling class of the *ancien régime*, largely satisfied with evoking its commitments to diversity and inclusion as evidence of its enlightenment and concern for equality and justice. I don't want to be misunderstood as denying the justified and necessary commitment to racial equality and respect owed toward people who have been historically marginalized and excluded. However, the institutions most responsible for winnowing the social and economic winners from the losers have left largely unquestioned their own role in perpetuating structural inequality and even fostering a broader social ecology in which those who are not among the ruling class suffer an array of social and economic pathologies that are increasingly the defining feature of America's underclass, regardless of race. Such questioning would, of necessity, include hard questions about the agenda underlying commitments to "diversity, equity, and inclusion"—efforts that are being advanced on every campus. And yet, this is today the one set of beliefs that is off limits to the supposed "critical thinking" that such institutions claim to promote.

Contemporary commitments to equality that focus especially on the inclusion of historically marginalized groups, and that generally exclude considerations of class, permit an extraordinary lack of curiosity about the complicity of elites in a system that increasingly resembles the old aristocracy in perpetuating generational class differentiation. Elite concern for "diversity and inclusion" applies to members of groups that have been historically marginalized or excluded from America's elite due to "ascriptive" features—race, gender, disability, or sexual orientation, or what today generally are understood under the rubric of "identity." They are characteristics that are lodged in the human body, understood to be biological facts that should be irrelevant in considerations of one's status or position in contemporary liberal society. As "ascriptive" forms of identity, these features are understood to be unchosen, and any historical or current obstacle the result of prejudice in the form of racism, sexism, homophobia, transphobia, and so forth. "Diversity" and "inclusion" are, on the one hand, commitments to equality, but ones that fit neatly into the meritocratic structure, and leave the winnowing structures of the new aristocratic order firmly in place and allow them to go largely unquestioned. The growing institutional adoption of homogenous and uniform policies of "diversity, equity, and inclusion" tracks quite closely to the increasingly prominent role played by elite colleges and universities in this winnowing process—and coincides all too strikingly with an intensifying divide between haves and have-nots that our elite educational institutions play so prominent a role in determining and perpetuating.

Thus, we are witness to a strange and often hysterical insistence upon equality emanating from our nation's most elite and exclusive institutions, such as Harvard University's recent recommendation to eliminate all social clubs due to their role in "enacting forms of privilege and exclusion at odds with our deepest values," according to former Harvard president Drew Gilpin Faust.[21] Those values include an admissions rate of 5 percent—a rate that makes Middlebury appear profligate—or two thousand out of forty thousand applicants in 2017, and a record low of 4.59 percent of admitted students in 2022.[22] The numbers suggest, contrary to President Faust, that the deepest value of Harvard appears to be "privileged inclusion." Yet, not only do the institutionalized and highly touted commitments to diversity, equity, and inclusion that extend to historically marginalized groups allow a veil to descend over institutional participation in fostering a new elite, but by extension, there is the implicit if submerged and only rarely stated belief that anyone who is not included *deserves* their lower status.

As political philosopher Michael Sandel has written, this generates a deepening of the class divide, in which success and failure are internalized by each class. The result is a politically destabilizing "toxic brew of hubris and resentment," a fair summary of today's politics in the Western liberal democracies.[23]

Identity Politics and the Will to Power

Many students at elite institutions frequently combine two courses of study: one, in the softer humanities or social sciences, often in order to pursue a genuine interest in literature, philosophy, sociology, politics, and so forth; and a more "practical" major, often in the STEM disciplines, economics, business, accounting, and the like—in part to satisfy parents as well as the broader demands of a pitiless economic order. The two kinds of majors seem to reflect opposite approaches and outcomes—the one, more humanistic and cultural, the latter conforming to the harsh demands of the modern economy. Yet, far from opposites, the lessons learned in these seemingly contrasting curricula are actually the same—and are mutually reinforcing as a preparation for lives in either corporations, consulting, academe, media, or entertainment. As David Brooks pointed out several years ago in his book *On Paradise Drive*, the postmodernist major and economics major hold the same views, namely, that "truth is indeterminate. . . . Every point of view deserves respect. The enlightened person should be open to everything—opinions, lifestyles, and ideologies—and closed to nothing."

The displacement of questions of *truth* for the advantages of flexibility naturally contributes to the central ambition of elite education in preparation for life in the managerial class: power and status maintenance. But because the power elite claims to *eschew* raw assertions of power and the embrace of inequality, its embrace of "flexibility" actually becomes a main source of its exercise of power. Hence, the intense attraction of identity politics as a source of implicit power.

A main reason to displace the traditional education in the classic texts of the Western tradition is not only the elimination of a cultural inheritance—the liberation to be a free agent, unmoored by a tradition—but one particular aspect of that inheritance: the long-standing effort to restrain tyranny. A main line of thinking from the inception of the Western tradition of political philosophy was the effort to limit the unjust and tyrannical exertion of political power, a project that links thinkers as widely disparate as Plato and Aristotle, Augustine and Aquinas, the authors of *The Federalist Papers* and Tocqueville. In the classical and Christian tradition especially, the attraction to tyranny was challenged by appeal to objective conditions of justice. This effort famously underlies Socrates's condemnations of the sophists in the Platonic dialogues and was especially pursued in one of the West's foundational texts, *The Republic*. In that work, Plato portrays his teacher Socrates combatting those who urge tyranny as the best form of rule for those who are willing to seize power, arguing instead that only a society formed around principles of justice, knowable through philosophic exploration of truth, can provide a genuine alternative to the tyrannical impulse. Such norms of justice articulated in antiquity, variously developed in the classical tradition based upon appeal to reason, or, in the Christian tradition, based in rational knowledge of the natural law but also reinforced by appeals to faith, were understood to be the ultimate forms of limitation upon the tyrannical exercise of political power.

For this reason, a liberal education—the education of a free person—necessarily placed heavy focus upon the study of philosophy and theology. From the inception of Western political philosophy, inaugurated in the work of Plato, the effort to discern the nature of justice—the basis on which to organize our political and social lives—was closely linked to a requirement to attain knowledge, wisdom, and prudence. Justice was understood to be an objective criterion of proper valuation—thus requiring extensive knowledge—as well as the weighing of often incommensurable goods, e.g., equality vs. unequal merit, or just deserts against clemency, and accompanying demands for prudence and good judgment (judgment and justice, after all, are not only etymologically but substantively related). The question of justice was more than merely "theoretical," for at its heart was the question of on what basis, and toward what end, public authority should be established, and political power exercised. The Western philosophic tradition is, in part, a long, often contentious but largely consistent effort to ascertain the nature and requirements of justice, understood as an objective standard requiring rigorous education in the pursuit of knowledge, the aspiration to wisdom, and the cultivation of a judicious character.

In America and throughout the West, this education in a liberty grounded in an ideal of self-governance, and a corresponding aspiration to constrain the tyrannical impulse that often animates the actions of both individuals and entire societies, has undergone sustained attack and has been extensively displaced. In its place, an education in "multiculturalism," "diversity," and so-called "identity politics" has taken root. These approaches not only deny that there is rational recourse to universal appeals to justice but insist that an individual or group's perceptions of offense ought to replace appeals to any shared understanding of justice as a constraint upon tyrannical power. This effort has led inevitably to the rise of "identity politics"—the assertion of the priority of individual and group experience of offense, harm, and injury as the criterion for assessing how to allocate political power and resources.

Because higher education has largely abandoned a grounding in philosophical and theological inquiry—indicated in part by the abandonment of those disciplines as requirements for a degree on most campuses, and, at a growing number of schools, a significant reduction of such faculty and even elimination of those disciplines and their replacement by various departments of identity "studies"—institutions are now subject to a different set of philosophical currents without comprehending their sources, their trajectory, and the profound danger they present to self-government and avoidance of tyranny. The dominant appeal to "harm" by identity groups indicates the displacement of "justice," and thus the replacement of Plato, Aristotle, and Aquinas by the philosophical currents inaugurated especially in the nineteenth century by the paradigmatic liberal philosopher John Stuart Mill. The consequence of this displacement—increasingly visible through-out academe—is the abandonment of the effort to cultivate standards of justice. Such efforts have been replaced by a form of increasingly ty-rannical liberalism, a tyrannical form that is not a contradiction of lib-eralism, but its fulfillment.

John Stuart Mill famously sought to replace justifications for the exercise of political power based upon appeal to objective standards of justice and right with more minimalist justifications based on the stan-dard of perceived harm done by one person to another. Thus, laws and norms based upon an appeal to objective standards of how one *ought* to live were to be replaced by minimalist standards arguing that all beliefs, words, acts, and deeds should be allowed until and unless someone or some people were *harmed* by such activities. A hero of libertarianism, Mill's principle promised a radical reduction of laws and even informal customary norms that existed due to moral codes based on a belief in the Right or Good or Just. In this famous passage of his 1859 essay *On Liberty*, Mill wrote:

> The object of this Essay is to assert one very simple principle, as entitled to govern absolutely the dealings of society with the indi-vidual in the way of compulsion and control, whether the means used be physical force in the form of legal penalties, or the moral coercion of public opinion. That principle is, that the sole end for which mankind are warranted, individually or collectively, in interfering with the liberty of action of any of their number, is self-protection. ***That the only purpose for which power can be rightfully exercised over any member of a civilized community, against his will, is to prevent harm to others.*** His own good, either physical or moral, is not a sufficient warrant. He cannot

rightfully be compelled to do or forbear because it will be better for him to do so, because it will make him happier, because, in the opinions of others, to do so would be wise, or even right. . . . The only part of the conduct of anyone, for which he is amenable to society, is that which concerns others. In the part which merely concerns himself, his independence is, of right, absolute. Over himself, over his own body and mind, the individual is sovereign.[24]

Mill's argument has become instinctively embraced by nearly every modern human living in a liberal democracy. Any law, policy, or norm that would constrain or direct individual behavior in the name of some objective good is immediately challenged on the grounds that no one is "harmed" when individuals act according to their preferences. Whether in the economic realm (should there be constraints on economic choice, such as Sabbath laws?), the social realm (should pornography be restricted?), and especially today in the domain of human sexuality (should homosexual marriage be granted equal legal status to marriage between a man and woman?), the challenge issued to any efforts at constraint or direction inevitably takes the form of Mill's "harm principle": the demand for proof that people are likely to be hurt by another person's individual choices. In the absence of such proof, we expect a maximal libertarian order to emerge in both the economic and social domains.

Mill's aim was thus to shift from a society thick with social norms, and even laws that sought to "make men moral," to one in which individuals would be maximally free from the judgment of society altogether. His goal was to promote, as he called it, "experiments in living" to fulfill "utility in the largest sense, grounded on the permanent interests of man as a progressive being." Mill held that the creative individual needed protection from the constraints of "custom" and the "mass"—that is, the freethinking, free-acting individual was to be liberated from nearly all forms of social constraint and order. Within an increasingly

individualistic ethos, any "objective" claim of "harm" came to be suspect, including all but the most obvious forms of harm, such as physical
injury.[25] While, for a time, the social and political order looked to the
social sciences to provide information about social harms resulting
from unrestricted individual liberty, eventually even invocations of
such "scientific" findings would be largely rejected if they ran counter
to the primary goal of advancing "experiments in living."[26] Ascertain-
ment of "harm" was a task increasingly determined in the eyes of the
beholder—or accuser—with special advantage given to identity groups
whose underlying philosophy could be shown to align with Mill's endorsement of "experiments in living." While some individuals belonging to historically oppressed racial groups doubtless have a profound
moral claim due to collective harm, the effort to align these groups
with claimants of harm due to libertarian sexual identities—namely
through theories of "intersectionality"—fall in line with the liberationist, Millian direction of our current educational and political system.
The attraction of identity as increasingly the sole means of invoking the
presence of "harm" follows the abandonment of efforts to define the
"good" through philosophy and theology; of successor efforts to determine collective harm through empirical studies in the social sciences;
and, instead, to locate harm in the eyes of the beholder.

    This was always the actual and ultimate source of power for the
most radical expressions of "experiments in living": the accusation of
harm not only against anyone who was perceived to be judgmental, but
also against anyone who does not openly and publicly approve of any
and all "experiments." The "harm principle" was once believed to be
the redoubt of libertarian freedom, a minimalist appeal that would
mostly be deployed to prevent exercise of political power in the moral
domain. However, embedded in its deepest logic was its potential, and
inevitability, of being wielded as an aggressive tool of domination and
even tyrannical power. Far from being a brake on tyrannical power, it

was the ultimate means of empowering the "experimental" over those who believed there ought to be limits to the libertarian dismantling of all norms, and the resulting social disruption caused by ever more extreme forms of experimentation.

Witness how the "identity politics" movement has gravitated toward Mill's criterion in expanding efforts to invoke institutional power on behalf of advancing its liberationist ethos. Students' frequent resort to the language of "harm," fear of "microaggressions," need for "trigger warnings," requirements of "safe spaces," and general anxiety about feeling "safe" on college campuses has pervaded the general cultural milieu. These invocations appear on the surface to be *defensive*, echoing minimalistic invocations of the "harm principle." But in fact, their invocations are discernibly *aggressive*, specifically calling upon the intervention of power—whether semiprivate (e.g., corporate or collegiate) or public—to prevent highly subjective claims of psychological or perceived "harm" and thereby enforce an increasingly liberationist ethos. The increasingly visible willingness to *enforce recognition* of "experiments in living" is experienced by those who refuse, or even mistake, the preferred pronouns of their interlocutors. To be "mispronouned"[27] or "deadnamed"[28] is to be *harmed*, and—in keeping with the Millian ethos—the full force and power of the state and its semipublic, semiprivate agents can be brought down upon the malefactor.

The deepest irony is that Mill himself believed that the replacement of the criterion of "one's own good—moral or physical" with a more minimalist standard of "harm" would promote a society based in freedom requiring the exercise of only minimal forms of coercion. *What Mill's heirs have discovered is that their very ground for justifying political power—the invocation of "harm"—can be extended nearly without limit when invoked as subjective claims based in identity, particularly inasmuch as identity could be linked to advancing an individualist ethos of "experiments in living."* These claims, in turn, are used now to deploy the power of the state as well as a growing number of powerful private entities, such as corporations, to dismantle every last vestige of traditional norms, and increasingly are directed at delegitimizing the very *expression* of belief in limits to "experiments in living." These efforts are especially and tirelessly directed toward conservatives of various kinds, and especially orthodox Christians of various denominations, who remain nearly the only existing group that rejects in part or in whole the individual liberationist ethos and the paramountcy of choice and self-fashioning. The result is the rise of a visible new form of tyranny, apparently paradoxical: an illiberal liberalism that demands and is willing to exert power without any internal limit.

Universities that were created in the belief that a civilization must protect liberty through the cultivation of principles of justice and virtue are today in the forefront of advancing new principles of despotism. But they are only the launching pads for those who will carry those teachings into the wider society.

A New, Doubtless Very Different Kind of Tyranny

Elite universities and their imitators are the training grounds of the new elite but, for most graduates, not their final destination. Rather, these credentialing centers are the launching pads for a managerial elite who will go on to occupy critical positions in key institutions, ranging from bureaucracy to business, from entertainment to NGOs, from media to journalism, from art to architecture. Some will remain in academe, a place of remarkable intellectual conformity, where they will assume the role of elite formation. These educational institutions help shape the worldviews and expectations of the managerial ruling class, who then deploy to a variety of settings where those lessons come to shape most of the main organizations that govern daily life: government bureaucracies, law firms, media, journalism, corporate sports management, philanthropic institutions, and corporate offices and boards. As Andrew Sullivan has written, "We all live on campus now."[29]

The form of governance exerted by these leading institutions tracks with the dominant commitments reinforced in elite university settings. Meritocrats have earned their status, overcoming obstacles through successful negotiation of a rigorous credentialing process, the necessary discipline to perform in both academic and preprofessional settings, and early years working down debt while continuing a postgraduation collegiate lifestyle. Meanwhile, the noncredentialed, the working class, the denizens of the service economy, servant class to the neo-aristocrats, and generally engaged in nondegreed work, have earned disdain for a variety of moral failings related to their economic status resulting from failure to make the cut, social pathologies that are deemed to be deserved, and most fundamentally for benighted views on race, gender, sexuality, and reproduction.[30] The aim of modern liberal civilization is individual expressivism and self-creation, and those who fail to achieve this status receive their just deserts; whereas, those who expressly reject these aims in the name of older norms are summarily branded as bigots and zealots. As the remaining resistance to this civilizational project has been increasingly isolated to various Christian and other orthodox religious traditions, a distinct animus has developed against religious believers, with an increasingly open display of cultural disapproval and power directed against these more traditional beliefs. From the pages of J. S. Mill's discussions of "harm principle" has arisen a new titanic form of power and control in which the most powerful individuals of modern liberal society, controlling the main levers of social, political, and economic control in its main institutions, extend and expand their power through domination over those at the periphery by claims that they are the true oppressors.

This power increasingly combines the forces of liberalism's progressivism in both its economic and cultural dimensions. We witness this combination in the rising use of direct economic power to advance culturally progressive and liberationist positions. In the early stages of liberalism, "the market" exercised indirect influence through the "flattening" of boundaries and borders, the commodification of all cultural forms, and the introduction of market forces into every area of life.[31] In recent years, leading economic actors have increasingly exercised hard, direct power in order to advance and effect cultural change. The two sides of liberalism—economic and social libertarianism—are revealed to be identical, monolithic, and eager to deploy power in the name of enforcing individual expressivism. Their power perceptibly takes the form of unassailable force by an oligarchic minority capable of the effective destruction of opponents through exertion of economic power, sanctioned public opinion, and professional reputation. Actual control of political institutions is adjacent to this power, and where democratic resistance is encountered, it meets this new hegemony on an uneven battlefield.

A particularly instructive example of the new hegemony was on display in 2015, when the state of Indiana passed a Religious Freedom Restoration Act that was modeled on an existing federal law and similar state laws in twenty other states.[32] RFRA laws extended what had been extensive protections for religious groups from undue burden of government legislation, beginning with a nearly unanimous passage of the federal RFRA in 1993 in response to the Supreme Court's decision in *Employment Division v. Smith*—a case holding that Native American groups were not exempt from general application of legislation forbidding ingestion of illegal drugs, including hallucinatory drugs such as peyote, which was used in traditional Native American religious ceremonies. RFRA thus "restored" what had been a presumption that religious groups should not be unduly burdened by government legislation or administrative diktat, effectively constraining the presumption of government authority over religion that followed from the *Employment Division* decision. Indiana passed a similar version of RFRA in 2015, but by that point, religious liberty had become a flash point in the culture wars, interpreted by advocates of gay marriage to be a way of protecting Christians from offering commercial services to gay marriage ceremonies. A number of high-profile cases, some involving bakers and photographers who cited their faith as reasons not to participate in and thereby sanction homosexual marriages, had decisively moved progressive opinion against RFRA laws in the intervening years.[33] Indiana's passage of a state RFRA became a national controversy.

A number of political leaders condemned Indiana's decision, including Connecticut governor Dannel Malloy, who banned state-funded travel to Indiana—in spite of the fact that Connecticut had a RFRA law on its books.[34] But it was not the political condemnation from other states or even national political figures that put Indiana's RFRA in jeopardy, but the reputational and economic threats. Major corporations, including Apple, Salesforce (with a substantial presence in Indianapolis), Eli Lilly, and Angie's List, among others, threatened to diminish or withdraw their economic presence from the state.[35]

New York Times columnist Frank Bruni noticed the general trend of corporate support of progressive causes—including gay marriage and permissive immigration practices and policies—and spared no praise for such corporate behemoths as Apple, Amazon, and Facebook in a 2015 column entitled "The Sunny Side of Greed."[36] He noted that these companies were acting in their best interest by ensuring that "laws and local customs don't prevent them from attracting and retaining the best work force." Bruni recognized that capitalism necessarily displaces local practices and beliefs in favor of a universalized commercial ethos, and approvingly noted that corporations were often more progressive than the places they were quartered and to whom they sought to sell their goods and services. In such cases, the exercise of raw corporate power was to be preferred to legitimate political governance; thus, the spectacle of a left spokesman praising corporations over democracy, since they exhibit "greater sensitivity to diversity, social justice, and the changing tides of public sentiment than lawmakers often manage to."

Bruni approvingly quoted consultant Bradley Tusk, who noted that such corporations are "ultimately more responsive to a broader group of voters—customers—than politicians are." A consumer ethos, fed and shaped by corporate commitments, was now seen as more fundamental than the kinds of beliefs and dispositions necessarily shaped by a shared civic and political life. It was an endorsement of corporate influence and even rule when democracy does not conform to liberal priorities.

This praise of enlightened corporate policy can be valuably juxtaposed with the vilification of a small family-owned business that found itself on the other side of approved narratives. While Apple and Amazon received fawning praise of *New York Times* columnists, a family-owned strip-mall pizzeria in economically challenged Walkerton, Indiana, became the public face of the kind of "hate" that people like Bruni believed would be protected by Indiana's RFRA law. Searching for a "smoking gun" that Indiana's RFRA was nothing more than a cover for "bigotry," an enterprising local reporter traveled to the downtrodden small town of Walkerton outside of South Bend, where she reported on the response of the owners of Memories Pizza about their views of RFRA. While stating clearly that the business would not deny service to anyone, a daughter of the owners stated that, as Christians, they would not want to cater a gay wedding. The report relayed the response of the owner's daughter to a purely speculative question. No one had requested catering from this restaurant. Unstated was that if they *were* to decline catering a gay wedding, RFRA would merely give the courts a means of balancing the legal claims of Memories Pizza against any couple (gay or straight) that might—in a bizarro world—request that a strip-mall pizzeria cater their wedding. Immaterial was that the entire "story" was manufactured around an implausible hypothetical. The outpouring of fury and denunciation on the various websites connected to the restaurant was swift, relentless, vicious, and devastating.

Unstated was that this business operated in a decayed and impoverished town that had seen corporate America and both parties lay waste to its economic base. Corporate powers, in combination with the globalizing ideology in both parties, advanced economic policy that helped gut America's manufacturing heartland in favor of low-wage labor markets abroad, low-wage immigrant labor domestically, and automation. Progressives from around the country posted Yelp reviews of a marginal restaurant thousands of miles from their homes, describing its owners as "in-breds," and living in what another poster called "BFE, Indiana between WhoGivesASh!t and AintNobodyGahtTime4Dat."

An online mob called for the economic destruction of a family-owned strip-mall pizzeria for an incident that never occurred, and that might or might not have passed judicial test. More broadly, the combined weight of the nation's wealthiest and most powerful corporations was brought down upon the state of Indiana in response to a legitimate, democratically enacted piece of legislation that existed in many other states and the nation. In both cases, the power elite demonstrated that the "traditional values" of the working-class electorate were to be destroyed, whether they were expressed through legislation, a small business, or even a passing comment captured by a reporter or in a video. In each case, even to intimate support of the belief that had been operative in Christendom for almost two millennia, and additional millennia before Christianity—marriage is an estate of a man and woman—a family, a business, and even a politically sovereign state was threatened with destruction. The asymmetry of power was astonishing, yet the likes of Salesforce and *The New York Times* imposing the power claimed to be combatting the oppressors—oppressors such as the family who owned Memories Pizza.

The decision by corporate leaders to take a political stand over a controversial issue is therefore of great moment. Corporations and business leaders have historically sought to avoid political statements and announcements, recognizing that such declarations have the effect of unnecessarily alienating potential customers. Corporations live in constant fear of bad publicity that can ruin a brand carefully erected through millions of dollars of advertising and publicity. Why step into a heated political debate and unnecessarily turn half of your customers away?

Through this episode, and an expanding number like it, we witness the deepening alliance between the libertarian economism of classical liberalism and experimental social libertarianism of progressive liberalism—the wedding of John Locke and John Stuart Mill, as it were. A progressivist ideology that is increasingly manifest in the world's most wealthy and powerful economic actors is deeply aligned with, and seeks to promote, the individual expressivism of a managerial class that is defined by mobility, ethical flexibility, liberalism (whether economic or social), a consumerist mentality in which choice is paramount, and a "progressive" outlook in which rapid change and "creative destruction" are the only certainties. They successfully overturned a legislative act by a sovereign political entity, not by persuading its citizens, but by strong-arming its political leaders with the threat of economic devastation and heedless destruction of reputation. They succeeded in circumventing the democratic will of the citizens of Indiana in the name of "democracy." They did so to advance the vision of human good among the managerial class at the expense of, and intended destruction of, the "traditional values" of disadvantaged, poor, average citizens in an economically tenuous situation in the Midwestern town of Walkerton. They did so by claiming they were protecting the powerless while threatening destruction of those clinging to a precarious life on the periphery of modern American progress. Memories Pizza was condemned for even notional support of "traditional marriage"; Apple and Eli Lilly were praised for undoing a duly enacted piece of democratic legislation. A complete asymmetry of power existed between the progressive elite and those entities that supported "traditional values"—whether they were relatively weak states, like Indiana, or small, family-owned businesses, like Memories Pizza. The powerless were tagged *as the oppressors* by the likes of Apple, Amazon, Microsoft, and *The New York Times*.

Even as the power, wealth, and influence of those in the "party of progress" have penetrated every human institution, it has become paramount to eliminate every vestige of opposition. What had been presented as a "choice" at the early stages of progressivism—the choice to be free and a self-making individual—was now increasingly a requirement, one that was now *imposed* on the last resistance to this imperative. Corporations threw off their traditional avoidance of political stances in support of autonomy and self-making. This was especially the case at the front lines of the culture wars over human sexuality, with corporations lining up in favor of gay marriage, transsexual rights, and "reproductive health." Mill's efforts to *protect* "experiments in living" by limiting the "despotism of Custom" became a positive *requirement* to force all into expressivist beliefs by *eliminating* any vestige of self-limiting belief. All were now aligned against the "traditionalism" of the natural family.

This last stage of modernist and progressive revolution is especially visible today in the rise of "woke capitalism," combining the radical individualism, anti-culture, and revolutionary overthrow of traditional institutions in contemporary corporate political power exercised not only against religious believers, but even sovereign political actors. These powers operate as an unofficial political regime, shaping the horizon of contemporary humanity while marshaling its resources and power of shaping perception to demolish political opposition. Whereas an earlier generation of corporations such as Standard Oil and Carnegie Steel were at the forefront of extracting resources and conquering the natural world, today's corporations such as Apple, Netflix, and Facebook (or Meta) at once advance a disembodied experience of the world and each other, while supporting political causes whose ultimate outcome is the conquest of the last frontier of nature—the human body. What the extraction of fossil fuels offered to humanity, the liberation from place, from menial tasks, from our experience of the world in its diurnal and annual forms—is today advanced through the technologies of virtual reality, gnostic minds no longer needing the body for communication,

a constant stream of titillation and distraction. Their forthright commitment to causes of sexual liberation is a further extension of the de-
racination inaugurated by earlier technologies of progressivism. And,
like the confidence of those progressives of several centuries ago who
believed that no dire consequences would arise from the constant burn-
ing of fossil fuels, so too progressives today embrace and cheer the new
liberationist ethos—even lauding "the sunny side of greed"—as a morally pure route to progress and perfectibility.

We are witness to the emergence of a perverse combination of the
new and older forms of tyranny: neither the raw imposition of power of
few resulting in the misery of many, nor the soft despotism of a pater-
nalistic state that keeps its citizens in a state of permanent childishness,
but the forced imposition of radical expressivism upon the population
by the power elite. In a marriage of classical and progressive liberalism,
required indifference toward the views of others becomes mandatory
celebration of individual expressivism, the ultimate coalescence of anti-
cultural, revolutionary consumer choice as the default human philosophy. An unholy alliance of progressive state and libertarian market
today enforces the adoption of capitalist consumer choice over every
aspect of life; radical individualism and expressivism as the marker of
human liberation; and a constant revolutionary ethos that unsettles and
destabilizes prospects for order and stability, particularly among working classes.

Strikingly, the opposition to this new tyranny comes broadly from
the working class, especially those whose work tends to be tactile and
embodied—in contrast to the "laptop class"—and who tend not to view
the world as fungible launching pads, but, rather, one of inherited homes.
This clash is not between the two parties of liberalism, but between a
broad party of progress and a broad party of conservatism. The party
of progress—as the party defined by its commitment to a rule by enlightened elites against the threats posed by "the many"—today seeks
the outright political, cultural, economic, and social suppression of its

opposition. From the viewpoint of this nascent party of conservatism, the answer is not the elimination of the elite (as Marx once envisioned), but its replacement with a better set of elites. Most needful is an
alignment of the elite and the people, not the domination of one by the
other. To this end, what is needed is a renewal of an older and forgotten
but better form of conservatism, one that seeks the mutual betterment
of both the elite and the people.

PART II

COMMON-GOOD CONSERVATISM

3

A Good That Is Common

Conservatives enjoy few things more than to debate the nature of conservatism. Libertarians debate social conservatives; military hawks disagree with isolationists; right liberals argue intensely with postliberal critics of liberalism. A conclusion one might easily draw from these interminable debates is that conservatism is a chameleon, taking on the features of the surrounding society and political order. It appears to be nothing more than a label for an incessantly shifting position, one that gauges its positions in relationship to changes taking place in different times and places. Unlike liberalism—which, for all its manifold meanings, can point to a distinctive philosophy, particular philosophical architects, and enduring principles—conservatism is not infrequently described as more of a mood or a disposition.

Conservatism further appears to describe merely a relativist stance in relation to the nature and speed of existing currents. What is "conserved" will depend on contemporary challenges. Thus, while in the 1970s American conservatives sought to protect public forms of religious expression—such as prayer in school and the display of the Ten Commandments or nativity scenes in public buildings—today one is more likely to encounter self-described conservatives who defend "religious liberty," that is, the defense of relatively private forms of religious expression that should be free from state interference. Similarly, in pre-vious generations, "conservatism" might have meant strict patrolling of comportment and speech, including limits on blasphemy, obscenity, and pornography, while today many conservatives are ardent defend-ers of "free speech," taking as their main inspiration the arguments of arch-liberal philosopher John Stuart Mill.[1] What is being "conserved" will tend to depend on contemporary developments more than an en-during set of positions or commitments.

Thus, following the triumph of the United States and liberal de-mocracy over fascism in World War II and subsequent US opposition to the communism of the Soviet Union, the evolution of American con-servatism during the decades of the Cold War came to fashion a posi-tion relative to developments *within* liberalism. What came to be known as "conservative" were positions that were not aligned with progressive liberalism, socialism, or communism. Against socialism and commu-nism, American conservatism adopted the classical liberal view of property as a prepolitical, inviolable individual right; and against leftist "softness" toward communism and its criticisms of the Vietnam War, conservatism came to embrace more aggressive forms of anti-communist militarism often draped in the red-white-and-blue garb of garish patri-otism. Postwar American conservatism not only embraced liberalism; it developed a set of positions and a variety of institutions that pro-pounded the position that the United States was *originally*, and thus most truly and in essence a "classical" liberal nation. Conservatism could declare allegiance and patriotic fealty to America not as it existed then, or even as it might have existed in the past, but to a set of liberal ideas and principles that it claimed constituted the true animating philoso-phy of America.

This self-described "conservatism" in the United States was wed to American narratives of national exceptionalism, progress, and a mani-fest destiny that now took on global aspirations. Its basic philosophy often governed in the years of American-led globalization, whether the creation of globalized markets or the extension of American military, financial, and cultural power around the world. While conservative rule was occasionally interrupted by periods of governance by moderate progressive liberalism, its representatives—such as Bill Clinton and Barack Obama—shared basic core beliefs spanning the varieties of liberalism, and, above all, the aspiration of a humanity constantly progressing in liberty, prosperity, and happiness, whether variously pursued in economic, social, biological, therapeutic, or moral terms.

In fundamental respects, then, American conservatism—as a form of liberalism—was effectively a progressive philosophy that urged a slower pace of change in the social domain, often stating its commitment to various social conservative positions. Yet such a stance also entailed gradual modification as liberal norms advanced, exemplified in the abandonment of conservatism's onetime opposition to no-fault divorce, which ceased to be a central conservative tenet when, under the logic of liberal principles, the practice became widely accepted as a basic feature of a liberal regime. Today—with a sizable number of Republican politicians voting in favor of the legislative codification of the Supreme Court's decision to require all states to recognize marriage between two homosexuals—the goalposts again seem to have moved as a reflection not only of changed public opinion but also the underlying liberal basis of American conservatism.[2] Moreover, right liberalism's unwavering support for a free market, ideally unhindered by regulation and political limits, frequently resulted in economic disruptions and dizzying change that undermined the stability of the very social institutions that conservatives claimed to prize, including family, community, and religious institutions. Conservatism thus appears to be nothing other than a commitment to a slower rate of change—albeit largely in the social domain—while, at the same time, insisting upon conditions of accelerating change in the economic domain.

Such a conclusion—that "conservatism" is largely a variable label reflecting a relativist stance that cannot, in fact, lead to commitments

or efforts to conserve anything substantive—might incline anyone
with an interest in "conservation" to eschew the label. Moreover, its
political baggage today—associated with political figures such as Donald Trump, who repulses at least half of the population not only of the
United States, but the world—and its overall disreputable status in elite
circles would suggest that such a polarizing label should be abandoned
by anyone wishing to explore an alternative to liberalism.

Yet it remains, for better or worse, the best descriptor of a position
that, understood as a set of substantive commitments, is fundamentally
opposed to liberalism—including the "classical liberalism" that assumed
the label "conservative." While that usage may have permanently linked
the concept of "conservatism" with a variant of "liberalism," the growing recognition that such "liberal conservatism" does not in fact "conserve" very much opens a prospect for redefinition. The very label might
be repurposed in the effort to *reconstitute* the conservative elements of
the preliberal tradition—the "common-good" political tradition of the
West. This tradition, of course, did not describe itself as "conservative";
it was simply the tradition of the West itself. But it was, by definition,
"conservative" in the sense that it sought guidance from the past, both
philosophically, historically, as well as from the well of experience. This
tradition perpetuated itself through time and across generations, seeking to pass along wisdom of the past to the present and the future. It
encouraged human projects that transcended life spans, exemplified in
the great cathedrals of Europe. But above all, because this tradition was
antecedent to any ideological belief in the promise of *progress*—which
would become the hallmark of modern philosophy beginning with the
advent of liberalism—the label "conservative" reflects the original es-
chewal by the common-good tradition of a social order that uproots,
transforms, and destabilizes. Continuity, balance, order, and stability,
grounded in the unchanging truths knowable through human reason
and also present in the Christian inheritance of the West, were among
its constitutive political commitments.

Understood as a *contrast* to the modern liberal tradition as a whole—and not as one expression within it—we can begin to see clearly how the modern project pursues the same end: transformative progress. By means of a contrast to "common-good conservatism," it's possible to see clearly that even apparent differences of various modern, progressive traditions are bound together by fundamental agreement over the ends of political life: progress. What I seek to distinguish as "common-good conservatism" starkly highlights several consistently similar features of the three main progressive political traditions of modernity—classical liberalism, progressive liberalism, and Marxism.

If the end is consistent, these modern political strands embrace different paths to transformative progress. In this chapter, I explore how the three great progressive political traditions of the modern age—classical liberalism, progressive liberalism, and Marxism—at once differ but also overlap. Most fundamentally, each is opposed to the premodern common-good conservative tradition, even more than differences that they have in relation to one another. Thus, while uncoordinated, these progressive traditions have nevertheless in effect worked in combination to hold at bay the premodern expression of this common-good political tradition (including an implicit agreement to describe one of their number by the name "conservative").

Classical liberalism, progressive liberalism, and Marxism, all of which have been in various ways locked in contention with each other in the modern age, nevertheless all share the basic feature of advancing forms of transformative progress. They divide not over the *goal* of politics, but over the *means*, which has inescapably involved taking sides between "the many" or "the few." The liberal order begins with a preference for the "few" against the "many," since it holds that "the many" will prove the greatest obstacle to either economic or social progress (in the respective views of classical and progressive liberalism). Thus, the rise of the "power elite" is not an accidental "bug" of the ascendancy of a liberal order, but its inevitable feature. While Marxism arose in rejection of the liberal preference for "elite" rule, it retained liberalism's commitment to transformational—indeed, *revolutionary*—progress, which it believed to be primarily driven by the *people* against the *elite*. These three versions of modern progressivism *encouraged* the division of society—many against the few, elites against the people—that the classical tradition had sought to reconcile.

The fundamental similarity between these three progressive traditions is only genuinely visible from a standpoint outside of them—namely, a predecessor preprogressive tradition. I will conclude a discussion of these three "progressive" traditions by arguing that a genuine alternative is not to be found among these three dominant modern traditions, but outside them—in a renewed conservative common-good political tradition whose roots predate all these iterations of the modern progressive project.

The First Progressivism: Classical Liberalism

Modern thought rests on a core assumption: transformative progress is a key goal of human society. Humans can only realize their potential for individual happiness and collective satisfaction through the workings of progress—economic, social, or otherwise. According to all three progressive versions of modern political philosophy, *only one segment of the political order is oriented to advancing progress*—either the "few" or the "many," the elites or the populace—while the *other* element is suspect for its tendency to resist the changes wrought by progress.

Broadly speaking, the modern world split politically over the question of whether the *people* or the *elites* were likely to resist progress, either as forces of radicalism or conservatism. Depending on differing conclusions on this question, the different traditions divided over which segment of the political order ought to govern with the aim of advancing progress. Liberalism, of both varieties, is the political tradition that inaugurates the new framing—and answer—to the ancient problem of the relation between the classes. Liberalism becomes the dominant tradition, and practice, throughout the modern West through its apparently successful claim that "the people" pose an obstacle to progress and, therefore, that new institutions must either be devised, or old institutions reinvented, to restrain the baleful tendency of ordinary people to hold back hoped-for advances. Marxism disagreed with both variants of liberalism, holding the view that the progressive force in society was "the people," who must overturn the conservatism of the "few."

But to focus on liberalism's two variants, first it's essential to recognize that, in spite of its reputation, liberalism is not an egalitarian political philosophy. While we tend to think of liberalism as the regime that overturned ancient privileges, particularly the old aristocracy, it not only sought the elimination of the *ancien régime*, but the creation of a new governing class. As such, it was arguably born as fundamentally out of a decisive fear and even loathing toward "the many" who posed at least as great a threat as the old aristocracy, if not a challenge that would prove to be more permanent. In the eyes of early liberals, ordinary people bore as much hostility toward the new wealth and position of those leading a nascent capitalist system as many previously bore toward rulers of the *ancien régime*. Early liberals—concerned especially about the threat "the many" posed toward a regime that prized the prospect of unequal economic outcomes—would often appeal to the *theoretical* consent of the people in order to *limit* popular ability to limit individual rights. To this day, "classical liberalism"—which bears the strongest resemblance to the foundational liberalism of the early modern tradition—is especially suspicious of majoritarian democracy, with some of its most libertarian-minded thinkers consistently revisiting doubts about the governing abilities and apparent ignorance of ordinary people, with accompanying calls to restrain their participation in politics, whether institutionally or informally.[3] Thus, a hallmark of liberalism was its effort to inaugurate a new ruling elite and to develop strategies—institutional, cultural, and otherwise—to constrain "the many" who would likely not be as enamored of the consequences of unfettered economic liberty.

Liberalism was unified in its view that a new elite would and should be a force for advancement and progress in a modernizing world. Classical liberals believed in unleashing the energy and talent of gifted people—especially in economic affairs. John Locke, for instance, believed that society would benefit if governments protected the essential right of property, allowing for the differentiation between "the industrious and rational" from "covetousness" of "the quarrelsome and contentious." Locke observed an existing society in which the differentiation between the many and the few, aristocrats and peasants, failed to identify and reward "the industrious and rational."[4] By reordering society on the basis of talent and success, and thus adding value to the otherwise dormant value of the material stock of the world, Locke believed that a new and different elite might emerge. The protection of the rights of property became paramount, thereby promoting the differentiation of talent and inequality of property that Locke expected to develop.

The members of the new ruling class were to be elevated for their productivity and inventiveness. No longer was ownership of property to be conferred simply as a matter of inheritance; rather, property was to be dynamic, less a static anchor for family stability than substance whose value could be increased by creative and industrious development. The value lay less in the *property* than the intellect that sought to unlock its potential value—hence, why Locke supplied a radical new definition of property that extended not only to material objects, but to ownership of *self*. The liberal regime came into being not mainly to protect property rights—though that was an important political imperative—but to legitimatize the ruling principle that would encourage the formation and ascendancy of "the industrious and rational."

The cognitive basis of the new ruling class would eventually manifest itself in a set of distinct philosophical and political positions, a comprehensive worldview increasingly *required* as a basis of the social, political, and economic order. Primary was a belief in self-making, demanding a social order that allowed the greatest possible freedom—even liberation—from unchosen commitments. This imperative required a highly mobile social order, allowing "the industrious and rational" to pursue and realize their talents wherever they were most in demand and rewarded. Borders of all kinds would be challenged as arbitrary limitations upon the pursuit of one's preferences. Family duties and formation would increasingly be seen as a burden upon personal autonomy, rather than a core institution of civilization. Cultural constraints—whether upon individual or economic liberty—were to be largely eviscerated. Religion must necessarily recede as a domain of constraint (or "interdicts," to use Philip Rieff's formulation), instead becoming a form of personal belief and thereby losing any broadly social or political status as a governing authority that could impose "interdicts." The measure for success would be increasingly materialistic, shifting resources and attention away from formation through humanities and toward the control of the natural world through science and technology. A complete social, economic, educational, and political order would necessarily arise in conformity with the ruling claims of the new elite—a regime of, by, and for the industrious.

Classical liberalism thus sought to promote a new elite that would advance economic progress. Such progress would necessarily require a new, and potentially extensive, differentiation between the many and the few. Theories of property rights were developed to provide government support and sanction to this form of inequality, even as Locke (and later classical liberals) also hoped that "the many" could be persuaded that they would be materially better off in a dynamic economic order that increased the general stock, even if it resulted in an expansive

divide between the many and the few. Locke feared the people as a potentially "radical" force, particularly for the tendency of envy and resentment to undermine liberal rights of property. In the eyes of classical
liberals, this potential "radicalism" would actually have the effect of
undermining progress, leading instead to the decline of economic dynamism and prosperity. One need only read the novels of Ayn Rand for
an unsubtle set of portrayals of how the interventions of a politically
potent rabble could derail the efforts of a small minority of geniuses
whose ingenuity and inventiveness would increase the gains that can
be enjoyed by everyone, including ordinary people. A central aim of
classical liberalism thus became a project of insulating the economically successful few from the average and "querulous" many, especially
through constitutional constraints, economic incentives, as well as social and cultural arrangements that would tamp down the development
of a powerful class of "the many."

A helpful way of differentiating the various traditions being discussed is a classic four-part box that distinguishes four categories
separated along two axes. "Classical liberalism" is the first category, distinguished as a liberal philosophy that fears "the many" as
a potentially destabilizing, "revolutionary" force, and thus one that
seeks to devise ways to ensure the ascendancy of a political and
economic elite.

	PEOPLE AS REVOLUTIONARY	PEOPLE AS CONSERVATIVE
Favor Elite— **(Liberal)**	Classical Liberal (John Locke)	
Favor People— **(Nonliberal)**		

Today, this political philosophy goes by the name "conservative," but as its origins disclose, its aim was anything but the "conservation" of a settled political, social, and especially economic order. Instead, it sought to shape a political, social, and economic order that would be dynamic and ever changing, in which the experience of the world by one generation would be almost unrecognizable to the experience of a successor generation. Classical liberals typically laud the success of this so-called conservatism not in accordance with what has remained the same, but with the transformational effect it has had upon the world. A characteristic expression by a so-called conservative lauding the trans-formational aspect of modern economic progress can be found in a re-cent book by "Never Trumper" Jonah Goldberg. Goldberg celebrates the rise of what he calls "the Miracle," in which "nearly all of human prog-ress has taken place in the last three hundred years." Goldberg extols this period—marked primarily by a rapid increase in economic prosperity—as the result of "a revolutionary way of viewing the world," "a profound and unprecedented transformation," a "Lockean Revolution" in which "it was as if the great parade of humanity had started walking through a portal to a different world."[5] By a fluke of history, "classical liberals" claimed to be (and were consistently described as) "conservative," but—as these passages, and similar arguments by such liberals attest—what classical liberals hope to "conserve" is a revolutionary doctrine that aims at the constant transformation of all aspects of human social organization.

For decades in the United States, Goldberg has been considered one of the leading "conservative" intellectuals, even writing until recently for the premier conservative American journal, *National Review*. Yet, as the conservative movement he once claimed to champion has become less dominated by classical liberalism, he has increasingly shed his identifi-cation as a conservative, instead identifying with the label that was once cast as an aspersion upon political candidates such as Michael Dukakis—a *liberal*.[6] Many of the self-described "Never Trumpers"—

including the likes of William Kristol, Max Boot, and Goldberg—today openly acknowledge that their political philosophy is most fundamentally liberal, and that, whatever their antipathy to Trump the person, more fundamentally, they embrace the nonconservative principles of classical liberalism against what they view as a more economically "statist" and socially "authoritarian" set of social commitments. The label "conservative" is beginning to separate from classical liberalism inasmuch as the liberal tradition was never fundamentally about "conservation" of a stable order that sought continuity and balance between the concerns of the many and the few.

Still, the confusion persists. One need only open one of George Will's recent books—rather astonishingly titled *The Conservative Sensibility*—to encounter an argument on behalf of a progressive and transformative economic program that seeks to refute nearly every claim he made in an earlier work, *Statecraft as Soulcraft*. While the Will of 2019 argues that a maximally minimalist state will result in the "spontaneous order" that allows the unleashing of dizzying economic progress and change, it was the author of the 1983 book *Statecraft as Soulcraft* who argued that such a view was decidedly *not* conservative. Instead, the younger, more Burkean George Will of 1983 held that government needs to play a positive role in supporting the social institutions that a dynamic society consistently undermines, arguing that liberal American society draws down a "dwindling legacy of cultural capital" that cannot "regenerate spontaneously."[7]

Classical liberalism—beginning with Locke, advanced by some of the most prominent of America's Founding Fathers, instantiated in our Constitution, and today defended by libertarian liberals who are mistakenly called "conservative"—seeks, above all, a dynamic economic order in which the achievements of the few are maximally protected from the potential discontents of the many. Partly by calling itself "conservative" during its rise in the decades of the Cold War, it was able to appeal to a working class suspicious of the more explicit progressivism of the liberal left that sympathized with Marxism. All along, however, classical liberalism too was a progressive political philosophy that arose from a vision of a dynamic and transformative order that would generate even more titanic inequalities than the system it displaced. Its architects recognized that this philosophy would be unlikely to appeal in the long term to the "many," and, as a result, developed a theory of constitutionalism that would provide maximum protections to individual liberty and property rights at the expense of concerns for the common good. This philosophy, peculiarly described as "conservative" for a brief period at the end of the twentieth century, momentarily enjoyed the widespread support of working classes. Today that support has dissipated— a result, ironically, of classical liberalism's very success in advancing a globalized form of market liberalism that has proved to be unbearable, and no longer acceptable, to ordinary citizens who rejected it at the ballot box.

The Second Progressivism: Progressive Liberalism

Progressives—as their name suggests—believed that a truer and better liberalism could be advanced through setting society on a progressive course. Rather than locating the primary human motivation in self-interest and greed, progressives believed that a social spirit could introduce a national and ultimately global solidarity, allowing everyone to benefit from the economic, social, cultural, and moral fruits of transformative societies. In the United States, figures such as John Dewey, Herbert Croly, and Frederick Jackson Turner believed that the early liberalism of the Founding Fathers had reached its limit, bequeathing upon the nation a widening web of interaction and relationality that now required moving beyond the selfish individualism of Lockean liberalism. They called for a national spirit and widening solidarity to replace the

parochial identities that limited people's capacity to understand themselves as part of something larger. Rather than relying on individual
initiative for progress, they called for a national (and, later, international and global) project to advance the progress of human connectiv-
ity, morality, and an expansive understanding even of one's very sense
of self.

The greatest obstacle to this advance was *not* foremost the individualist beliefs of classical liberals—though progressives were often critical of their classical liberal forebears—but the parochialism of ordinary
people. For this reason, like their classical liberal forebears, progressive
liberals greatly feared and even loathed the people. Now, however, it
was not because they believed that "the many" were a *revolutionary*
force, but, rather, because they suspected that "the many" were a *conservative* damper who were likely to oppose the transformative ambitions
of progress as moral transformation. Unlike their classical liberal op-

The second category of "liberalism" shares with its forebear an embrace of a progressive project advanced by "elites" but differs inasmuch as it seeks the moral transformation of humanity. As such,
progressive liberalism views "the people" as a conservative rather
than revolutionary force, needing to be guided and even politically
dominated—often against its will—by a more visionary, if smaller,
revolutionary elite.

	PEOPLE AS REVOLUTIONARY	PEOPLE AS CONSERVATIVE
Favor Elite— (Liberal)	Classical Liberal (John Locke)	Progressive Liberal (John Stuart Mill)
Favor People— (Nonliberal)		

ponents, they did not see "the many" as a potentially radical and revolutionary threat against rights of property; rather, they saw "the many"
as traditionalists who constituted an obstacle to the realization of progress. While the two sides of the coin of liberalism disagreed on the
threat posed by "the many"—whether they were too radical or too
conservative—they agreed that ordinary people posed a threat to their
vision and ideal of progress.

The intellectual progenitor of progressive liberalism was John Stuart Mill, a figure often mistaken as a "classical liberal." In his influential book *On Liberty*, he acknowledged the achievement of his liberal
forebears (such as Locke) who had created constitutional liberties that
limited government and secured the rights of individuals. But this
achievement, he believed, was ultimately insufficient in failing to take
into account the threat to liberty that was posed by "the many." The
demos posed an even greater threat to liberty because ordinary people
were most likely to hold conservative and traditionalist views that would,
in a democracy, politically dominate through a "tyranny of the majority." Through the tyranny of numbers, the *demos* was enabled to attain
a form of social control through "the despotism of Custom." Mill's famous argument in favor of the "harm principle"—which disallows legal
as well as social limits on free expression, inquiry, and action, so long as
no one is harmed in their pursuit—was not made merely for the sake of
advancing liberty in itself, but in order to provide liberty to "individu-
ality" and nonconformists who were most likely to spur transformative
change. Mill famously justifies near-complete freedom of speech, opinion, and expression as an essential means of liberating a small number
of unique and nonconformist individuals from the bondage of custom
that tends to dominate the habits and thinking of most ordinary people. Only by subjecting all beliefs and opinions to ranging skepticism
and alternative viewpoints might blind adherence to tradition be discarded and society be set on a trajectory of progress.

Until liberty becomes sufficiently widespread, Mill argued, humans

exist otherwise in bondage to unexamined opinion. As a result, societies remain static and unchanging. While time passes in such societies,
they do not progress. "The greater part of the world has, properly
speaking, no history, because the despotism of Custom is complete."[8]
To participate in "history" means more than merely for time to move
and events to accumulate; rather, to be "historical" means that a certain
temporal trajectory must be achieved, namely, one of progress and improvement. Liberty is the necessary means to initiating the movement
of a progressive history.

Only a society led by a small minority of creative nonconformists
might lead not merely to material improvement—the main aim of classical liberalism—but moral and psychic improvement of humanity itself.
Mill hoped that progress would not be limited to measurable material
advances, but ultimately would be reflected in the moral improvement
of humanity itself:

> It is not by wearing down into uniformity all that is individual in
> themselves, but by cultivating it and calling it forth, within the
> limits imposed by the rights and interests of others, that human
> beings become a noble and beautiful object of contemplation;
> and as the works partake the character of those who do them, by
> the same process human life also becomes rich, diversified, and
> animating, furnishing more abundant aliment to high thoughts
> and elevating feelings, and strengthening the tie which binds ev-
> ery individual to the race, by making the race infinitely better
> worth belonging to.[9]

While Mill recognized that "the many" should be accorded political voice and representation, he sought to limit their influence—at
least so long as they constituted a potentially conservative obstacle to
progress. For nations such as England—already relatively liberal—Mill
proposed a system of "plural voting," in which people with more educa-

tion would be accorded a greater number of votes.[10] In this way, he believed, those more sympathetic to progress and transformative social change would repel any conservative leanings of the general population. Because of their fear of change and progress, Mill held that the "conservative party" was constituted by people who were, by definition, "stupid"—that is, unwilling and unable to initiate, accept, or understand the advantages of change and progress.[11] Mill's modern heirs are today just as likely to criticize such people for their propensity to "cling" to backward beliefs, making them a "basket of deplorables."

For those who lack even the benefit of living within a broadly liberal society, Mill believed more extreme measures were in order. In the opening pages of *On Liberty*, Mill points to the need for more advanced people—progressive people—to intervene in societies that have "no history." In societies that are entirely dominated by the "despotism of Custom," a form of enlightened rule from outside that society is necessary—a view that was fitting for a man who spent thirty-five years as an employee of the East India Company. In such situations, Mill wrote, "the early difficulties in the way of spontaneous progress are so great, that there is seldom any choice of means for overcoming them." The only choice to be made is to enforce their progress: "A ruler full of the spirit of improvement is warranted in the use of any expedients that will attain an end. . . . Despotism is a legitimate mode of government in dealing with barbarians, provided the end be their improvement, and the means justified by actually effecting that end."[12]

This "improvement" consisted especially in changing the conditions of those otherwise settled within the boundaries of traditional societies—in which the future could be expected to largely resemble the past and present—by forcing them into a "progressive" society in which change will become the norm. Indeed, Mill suggests, but for the external intervention of a suitably progressed society, such traditional cultures might never enter the flow of history. For Mill, this external, enforced change consisted especially through enforced labor, with participation in a dynamic economy the base condition for a progressive society. Thus, echoing his argument on behalf of slavery in *On Liberty*, he wrote in *Considerations on Representative Government* that

> uncivilized races, and the bravest and most energetic still more than the rest, are averse to continuous labor of an unexciting kind. . . . There needs a rare concurrence of circumstances, and for that reason often a vast length of time, to reconcile such a people to industry, unless they are for a while compelled to it. Hence even personal slavery, by giving a commencement to industrial life, and enforcing it as the exclusive occupation of the most numerous portion of the community, may accelerate the transition to a better freedom.[13]

Mill's arguments on behalf of slavery today hold little sway or attraction to progressive liberals, but his deep hostility to traditional society remains a powerful and even dominant viewpoint among progressives. So, too, his argument on behalf of strenuous exercise of state power to enforce progress if a population is recalcitrant—whether domestically or internationally. Today, the path to such enforcement eschews arguments in support of enslavement, but is rather pursued through elite-controlled avenues such as courts, administrative fiat, corporate pressure, manipulation and control of technology and "social media," and rarely, if occasionally, outright force. Internationally, progressivism is similarly advanced by a set of global elite actors such as economic agencies and NGOs, though at times outright invasion has been the ultimate recourse (especially by those who championed the military imposition of liberalism, sometimes called "neoconservatives"). While pursued often in the name of "human rights," the aim of transforming societies "without a history" into progressive populations or nations remains very much animated by J. S. Mill's abiding fear that "the people" represent the greatest obstacle to a liberty that ensures progress, and thus need at times—even often—to be "forced to be free."

Progressive liberalism was at once an apparent rejection but deeper fulfillment of the main aims of classical liberalism. On the one hand, its proponents rejected classical liberalism's anthropological individualism and its endorsement of economic inequality as a beneficial driver of progress and advance. On the other hand, it embraced classical liberalism's core belief that progress could be achieved by liberating people from the bonds of tradition, custom, and stability, but replaced the faith in material progress with a faith in moral transformation. However, because it viewed people as potential obstacles to progressive transformation, it required again the need for their ongoing consent while insulating the actual transformative work of governance to a cadre of enlightened experts. The experts were to be deployed to transmute untutored hayseeds into the gold of progress and advance—unless the people proved to be altogether unenlightened, in which case, enlightened progressives were simply to rule outright.

Progressivism of the People: Marxism

Against the liberals—classical and progressive alike—there arose a countervailing tradition that argued for the progressive potential of the people against the elites. Marxism is forthright in its hostility to the economic inegalitarianism of classical liberalism, and the two are adamant foes. In its commitment to economic equality, Marxism cleaves closer to, and has formed stronger alliances with, progressive liberalism, though it is impatient with its reformist tendencies, its acceptance of the basic frame of market economies, and its technocratic elitism. We can think today of the disdain of Bernie Sanders toward the likes of Hillary Clinton, or earlier, Karl Marx toward Eduard Bernstein.[14]

In *The Communist Manifesto*, Marx and Engels described how the dynamics of advancing capitalism were upending all the premodern traditional forms of society, transforming formerly religious, patriarchal, and traditional culture into a mere "cash nexus," dissolving all romantic and "idyllic" relations in the "icy water of egotistical calculation." The new conditions of instability and constant churning change—recommended both by classical and progressive liberals—had disrupted all previous relations and thrown people living in traditional societies into a condition of disarray and uncertainty.

> Constant revolutionizing of production, uninterrupted disturbance of all social conditions, everlasting uncertainty and agitation distinguish the bourgeois epoch from all earlier ones. All fixed, fast-frozen relations, with their train of ancient and venerable prejudices and opinions, are swept away, all new-formed ones become antiquated before they can ossify.[15]

Marx and Engels here echo similar lamentations found in an earlier form of conservatism, bemoaning the coarsening utilitarianism and materialism induced by capitalism across every sphere of life. But unlike conservatives, Marx and Engels saw these unstable conditions as forming the cradle of revolution, developing through an inexorable historical process the class consciousness of an awakened proletariat. A long-standing division between "many" and "few" was developing in a new and intensified form, with society "more and more splitting up into two great hostile camps . . . directly facing each other: Bourgeoisie and Proletariat."[16] Marx anticipated that the growing divide between these two eternal classes would lead finally to the full awakening of the latent power and radicalism of the working class. The proletariat would advance the revolution, overturning all previous relations, culminating in the final elimination of the class divide. "Of all the classes that stand face to face with the bourgeoisie today, the proletariat alone is a really revolutionary class."[17]

Marx and Marxism critiqued the supposed progress of capitalism, but in the name of a better progress: communism. Unlike liberalism—which sought to protect an elite from the people—Marx believed that the dawning "revolutionary" nature of the people would become the progressive force in history, leading eventually to dictatorship of the proletariat and finally the "end of history."

	PEOPLE AS REVOLUTIONARY	PEOPLE AS CONSERVATIVE
Favor Elite— (Liberal)	Classical Liberal (John Locke)	Progressive Liberal (John Stuart Mill)
Favor People— (Nonliberal)	Marxist (Karl Marx)	

In a sense, the proletariat does not exist until it has realized this class consciousness. The working poor would have experienced their conditions as individuals, as parts of an extended family, as members of a community, and with these others, lamented their condition; however, they did not recognize their condition *as a class*, and thus were unable to recognize the systemic reasons for their condition.[18] The advent of capitalism thrusts into their cognizance the reality of their situation; as soon as they come to recognize their condition as a *class*, their consciousness is altered: individuals are now most essentially members of this class, and this class is necessarily a revolutionary agent on the world stage. Thus, Marx concludes, "The working class is either revolutionary or it is nothing"; it is either a class that is by definition a progressive revolutionary force, or it has not achieved a distinct status *as a class* and cannot yet play its destined revolutionary role.[19]

Awakened to its own existence, the revolutionary character of the proletariat is not theorized or philosophized. It is not a consequence of elite theory, but concrete activity. Marx famously opined, "The philosophers have only *interpreted* the world in various ways; the point is to *change* it."[20] The "change agent" is the awakened proletariat.

Thus, Marx conceived of the proletariat—"the many"—as inaugurating *the* ultimate and inevitable progressive age in the world historical drama, the final actor who will push forward the revolutionary spirit necessary to overthrow the ever-present contradictions at the heart of human civilization. Whether the "people" would remain "revolutionary" after the revolution, however, is a ticklish question.

Marx was famously opaque about life after the revolution, but among his most revealing and intriguing descriptions was to imagine a world in which there is no longer a division between classes, but in which there arises the elimination of the division of labor itself: the final overcoming of alienation. A key component of liberalism is its institutionalization of divisions and subdivisions of labor, relentlessly differentiating tasks in pursuit of efficiency, expertise, and increase of production. Marx, along with many early conservatives, was deeply critical of the resulting alienation of humans from the fruits of their labor, from knowledge of how their work contributed to a common good, and from each other. Writing of a time after the revolution, Marx imagined that the successful overthrow of the bourgeoisie by the proletariat, and the ushering in of a society of genuine cooperation, sociability, and expansion of capacities, eliminating remaining division between individual and individual and between individual and society, and, ultimately, the division of labor itself.

> In communist society, however, where nobody has an exclusive area of activity and each can train himself in any branch he wishes, society regulates the general production, making it possible for me to do one thing today and another tomorrow, to hunt in the morning, fish in the afternoon, breed cattle in the

evening, criticize after dinner, just as I like, without ever becoming a hunter, a fisherman, a herdsman, or a critic.[21]

Marx intimated that the final elimination of the division between the classes will result in the elimination of the division within the human soul. No longer will humans be required to limit themselves to a profession, a hobby, a narrow pursuit necessary to make a living or even craft an identity.

Yet, in this same work Marx insisted that there would be no final resolution, that the proletariat would initiate a new form of revolution that is potentially unceasing. "Communism is for us not a stable state which is to be established, an *ideal* to which reality will have to adjust itself. We call communism the *real* movement which abolishes the present state of things. The conditions of this movement result from the premises now in existence."[22] If the proletariat's existence was premised upon its self-realization as the antipode of the bourgeoisie, then its ongoing existence rests upon what one might describe as a kind of "institutionalized revolution," what political theorist Bernard Yack has called "the longing for total revolution."[23] Far from envisioning an end station of communist utopia, the very logic of the working class's existence requires the relentless and unceasing effort to eradicate every last vestige of a predecessor order—whether bourgeois, aristocratic, religious, or medieval. The revolution must be unceasing:

> Proletarian revolution, like those of the nineteenth century, criticize themselves constantly, interrupt themselves continually in their own course, come back to the apparently accomplished in order to begin it afresh, deride with unmerciful thoroughness the inadequacies, weaknesses and paltriness of their first attempts, seem to throw down their adversary only in order that he may draw new strength from the earth and rise again from

the indefinite prodigiousness of their own aims, until a situation
has been created which makes all turning back impossible, and
the conditions themselves cry out: *Hic Rhodus, hic salta! Here is
the Rose, here dance!*[24]

Deeply embedded in Marx's thought was a tension, if not outright
contradiction, between the aspiration for a settled and orderly condition of human happiness once capitalism was finally and thoroughly
overthrown, and the embrace of a revolutionary mindset and agenda
necessary for its realization. Indeed, while Marx might have yearned
for the postlapsarian establishment of the conditions that were comparable to those in Eden, he also yearned for "total revolution": the complete erasure of much of what we understand to exist in the world as we
know it. He held forth (at least on occasion) a profoundly "conservative"
vision for the resolution of modern ills by appealing to a revolutionary
fervor among the working classes. Yet, he was ultimately ambivalent
about what would attract and motivate the working classes to this vision,
whether a stable and unchanging resolution, or ceaseless revolution.
This tension at the heart of Marx's thought revealed a deep incoherence
that became more apparent both in theory and in fact: against the
ravages and instabilities generated by capitalism, the working classes
yearned not for a condition of constant revolution for the sake of revolution. That was the situation into which modern capitalism had already thrust them. If they longed for revolution at all, it was to effect
the opposite of a revolutionary condition. If they could be persuaded
to adopt revolution as a means, it was as likely for more "conservative"
aims rather than the radicalism of "total revolution." And if the working
classes could not be even persuaded to adopt a revolutionary mindset,
then their reluctance must have lain most fundamentally within the
system that conspired to debase and subject them. False consciousness
among the proletariat about what they should really *want* and how they

should authentically *act* was the culprit, and Marx and his epigones increasingly despaired of the revolutionary potential of the working class, turning their hopes instead to the cultivation of a revolutionary elite that could guide and incite the people to embrace their world-historical role. Thus, progress required (yet again) the embrace of an elite class to take over the reins—even if temporarily. Marx, and Marxists after Marx, called for the cultivation of a revolutionary intellectual class.

Marx and Marxism's dedication to the revolutionary potential of the people was ultimately qualified by its fear—like that of progressive liberals—that the people are not, in fact, sufficiently revolutionary. Without ever abandoning the *theory* of the revolutionary potential and even inevitability of the working class's revolt, Marx and Marxists were forced to confront the frequent reality that the working classes either were disinterested in, or outright hostile to, an ongoing revolution. Rather than proposing rule by technocratic experts, however, Marxism sought to establish an elite—even if temporary—that would, in theory, either shape the working classes into a revolutionary movement or advance the revolution in their place and name.

Marx himself finally recognized that the working classes were not practically reliable as the revolutionary element that his theory supposed. Remarking on his disappointment in the revolutionary potential of the British working class—indeed, its stubborn conservatism—Marx concluded that any revolution to occur in England would require the machination not only of the elite within the Communist party (the "General Council"), but a movement that could later be *attributed* to the working classes, and thus afford a form of post hoc legitimacy to Marxist theory.

> The English have all the material requisites necessary for the social revolution. What they lack is the spirit of generalization and revolutionary ardor. It is only the General Council which

can supply this deficiency, which can thus accelerate the truly
revolutionary movement in this country and consequently everywhere. . . . As the General Council we can initiate measures
which later, in the public execution of their tasks, appear as spontaneous movements of the English working class.[25]

In a remarkable concession, Marx acknowledged that the material
conditions were in place for the predicted uprising of the working class.
According to Marxist theory, it would be such economic conditions
that would finally push the proletariat to recognize the *objective conditions* that positively required their revolutionary action. Yet, in spite of
the theoretical conclusions, Marx recognized that, in fact, the working
classes lacked "the spirit of generalization and revolutionary ardor."
The revolution would have to proceed without them, led by an elite
class of "professional revolutionaries,"[26] and the outcome of the successful social, political, and economic transformation could be later
attributed—or even blamed—upon the working classes. The people were
simply not good enough for the anticipated utopia—and would have to
be pressed into its service if they refused to follow the playbook.

The Modern Nonprogressive Alternative: Common-Good Conservatism

Now we can answer the question—might conservatism, understood
as an inheritance of a premodern tradition, be more than an empty,
relativistic label? Might it have as robust and defined a content as
liberalism? And might there be a form of "conservatism" that is not
merely a makeweight *within* liberalism, but a distinctive tradition in its
own right?

Modern politics, shaped deeply by philosophical assumptions about
progress and how the divide between "the few" and "the many" was best

negotiated, have given rise to these four main possibilities, depending on whether one favored the ascendancy of either the party of the people or the party of the elite, and whether one was within or outside the liberal tradition.

Of the four main divisions that mark modern politics, only conservatism is the category that eschewed the modern embrace of progress as a main purpose and goal for politics. Conservatism was born of a skepticism toward modern faith in the unwavering beneficence and advantages to be reaped by constant transformation and advance of society, and the attendant belief that any temporary costs—especially those borne by ordinary people—were justified in the name of eventual betterment. While other ideologies advanced politically as belief in progress became the dominant ideology of the Western world, conservatism played a small but vocal role as critic within these regimes. Today it is newly visible as a viable political alternative for three main reasons: first, the resounding failure of the parties of "progress," liberal and Marxist alike; second, following the downfall of Marxism, the growing

The final category marks a departure from the previous three—it is the only **nonprogressive** category, in which the elite are expected to work on behalf of the conservative preferences of the many. As such, "conservatism" represents the modern articulation of the ancient ideal of the "mixed constitution."

	PEOPLE AS REVOLUTIONARY	PEOPLE AS CONSERVATIVE
Favor Elite— (Liberal)	Classical Liberal (John Locke)	Progressive Liberal (John Stuart Mill)
Favor People— (Nonliberal)	Marxist (Karl Marx)	Conservative (Burke, Disraeli)

awareness of the irresponsible and damaging rule of elites in liberal societies; and third, a growing self-realization that a true conservatism rests not with allegiance to liberalism, but a non-Marxist assertion of the political power of "the many" in defense of the conservative aims of stability, communal norms, and solidarity afforded by and protected within nations.

Like Marxism, conservatism arose against the currents of modern political theory and practice that dislocated the condition of the working classes and ushered in a chasm between the working classes and the "bourgeoisie." While at first glance conservatism would seem to have little in common with Marxism, in fact, we can see clearly that they share a deep hostility to the arrangements of modern liberalism. As Marx scholar Andrew Collier has written, "It is thought that [Marx] is asking the same questions as liberals and giving different answers, whereas . . . it is closer to the truth to say that he is asking the same questions as conservatives and giving different answers."[27] Those questions would include: How can society best secure the advantages of "the many" against "the few"? How can we best overcome the alienating effects of modern liberal politics, society, and economics? What is the proper relationship between the working classes, the growing power of capital, and the intellectual elite? For Marx, the answer lies in the revolutionary potential of the working classes; for conservatives, it lies in their yearning for stability, tradition, and custom—in short, in their conservatism.

Recent political developments allow us again to recognize the outlines of this tradition in its contemporary form. Rather than intentionally and institutionally arranging a political order that pits "the many" against "the few" for the purpose of advancing the main aim of *progress*—whether economic, moral, or both—instead, it seeks their mutual cooperation with the end of defending *a good that is common*. This good partakes of insights and experiences of both "the many" and "the few," grounded both in the "common-sense" experience of ordinary people, as well as the more refined, even philosophic understandings that are more available to the "few" through a liberal arts education. This anti-progressive alternative—drawing implicitly on the wisdom of ancient theories of the "mixed constitution"—rejects both liberalism's commitment to progress advanced by the elite (whether classical or progressive), but also Marxism's identification with "the many" as a fundamentally *revolutionary* force. Rather, common-good conservatism aligns itself in the first instance with the "common sense" of ordinary people especially because they are the most instinctively *conservative* element in a social and political order. They seek stability, predictability, and order within the context of a system that is broadly fair—and, in particular, arrangements within which prospects of life success do not merely hinge on wealth, education, or status. A "common-good" order is arranged as a kind of "public utility," with its stabilizing norms and order making a flourishing life not only possible, but likely, to the broad base of a social pyramid. Social, political, and economic arrangements ordered to the "good that is common" will necessarily and inescapably have elites—whose responsibility is to give voice to the nature of the good itself, within the particular historical, geographic, and political context in which they find themselves—but they will be entrusted to be stewards and caretakers of the common good.

In recent years, a profound reassessment of conservatism has arisen not mainly from high-level debates among the intelligentsia, but due to a chorus of demands from working- and lower-class voters across the developed world. Described as "populism" or "nationalism" by its classical and progressive liberal opponents, the rejection of elite class commitments found in liberals of both stripes—such as libertarian free markets on the right, and sexual libertarianism on the left—has resulted in the practical political manifestation of a "new" conservatism. This "new" conservatism is, in nearly every respect, the opposite of certain core commitments of modern liberalism. It is pro worker, favoring policies that protect jobs and industries within nations, urging more controlled immigration policies, supporting private-sector unions, and calling upon the power of the state to secure social safety nets targeted at supporting middle-class security. It rejects the progressive commitment to "identity politics," in which the human essence is reflected in racial or sexual identities. It is socially conservative, preferring "traditional" marriage, rejecting the idea that gender is elastic, opposed to the sexualization rampant in modern culture and especially that aimed at young children. It is increasingly supportive of public encouragement and maintenance of the family, and in some countries, such as Hungary, has effected legislation to encourage and support marriage, family formation, publicly funded child support, and increasing birth rates. This conservatism is generally patriotic and supportive of distinct national identities and cultures, rejecting the ethos of cosmopolitanism. It rejects globalization both as an economic and cultural project. In its valorization of stability, continuity, cultural inheritance, and national heritage, it is a rejection of the broader modern commitment to a project of *progress* that seeks to displace, dismantle, and overcome all boundaries and limits to infinite choice and self-creation.

In fine, this "conservatism" is not a species *within* liberalism but opposes liberalism's main commitment of liberty understood above all as individual choice, which treats the political and social sphere as a marketplace, and an instinctive anti-traditionalism. It begins with the primacy of the family, community, and the human goods that can only be secured through efforts of the political community—and not with primacy of the individual. It has, predictably, met with ferocious opposition by today's liberals, both "classical" and "progressive." In the United States, it is associated with the historic American tradition of "populism," and has resulted in a new oppositional coalition comprised of progressive leftists and "neoconservatives"—that is, "Never Trumpers" who were all along classical liberals. At its core, this "new" conservatism represents a genuine alternative to the two branches of liberalism—classical and progressive—as well as Marxism's revolutionary commitments, rejecting the primacy of "progress" (variously defined, whether economic libertarianism or social revolution) as the main aim and purpose of modern politics. Instead, it stresses stability, generational continuity, and an economy and social conditions that support traditional ways of life over the primacy of "creative destruction" advanced by its more progressive alternatives.

This "new" conservatism is, in fact, quite old: it is a new manifestation of "original" conservatism, the conservatism that arose especially as a response first to Enlightenment liberalism, to the French Revolution, and to Marxism, in the eighteenth and nineteenth centuries. It has deep roots in the tradition of British conservatism, particularly as originally articulated by Edmund Burke and in later iterations, such as Benjamin Disraeli's "Tory Democracy" or one-nation conservatism, the "Tory socialist" tradition of English mutualism, the "Distributism" of G. K. Chesterton and Hilaire Belloc, and, today, "Red Tory" and Blue Labour philosophies and political programs. It has been articulated in the American tradition as well, particularly in a long line of "populist" political efforts that began with the opponents to the Constitution—the so-called anti-federalists—as well as in the populist movements of the nineteenth and twentieth centuries, and most recently has been powerfully resuscitated by the writings of the twentieth-century social historian Christopher Lasch. One of its features is that it defies easy political categorization along the left-right axis as defined by liberalism, and just as often can be seen as a "left" critique of capitalism as much as a "right" defense of a traditional, stable society of families, faith, and communities.

But its deeper origins lie in the classical and Christian tradition of the West—a common-good political order that aims to harmonize the various contentious elements of any human society. Its reappearance in modern times was given the label of "conservative," but its deepest origins lie in both the preliberal, as well as preconservative, thought of figures such as Aristotle, Polybius, and Aquinas.

A common-good conservatism—until recently, largely submerged by the appropriation of the label to describe right liberals, or "neoliberals"— combines the left's commitments to a more egalitarian and communal economic order with the right's support for social values that undergird strong and stable familial, communal, associational, and religious order. What modern liberalism—in both its right- and left-wing forms—tore asunder, a renewal of this older conservatism would put back together. Conservatism was initially born of a skepticism toward modern faith in the unwavering beneficence and advantages to be reaped by constant transformation and advance of society, and the attendant belief that any temporary costs—especially those borne by ordinary people—were justified in the name of their eventual betterment. While other ideologies advanced politically as belief in progress became the dominant ideology of the Western world, a common-good conservatism that drew on preliberal and preprogressive tradition played a small but vocal role as critic within these regimes. Today, with the declining fortunes of liberalism now evident to most observers, it is poised to assume a more dominant political role throughout the West.

The "contemporary" aspects of this more ancient tradition can be discerned in interconnected features that I will explore in the next two chapters:

- The Wisdom of the People
- Reviving the Mixed Constitution

Each focuses on securing the common good in all senses of the word "common"—ordinary, shared, and especially needed by average people. Each also seeks to secure the shared "good" for every human being—not simply a select elite—through the concrete expressions of human flourishing secured through the accumulation of human experience over time, consonant with the unchanging nature of the created order itself. Thus, each rests on and constitutes a wholesale rejection of both the progressivism and elitism of liberalism, and the revolutionary populism purportedly advanced by Marxism. Because this tradition has been submerged by the progressive commitments of modern times and obscured by the theft of the label "conservative" by classical liberals over the past half century, a recovery of this tradition—one that largely unconsciously undergirds the modern political realignment—is essential.

4

The Wisdom of the People

In the shadow of the pandemic, humanity has everywhere just lived through an intensely contemporary version of one of the most ancient debates in the West: Who is best capable of rule on behalf of the common good—a well-qualified few, or the general mass of the people? This debate can be as readily found not only in today's headlines, but in the yellowed pages of Plato's and Aristotle's political writings. Writing centuries before the birth of Dr. Anthony Fauci, Plato argued on behalf of rule by the knowledgeable few, whereas Aristotle was more cognizant of the collective wisdom of the many. Recognizable elements of this ancient debate have played out on recent reporting of the evening news, over kitchen tables, over beers and cocktails in bars (once reopened), and in the streets of cities around the globe. The increasingly contentious debates over the economic, social, and political constraints imposed during the COVID-19 pandemic at times led to new articulations of ancient arguments, with one side making the case for the preeminent role of *expertise* (and, thus, governance by a specially qualified few), and others making the case for the preeminent role of "common sense" (and, thus, deference to the accumulated experience of the many).

The outbreak of COVID occurred at the very moment in which there was already a growing division between those calling for deference to expertise, on the one hand, and on the other, a more "populist" resistance to governance by "elites." The reputation of expertise in the United States and across the Western world had been steadily declining due to a succession of crises and disastrous projects by the governing class, ranging from the financial crisis of 2008, the poorly executed occupation following the invasion of Iraq, the general failure to secure the end of war in Afghanistan and the debacle during the US withdrawal from Kabul, and elevated rates of inflation around the globe that have especially diminished the financial condition of the least affluent. At the same time, the results of the Brexit referendum, the election of Donald Trump, and widespread populist resistance to pandemic mandates led the educated strata in ruling institutions to adopt a dim view toward what they perceived as the disrespect toward expertise by, and even ignorance of, average citizens.

In recent years, the growing call to exhibit deference to experts has become a touchstone in our daily politics. Reflecting the mixed legacy of the progressive tradition, deference to expertise is not only a staple on the left, but a core position of anti-populist conservatives. One "Never Trumper," Tom Nichols, sounded an alarm in his 2017 book, *The Death of Expertise*, over the stubborn ignorance and even recalcitrance of people refusing to be governed by the evidence and scientific knowledge of experts. Nichols lamented the fact that mistrust of expertise, while endemic especially in egalitarian societies, had become worse in the developed world in recent years. "The issue [today] is not indifference to established knowledge; it's the emergence of a positive *hostility* to such knowledge. This is new in American culture, [according to Nichols], and it represents the aggressive replacement of expert views or established knowledge with the insistence that every opinion on any matter is as good as every other."[1] The mantra "follow the science" is one legacy of a tradition that urges deference to evidence and fact, requiring only scientific discovery, political application, and civic acceptance.

Lost entirely in this purported governance by "the science" is the yawning gap that always exists between discoverable facts—which, even by the annals of science, are always provisional, subject to further investigation and revision—and the necessity for complex, challenging, and debatable political responses that arise even from widely agreed-upon, largely settled facts. Perhaps the most obvious example in recent years was the intense variety of political responses to the COVID epidemic. The political debate in the United States, and increasingly around the globe, tended to divide *not* over the fact of the virus itself (though, here, as in any politically fraught climate, there were outliers either seeking attention or, drawn to data or theories at the fringe, seeking to stoke outrage), but rather, the crux of the debate centered on the appropriate political response. One side—more cautious, and believing in a high degree of human control over the course and impact of the virus—regularly declared, in defense of lockdowns, masking, and social distancing, that "the science" ought simply to be followed. The other side—more likely to feel the direct impact of the shutdowns, and less trustful of the leadership class as a whole—argued that masking, distancing, and shutdowns were excessive reactions, particularly given certain known facts about the virus's threat depending on age and co-morbidities. Both sides invoked a set of facts, all the while arriving at policy conclusions that reflected a deeper underlying set of political and personal commitments. The invocation simply to "follow the science" was, of course, a frequent refrain by one side of the debate on behalf of debatable political and social decisions—"values"—that, it was pretended, were indisputable. The appeal to expertise increasingly elides the distinction between the realms of empirical data and the kinds of prudential decisions that such empirical evidence always requires.

People today broadly intuit that deeper and more comprehensive political claims underlie calls to defer to a knowledgeable class (e.g., experts), on the one hand, and the common sense of the people, on the other. The fact that these positions today increasingly reflect commitments of progressive liberals—who generally favor expertise—and of conservatives, who align with more populist intuitions, is more than merely coincidental. The divergent claims about who should govern, and why, lies at the very heart of a long-standing and foundational political divide.

For the Experts

In his most famous work, *The Republic*, Plato established some of the oldest sets of claims for why rule of a knowledgeable elite should be preferred over the rule of the many. Socrates is portrayed as favoring the formation and ascent of a "philosopher-king" who would establish a truly just political order. This individual, or a small number of *aristoi*, would be a person or people of special ability, knowledge, and understanding who had successfully completed approximately fifty years of education in order to attain knowledge of the Good. According to Plato's Socrates, justice could only be realized when a small number of individuals, or one person, had attained genuine and comprehensive knowledge about all knowable matters that might pertain to political decisions. The role of the populace was mainly to assent to the rule of the wise, follow the laws, and carry out their commands. Plato appeared to be so skeptical that people could attain even this minimal level of cooperative understanding that he deemed it likely that if such a qualified and unique ruler were to appear in the midst of a populace, the people would denounce, persecute, and execute that individual. Plato intimates that it was exactly the profound ignorance, parochialism, and mistrust of philosophic wisdom that led them to accuse, try, and execute his teacher, Socrates.

Plato was conscious of the utopianism of the recommendations he

portrayed Socrates making, and duly portrayed him as somewhat em-
barrassed by a recommendation of rule by "philosopher-kings." The
watershed transformation that marks the transition of modernity from
the classical and Christian tradition was the loss of embarrassment
over such claims, indeed, the certainty that progress could be achieved
through the exertions of an enlightened class and the willingness to
promote a cult of expertise. One of the first portrayals of such an enlightened society extensively governed by scientific expertise is found
in the pages of Francis Bacon's unfinished utopian novel, *The New
Atlantis* (1626), in which the learned scientists of a scientific institute
called Salomon's House are dedicated to the pursuit of knowledge that
culminates in beneficial practical applications. According to one of the
wise governors of Salomon's House, "The end of our foundation is the
knowledge of causes, and secret motions of things; and the enlarging of
the bounds of human empire." In this utopian vision of complete human
mastery over the natural order, the scientists of Salomon's House act as
the "lanthorn of this kingdom," a lantern that enlightens and guides
the political ruler, especially through the application of scientific tech-
nique and mastery in almost every domain, including not only mastery
in the natural world, but over human biology itself.[2]

Liberalism is the preeminent political manifestation of this progressive belief, and throughout its history it has sought to preserve the
role of a knowledgeable class in advancing progress against the threat
posed by the backwardness of ordinary people. Liberalism was a political philosophy that posited the *theoretical* equality of humankind in
order to justify a new aristocracy, an arrangement in which one's status
was achieved not by birth, but achievement. While liberalism sought a
combination with popular rule—"liberal democracy"—a main exertion of liberalism's architects was to contain the *demos* through constitutional constraints and the arrangement of social institutions that
would allow a new elite to arise as the main governing force in society.

A key feature of liberalism—whether in its classical or progressive form—becomes its efforts to ensure the ascendancy of a progress-seeking ruling class against the inherent conservatism of ordinary people. The respective differences between classical and progressive liberalism lie not in this preference for a progressive elite, but rather the emphasis on the nature and engine of that progress, and the best means of attaining this ascendancy.

On one side, a libertarian strand of liberal thinking—often called "conservative"—has often been insistent and explicit in its mistrust of the governing capacities of ordinary people. Preferring a government that largely advanced policies securing economic and personal liberty, and therefore mistrustful of populist interferences in both domains, libertarian thinkers such as Jason Brennan of Georgetown University have issued frank broadsides against the disadvantages of widespread political participation by ordinary people. In his 2016 book *Against Democracy*, Brennan celebrated declining levels of political participation and low levels of voting, suggesting that "this decline in political engagement is a *good start*." Brennan echoes the arguments of a generation of classical liberals who interpret *lack* of political participation as powerful proof of "tacit consent," arguing that people act rationally and essentially consent to the status quo when they eschew political involvement. Brennan's argument aims to *increase* this implicit form of tacit consent of ordinary people by *decreasing* their practical engagement to effect changes in politics. Calling for the rise of an "epistocracy"—rule by the knowledgeable, or a class of scientists of politics—he expressed his hope that politics will come to "occupy only a small portion of the average person's attention. Ideally, most people would fill their days with painting, poetry, music, architecture, statuary, tapestry, and porcelain, or perhaps football, NASCAR, tractor pulls, celebrity gossip, and trips to Applebee's. Most people, ideally, would not worry about politics at all."[3] While all these activities are doubtless enjoyable to people who think them worthwhile, the commendation to think about anything *but* politics is consistent with the classical liberal tradition that prefers for average people to be rendered largely passive. A condition of relative political muteness can then be interpreted as tacit support for the classical liberal order and the libertarian and economically progressive commitments of an epistocratic ruling class.

Reflected in this high regard for the rule of knowledgeable experts as well as skepticism toward the political capacities and wisdom of ordinary people, a number of today's classical liberals resemble those they purportedly oppose—the progressives who established the institutional role for expertise in politics. At the turn of the twentieth century, the first progressives called for the creation of an administrative state that would benefit from the ascendancy of a scientific approach to politics. While some early progressives believed that the *demos* might someday be made worthy of political rule, others were forthright in calling for strict limitation of popular governance in favor of rule by a small cadre of experts. Progressivism was in significant part a response to the populism of the last decade of the nineteenth century, an effort to *incorporate* the views of a discontented public while at the same time *taming* its influence. While calling for more immediate ways to register the opinions of the people, progressives also universally insisted on the essential need for expertise in politics. Thus, accompanying calls for *more* democracy (often celebrated by today's heirs of the progressives) were concomitant calls for *less* popular influence over policy making. Progressives sought the professionalization of government and a new "science of administration," above all civil service reform with corresponding examinations of and reductions in the numbers of political appointees within. They were in the vanguard of the promotion of the social sciences—including especially political science—as the best and most objective means of determining and implementing rational and objectively sound public policy in preference to the passing whims of the electorate. Major figures in the discipline such as Woodrow Wilson sought to advance the scientific study of politics in the early years of the twentieth century, laying the groundwork for the rise of social scientific methodology as the necessary replacement of value-laden policy. Many figures during this period echoed the sentiments of Elton Mayo—an influential social scientist in the 1920s—who wrote, "A world over, we are greatly in need of an administrative elite." Armed with data gleaned from early studies by the social scientists, a bureaucratic elite was expected both to respond to public opinion *and* to lead and direct democratic masses to accept objectively good public policy.[4]

While Progressive Era social science was conceived originally as a mechanism for translating the "voice of the people" directly into policy—in which social scientists would merely study political facts and eschew values—before long the siren call of expertise began to predominate.[5] The same social science that was to merely *serve* democracy began to elicit findings that people themselves did not have adequate political knowledge even to set the direction of the polity. Many of these findings convinced a growing cadre of social scientists that the people were not sufficiently capable of even modest self-government. A growing chorus of social scientists called for the dismissal of irrational "democratic faith" in favor of the rule of the knowledgeable. Thus, over time, the envisioned "servant" role among social scientists, administrators, bureaucrats, and the apparatus of "expertise" increasingly grew to mistrust the viability of merely following or fulfilling the will of the people and instead began to assert the need for the experts not only to devise policy based on popular preference, but to guide and even replace recourse to the popular will.[6]

It was the hope of progressive technologists since the beginning of the progressive project that the traditional divisions of politics would be superseded by value-neutral application of scientific findings. "Follow the science" is merely the most recent refrain of an older dream that reaches all the way back to the fanciful imaginings of a philosopher-king proposed in *The Republic* of Plato; the serious hopes of a "new Atlantis" by Francis Bacon; and the proposals for a regime of experts, today represented in the social sciences, whose findings would guide policy better than an ill-informed and easily misled *demos*. It was a hope encapsulated in a statement by John F. Kennedy in 1962, who believed that the modern era spelled the end of turbulent political disagreement, to be replaced by uncontroversial technical solutions:

> Most of us are conditioned for many years to have a political viewpoint, Republican or Democrat—liberal, conservative, moderate. The fact of the matter is that most of the problems, or at least many of them, that we now face are technical problems, are administrative problems. They are very sophisticated judgments which do not lend themselves to the great sort of "passionate movements" which have stirred this country so often in the past. Now they deal with questions which are beyond the comprehension of most men."[7]

Embedded in this apparently uncontroversial claim by Kennedy—one shared before and since by many—is a deeper set of philosophical and political commitments that deserve attention. A social and political order that insists on decisions and governance by *experts* isn't itself just a neutral or value-free position, *but generates a social order that requires ever-increasing expertise*, and, as a result, necessarily sidelines ordinary judgment. The increase of knowledge as power, and a social, political, and economic order requiring constant expansion of such knowledge and power, necessarily becomes overwhelmingly complex and incomprehensible. The growing complexity of this project in turn requires that political rulers increasingly defer to the "experts." A society *based* upon the progress of scientific expertise necessarily diminishes the governing role of nonexperts.

No one made this clearer than the "democratic" thinker John Dewey, who praised Francis Bacon as "the great forerunner of the spirit of modern life" and "the real founder of modern thought."[8] Dewey maintained that a growing role of science in education wasn't just to understand an increasingly complex and changing society, but to *accelerate change*. Only a society that was constantly changing and transforming could achieve what he regarded as the only desirable ends of politics: *growth*. Dewey's imprint on the American educational system reflects his rejection of an older view that education should be primarily organized around the practice of *cultural transmission*, which he regarded as passive and rearguard. In his extensive educational writings, Dewey instead called for education more in tune with assumptions of modern science—progress and change. Dewey argued that such education was needed not only as a *response to* a rapidly changing society, but that such in education would, in turn, generate *more* and *more rapid* change. For Dewey, such change was the essence of *growth*. "The criterion of the value of school education is the extent in which it creates a desire for continued growth," Dewey wrote; growth "has no end beyond itself." The formative institutions of a social and political order in which expertise would come to predominate rest upon the purpose of continual and unceasing transformation: "the educational process is one of continual reorganizing, reconstructing, transforming."[9] A social order devoted to constant turbulence and change would assure that "common sense" inherited from long-standing practice and past experience would no longer be relevant. Instead, the guiding role of the expert would necessarily ascend as the essential ruling element in any society dedicated to constant upheaval.[10]

One of the intended consequences of a social order that would generate unceasing change and even a constant "state of emergency" is the strong tendency to transfer political decision-making from those best placed to exercise political wisdom in conditions of relative stability—the "wisdom of the people"—to those not only with the incentive to dismiss such wisdom in the interest of generating more upheaval, but also most likely to benefit from unsettled conditions and to gain political, social, and economic power as a result of constant transformation.

Today that division is manifest particularly in a conflict between those who retain the optimistic belief that politics is best left in the hands of an educated elite who are positioned to continue progressive advance for the nation and the globe, and those who experience that claim simultaneously as an expression of condescension as well as in the form of social and economic turbulence that exacts a dire set of costs. The ancient divide between "the many" and "the few" has been exacerbated and deepened by an underlying theory of progress and a belief that the few are ideally charged to advance progressive transformation. Thus, this modern vision of progress, advanced by a vanguard of technocrats who master the necessary knowledge and circumvent those who lack the "comprehension" necessary for governance, exacerbates an endemic divide in politics, continuously fraying the fabric of the political order without prospect of reconciling the parties.

For the People

By contrast, there is an equally potent if, today, less dominant tradition that argues for the superiority of "common sense," the everyday knowledge that is more likely to be discovered as a collective knowledge embedded in the lives and practices of ordinary people. Plato's most famous student, Aristotle, inaugurated a tradition that not only criticized the frequent hubris of experts, but—at least in some of his writings—elevated the role of "common sense" as one potential claimant for social and political rule. His argument is among the few to be found in antiquity that make a positive case for democracy, a regime that was often criticized by ancient philosophers as likely to be among the most unjust.

Aristotle acknowledged that there was a strong claim to be made on behalf of democracy—rule by the many. Aristotle recognized that there are certain arts and disciplines that clearly require expertise, among them medicine, engineering, and piloting. Indeed, only those who have mastered those disciplines should themselves select who is qualified to practice them—experts should both train and credential experts. While these claims are self-evident, and continue to be practiced today—it is still widely the case that only those possessing doctorates may confer that degree upon candidates they deem to be qualified—Aristotle offered a key addendum. "There are some [arts] concerning which the maker might not be the only or the best judge, but where those who do not possess the art also have some knowledge of its works. The maker of a house, for example, is not the only one to have some knowledge of it, but the one who uses it judges [it] better than he does." Aristotle distinguishes a series of "users" from the "experts"—"a pilot judges rudders better than a carpenter, and the diner, not the cook, is the better judge of a banquet."[11]

Aristotle observed that those who *use* what experts make or design, or whom expert decisions *affect*, are often more likely to be better judges of the benefits and shortcomings of those decisions, plans, or products than the experts themselves. The wisdom of the multitude arises in the main not because they can claim to possess the kinds of specialized knowledge of experts, but because they have the benefit of "common sense" and experience—everyday interaction with the objects or practices of the world that are so often lacking in the theoretical evaluations by experts. Any family that has owned a home for a time quickly comes to recognize the deficiencies of the one who planned the house, whether in placement of light switches and outlets, room sizes, or even the entire layout. In many instances, nonexpert users have greater comprehension of the effects of such plans than the knowledgeable expert. The very phrase "common sense" captures the essence of this distilled wisdom: a "sense," or kind of understanding, that is both *ordinary* and *shared*. Against the claims of the rule of experts is the wisdom that arises from the experience of ordinary people in everyday life.

Plato and Aristotle thus articulated in their earliest forms some foundational differences between the two relative approaches to political knowledge that, in turn, point to three main areas in which claims to political deference to "common sense" derive their force:

First, "common sense" draws on a vast reservoir of traditional knowledge, the collective memory of ordinary people from the lessons drawn from daily life. As originally articulated by early conservatives such as Edmund Burke, a traditional society appears ignorant in the eyes of "experts," but in fact is constituted by a deep well of experience and common-sense wisdom.

Second, such knowledge resists the narrowness of specialization, instead drawing connections between the various phenomena of the world that more closely approximate the kind of wisdom and prudence necessary for just political rule. "Common sense" is more comprehensive than the narrowness of expert knowledge, and thus more relevant and illuminating as a form of *political* knowledge.

Lastly, the social and political conditions that benefit the role of "common sense" are distinct and even opposite to the conditions and aims that privilege the role of expertise. If expertise is especially prized in societies that seek and promote *progress*, change, transformation, and "growth," the role of "common sense" is especially valued and necessary in societies that are stable and in which continuity between generations is prevalent. In such societies, older generations pass down the wisdom of experience to the young, whereas, in progressive societies, any knowledge of the elderly is quickly superseded and they are rendered irrelevant. Thus, these respective forms of social and political understanding are not "neutral," but rather, both *contribute to*, and their relative statuses *result from*, the very nature of the social and political order.

Traditional Knowledge

In the early modern period, it was Edmund Burke who argued against the progenitors of modern progressivism on behalf of the invaluable

treasury of knowledge, experience, and wisdom, in the form of institutionalized common sense. Burke's conservatism was based on a confidence in the wisdom of ordinary people built up over time in the
practices, institutions, and traditions that gained favor due to experience over time and in place. He praised "prejudice" as an unintentional
collection of largely unexamined belief in the tried and true, putting
him in distinct contrast with later arguments made by John Stuart Mill,
who regarded custom as a form of despotism of the past over the present and potential future innovation. By contrast, Burke praised his
countrymen's "sullen resistance to innovation":

> Instead of casting away all our old prejudices, we cherish them
> to a very considerable degree, and, to take more shame to our-
> selves, we cherish them because they are prejudices; and the lon-
> ger they have lasted and the more generally they have prevailed,
> the more we cherish them. We are afraid to put men to live and
> trade each on his own private stock of reason, because we sus-
> pect that this stock in each man is small, and that the individu-
> als would do better to avail themselves of the general bank and
> capital of nations and of ages.[12]

The "general bank" of a nation was the total sum of the practical
and experiential capital of a people over time. This was the storehouse
of value that was increasingly maligned and discarded by the innovators.

In contrast to progressives of all stripes, Burke viewed efforts to
innovate and transform society not as a boon and benefit to the ordinary working person, but as a burden and punishment too often borne
by the people in whose name such changes were wrought. Those inspired by the "spirit of innovation" exhibit a "selfish temper and con-
fined views."[13] Discontent with what is inherited in hopes of an untried
and perfected future, they exhibit impatience and imprudence in a
willful destruction of the basic decencies that make life of ordinary

people stable, predictable, and livable. Invoking the language of "rights of the people," such innovators are instead more often the beneficiaries of their destructive course, "almost always sophistically confounded with their power."[14] Burke was suspicious of revolutionaries and reformers who claimed that the transformation of society was undertaken in the name of "the people." Such innovators "despise experience as the wisdom of unlettered men."[15] Listening closely to their claims, he often heard contempt toward the settled folkways of ordinary people. Such "democratists . . . , when they are not on their guard, treat the humbler part of the community with the greatest contempt, whilst, at the same time, they pretend to make them the depositories of all power."[16]

A healthy polity rests on foundations of widespread moral virtue developed through informal social institutions such as family, community, and church, as well as the formal legal establishment of a well-constructed government that erects "sufficient restraint upon their passions." The true "rights" of citizens are not reducible to individual rights but must foremost consist in the right to be well governed, a right that rests on an intergenerational capacity to develop virtues. The flourishing of individuals thus requires associational rights—rights not merely as liberties to do as one wishes, but rights to governance that restrains and directs damaging acts of freedom.[17] For this reason, Burke argued that the only legitimate and viable "social contract" was multigenerational: "Society is indeed a contract," he wrote, but a partnership "between those who are living, those who are dead, and those who are to be born."[18] A society oriented toward constant upheaval, innovation, and improvement is more than likely to dismantle the place and status of the elderly, to neglect children, to live riotously in the present while denigrating the past and robbing the future.

For an older generation to pass along hard-won knowledge to a subsequent generation, the social conditions must be largely stable and changing only slowly, with ongoing popular "consent." The past cannot inform the present, nor the present the future, if developments in every subsequent measure of time make the previous moment antiquated. In revolutionary times, it is the youngest in that household or society who are the most knowledgeable, since they are most attuned to the changed conditions of their time. The extent to which modern people in liberal orders are far more likely to be attuned to "youth culture" rather than "the wisdom of the past" reflects nothing more than the fact that we live in revolutionary times—indeed, a revolution whose only permanent feature is its constancy. Such a condition was feared by Burke, who believed such generations were less "liberated" than they were deprived of an inheritance. Having all the wisdom of mayflies, the young not only receive little from the past, but in turn understand that they will have little to pass on as they age. The result is a civilization that lives for the moment—one likely to consume and play "while the sun shines" and store up neither cultural nor financial treasure for the future. If several of the hallmarks of our contemporary civilization are societies of self-described "consumers" who own little, master few if any disciplines, accrue debt, and both inherit nothing and produce no legacy (not even in the form of a next generation), we should hardly be surprised that a society of mayflies should indeed be one that lives but for, and until, the end of the day.

Integrating Knowledge

The great shortcoming of expert knowledge derives precisely from its apparent strength: the specialization required to attain expert knowledge also requires donning blinkers about the wider implications and consequences of its applications.[19] The organizing principle not just of the modern economy, but modern society more generally, is the division and subdivision of labor, producing innumerable unbridgeable archipelagos of specialized expertise. Modern societies are organized around the *principle* of division of labor, prizing efficiency, concentration of focus, and expertise.

Expertise thus rests on *dis*integration. Problems, disciplines, and areas of inquiry are parceled out for concentrated focus by people who acquire specialized knowledge. On the one hand, this organization results in major advances of knowledge especially in technical areas across the natural sciences, including medicine, biology, chemistry, and physics. On the other hand, specialization leads to oft-observed decline in integrated understanding—not merely "interdisciplinary" approaches, but genuinely comprehensive understanding that comes from membership in a wider community of discussion and exchange. Such an approach "advances knowledge" in discrete areas, but overall, both individuals and the system as a whole become more blinkered, even, arguably, more ignorant. The image of the "absent-minded professor" is a play on this underlying truth, the specialist whose narrow focus distracts him from the basic ability to function in daily life. Such a focus often results in the loss of "common sense."

The commonplace figure of the "absent-minded professor" at once captures the comedic narrowness of the individual expert while obscuring its larger social dimension. Rather, writ large, a social and political order as a whole will tend in a distinct direction, depending on the relative emphasis upon expertise vs. "common sense." It's not merely that a few Jerry Lewis–esque nutty professors will be in our midst; rather, the whole of our shared existence will be shaped in deep and imperceptible ways by the dominance of one or the other approach to knowledge and human understanding.

There is perhaps no better and more concrete example of how these priorities will be reflected in our institutional and social reality than the changes that have taken place to the institutions most responsible for stewardship of knowledge in our world: colleges and universities. Universities today are driven above all by "knowledge creation," urging faculty through incentives of hiring, tenure, and promotion to "advance new knowledge" through the production of original work, based upon the experimental model of the natural sciences. Faculty are trained to become specialists within a structure that constantly encourages greater focus and concentration, a system in which the subdivision of labor dominates. Many faculty in the same departments are not able to understand each other's work—much less that produced in different departments and schools—and faculty come to have more in common, and communicate more about their work, with faculty working in similar areas at *other* academic institutions around the world, and have far less in common with the people whose offices might be across the hall. The metaphor of "silos" is often used to compare the situation of faculty working within the same institution, a collection of isolated researchers whose only shared commonality, according to one legendary half jest, is a universal complaint about campus parking.[20]

The frequently invoked word "colleague" to describe one's fellow faculty is a vestige of a different worldview. To be a colleague refers to shared participation in a collegium, a word meaning "community, society, guild," or "partners in office," and the root of the word "college." A "college" was understood to be a "community" or "society" of colleagues whose common purpose was the search for knowledge and truth. Because each person's particular area of research and teaching was necessarily limited, an emphasis in such institutions was placed on cultivating community among colleagues—as one still can visibly observe in the "high tables" at the various colleges of Oxford and Cambridge (and portrayed as well in the depictions of the various houses at Hogwarts). Knowledge was to be pursued not merely through a focus and concentration on one's specialization, but through the ability to communicate and share one's particular area of knowledge in combination with others. This activity rested on the fostering of an active community of scholars whose primary interaction was with colleagues across many different fields and disciplines, and not the geographically scattered fellow specialists.

Thus, writ large, a "collegium" models a different kind of society. Faculty have their various specializations—as all humans are attracted diversely to different kinds of work and hobbies—but in addition to the work required to master their area of expertise, a primary job within their community is *developing the ability to understand how one's own work and knowledge fits with the work and knowledge of others*. For this reason, the original "college" was also understood to be a concrete community in which knowledge was achieved neither through individual efforts, nor a generalized societal knowledge achieved through the "invisible hand" of specialization, but a conscious effort to cultivate the connections between various approaches to understanding. Its aim was to produce not just piecemeal knowledge, but the cultivation of more pervasive virtues of wisdom and good judgment that were to inform all members of the community—faculty and students alike, those who would make their home in the collegium as well as those who would go on to become leaders and stewards within society at large.

Thus, basic assumptions about the nature of knowledge shape an entire social and political order. As modeled by the modern research university, the advance of knowledge is undertaken as a project of the *whole*—the *universitas*—in which the individuals will all be extensively ignorant about the work and activities of their neighbors. Researchers will have expertise about their own particular area of knowledge, but will be utterly stunted when it comes not only to the connections of their area of expertise to other areas, but the implications of their own work to the broader educational, social, and political order as a whole. The result is the *fragmentation* of knowledge and its divorce from the ability to put various ideas and findings together—to achieve an integration of knowledge. Modern researchers are a version of "idiot savants": people with highly specialized knowledge but utterly devoid of any ability to combine their expertise with the understandings of those in their midst. If, according to the formula often attributed to Francis Bacon, "knowledge is power," then we are simultaneously more powerful *and* more stunted. As such, we are supremely dangerous creatures, possessing tools of mastery, but accompanied by relatively little wisdom for their employment. The accumulation of failures and debacles by a nation led by various experts—in economics, war, responses to disease, and deeply divided politics—are largely not in spite of an order based around the ascendancy of expertise, but because of the inevitable consequences of combining specialized knowledge and widespread ignorance arising from *dis*integration.

The great prophet of division of labor—Adam Smith—recognized this baleful fact. Smith noted that the worker on the assembly line would know a great deal about the limited task to which he had been assigned, but would likely know little about the actual product, much less its greater purpose, nor its sources or likely destination. The assembly-line worker would need to be purposefully limited in understanding, knowledge, and even curiosity.[21] This form of "separation" would tutor the citizenry in a societal diminution of horizons, and how to grow accustomed to a fractured and fracturing order. Ironically, while Smith believed this degraded condition would apply to the assembler of pins, increasingly we are all effectively assembly-line workers in the modern liberal order.

In such a way, the social organization itself "teaches" us without requiring explicit instruction. Over time, we learn to internalize our stunted condition as an unquestionable norm. By point of contrast, when Henry Ford began hiring for his assembly line in 1913, the company found it had to hire 963 workers for every 100 positions that needed filling, "so great was labor's distaste for the new machine system."[22] People who had once worked on a product from start to finish—often farmers or craftsmen from a preindustrial era—were ill fit for the narrowed comprehension of the assembly-line worker. One might say that the long process of discarding those people indisposed to assembly-line work acted in a kind of Darwinian fashion, sifting those capable of limiting their comprehension and curiosity about the nature of their work from those whose minds yearned to know and understand the deeper connections of their activities and the fruits of their work. Rapid acclimation to a new form of "division of labor" rewarded those who were capable of compartmentalizing their labor to ever more minute operations, while shutting down the natural human desire to see a project through from start to finish, and the desire to understand the connections of one's work and passions with that of one's fellows.

Extending these costs into the social and political realm, we can begin to see the attendant problems with applying "division of labor" to the citizenry at large. If the same "Darwinian" logic applies, the successful political order in liberal democracy necessarily shrinks the capacity of individuals to think and act as citizens. The learned capacity for civic concern shrivels, like that more capacious understanding that might have inspired a preindustrial worker to better understand the nature and object of his work. Smith recognized that economic progress would require the stunting of the reflective capacities of workers, and the same would be expected to occur in our civic lives—that sphere that relies upon a more capacious understanding of the common good, a willingness to work and even sacrifice on its behalf, and a learned ability to make connections between the good of individuals and the good of the social order as a whole. Smith admitted that such stunting was an inescapable cost of a prosperous economy—yet one he thought a society should bear, even though it would fall hardest on the reflective capacities of ordinary people.

A social and political order organized around the *dis*integration of understanding that a progressive society requires is destined for the consequences of such imposed ignorance. Few authors have better articulated those costs than the farmer and agrarian author Wendell Berry. Berry has been insistent that a society premised upon the centrality of specialization will, by definition, exclude any "specialist" who is capable of discerning the costs of specialization. Only a "coherent community" can attain such breadth of vision. As Berry has written,

> We seem to have been living for a long time on the assumption that we can safely deal with parts, leaving the whole to take care of itself. But now the news from everywhere is that we have to begin gathering up the scattered pieces, figuring out where they belong, and putting them back together. For the parts can be reconciled to one another only within the pattern of the whole thing to which they belong. The local businesspeople, farmers, foresters, conservationists, investors, bankers, and builders are not going to get along on the basis of economic determinism. The ground of their reconciliation will have to be larger than the ground of their divisions. It will have to promise life, satisfaction, and hope to them all.[23]

Stability and Virtue

A woefully neglected element in the current debate that pits claims of rule by "experts" against appeals to the "people" is the recognition that recourse to the "wisdom of the people" operates best and most authoritatively in conditions of relative stability and continuity. The appeal to "experts" and insistence that citizens "follow the science" is itself not only a *consequence* of the kinds of progress that render a society unstable and constantly undergoing the churning of new social, economic, and technological challenges, but one of the very *causes* of the accelerating change, and thus, the growing need for recourse to experts. A political and social order led by the progressive ethos of expertise will

inevitably reinforce transformative conditions that require more expertise. Controversies arising from transformative new conditions such as
climate change or a new disease such as COVID-19 make it particularly
challenging to make appeals to settled wisdom of the *demos*. Yet rather
than such challenges occurring as exceptions to the rule, in a progressive society, the default "ignorance" of the masses becomes the rule and
the norm.

We can valuably understand how the seemingly neutral appeal to
"expertise" in fact masks deeper assumptions that will shape the social order as a whole, again by recourse to the example of universities.
Today, the priority of expertise over collegium is ultimately reflected in
the very nature of the society in which it will in part arise, and which it
will in part itself shape. The modern research university is understood
to be one of the primary drivers of *progress*, advancing breakthroughs
of knowledge that increase human mastery over the nature world;
achieving constant new discoveries about humanity's mind, body, and
psyche; and accumulating ever greater stores of data that can be plumbed
for insights about social, political, and economic phenomena. By contrast, the "college" system focused instead on the transmission of knowledge from one generation to the next, with a particular emphasis upon
learning anew the ancient lessons of human limits, the importance of
stability and order for the continuity of a civilization, and the achievement of genuine human freedom within a world of constraints—that is,
a "liberal education."

Thus, universities are among the primary places where a pervasive
commitment to *progress* means that existing social institutions must
also be constantly upended, transformed, changed, and altered in line
with the fundamental aim of progress. The aims of scientific progress
are echoed and amplified by the main commitments in today's faculties
in humanities and the social sciences, from which many of today's most
revolutionary and "progressive" projects arise: gender ideology, "critical
race theory" including the 1619 Project and the wholesale repudiation

of the entirety of the American and Western tradition, and radical efforts to institute "equity." Institutions formed around the priority of
"expertise" are not inherently "neutral," but assume, as well as advance,
a social and political order in which change and transformation are a
main aim and purpose.

By contrast, the social and political order both *presumed by* and
supportive of the kind of community to which a collegium aspires is one
of stability, continuity, and tradition. The work of faculty includes passing on a tradition of knowledge to students, with the expectation that a
deeper lesson imbibed within such a community is gratitude for an inheritance, and the cultivation of obligation to leave as much if not more
for future generations. The primacy and beauty of many of the most
prominent college buildings such as the campus library and the chapel
reflect this original purpose of a collegium: the transmission of hard-
won knowledge from one generation to the next, a practice of utmost
seriousness meant to inspire awe and admiration. While today's campuses often still retain the remnants of the architecture of the collegium,
more often than not even these older buildings today house undertak-
ings inspired by a wholly opposite animating philosophy, and are almost always today overshadowed by the grotesque buildings that, we
are told, reflect progress and the abandonment of the backwardness of
the past.

In miniature, the two institutions might look the same to the visitor, and today, prospective students are inevitably led through the oldest parts of campus where the most beautiful buildings are meant to
inspire and impress. Yet, the two institutions in fact inevitably reflect
fundamentally different commitments and philosophies—a fact that is
rarely discussed on a college campus, much less the broader society. A
political and social order governed by the primacy of *expertise* is not
neutral: it will shape the deepest priorities, and thus the nature, of the
entire society.

A society premised on continuity, on the one hand, and revolutionary transformation, on the other, will necessarily prize and seek to cultivate a certain set of attributes in the citizenry. The latter will advantage a relatively small number of "progressives"—Mill's nonconformists, entrepreneurs, "Anywheres." A social order premised on tradition and continuity looks instead to fortify the average and "ordinary," especially to accentuate the more "homely" virtues that arise from, and are useful to, the daily rhythms of a predictable world.

Concern for such "ordinary virtue" lies at the heart of the original critics of the progressive liberalism of America's Founding Fathers. Fearing that the Constitution would, over time, give preeminence to a small elite who would accrue power at the expense of ordinary people, the Constitution's original critics—the so-called anti-federalists—argued for the close connection between a social, political, and economic order that valorized the wisdom of ordinary people, temperance in economic and martial pursuits, and the modesty of the republic as a whole. That is, only a nation that was more fundamentally governed by, and treasured, the "wisdom of the people" would be likely to be a virtuous republic rather than an ambitious and ultimately despotic empire, both internally and internationally.

In contrast to the Framers, whose system sought to encourage the great and ambitious to hold public office, and which promoted the superiority of good administration to local rule, the anti-federalists insisted upon the superiority of the common sense embedded in and derived from the variety of places throughout the confederation. A more local and modest scale would not only serve as the cradle of an education of virtue, but would offer only modest means that would, in turn, tame the temptation toward self-aggrandizement and overweening ambition.

> Those in middling circumstances have less temptation—they are inclined by habit and the company with whom they associate, to set bounds to their passions and appetites—*if this is not*

sufficient, the want of means to gratify them will be a restraint—
they are obliged to employ their time in their respective callings—
hence the substantial yeomanry of the country are more tem-
perate, of better morals and less ambition than the great.[24]

Such ordinary virtues, Melancton Smith insisted, do not require
extraordinary efforts. Rather, they arise organically from the modest
conditions of a stable and orderly society. Responsibility, frugality,
moderation, and good habits are not necessarily the stuff of epic poems,
but they are the virtues most accessible to, and of advantage for, the
mass of ordinary people. Embedded in the debate between those who
favor the "experts" vs. "common sense," the contesting claims reflect
differing visions of the nature of the social and political order, and the
kinds of people it expects to produce. One, characteristically, favors
"the few"; the other, "the many."

A social and political order that gives preference to "the wisdom of
the many" does not eliminate the need for expertise—within its proper
boundaries—or more broadly for an "elite." Such a social and political
order positively requires that those best positioned to support a stable
social and political order, and the virtues of the *demos*, are enjoined to
lend their energies to this main purpose. A virtuous people can only be
maintained through the energies and efforts of a virtuous elite, and
a virtuous elite must be oriented to supporting the basic decencies
of ordinary people. These sentiments, and this older system, took their
inspiration—even if implicitly—from a long-standing tradition in the
West: the ideal of the "mixed constitution," to which we now turn.

5

The Mixed Constitution

In a conservative order, culture largely arises from "the bottom up," the generational inheritance of learned practices born of local circumstances, accumulated experience, form, and ritual that are most richly expressed at the intersection of human nature and our natural inclination to develop conventions to mark and celebrate human rites of passage, the rhythms of nature, and reverence for the divine. Culture is a concrete form of "the wisdom of the people," the ongoing and living treasury that is at once authoritative yet profoundly egalitarian and democratic. Yet, even as the authority of a conservative order rests in a deference to "the many," a vital and essential role is played by elites who are charged particularly as the trustees, defenders, and protectors of culture, tradition, and of a long-standing way of life.

This key insight—that an elite can and should be a defender of the cultural traditions that are mostly a development of bottom-up practices—points to how democracy and a proper aristocracy are not contradictory, but, in fact, ought to be mutually supportive and beneficial. This key insight was well understood by classical thinkers, ranging from Aristotle to Polybius, from Aquinas to Machiavelli, from John Adams to Alexis de Tocqueville. Most shared a common insight: distinct virtues of the two respective classes ought ideally to correct the vices inherent to its opposite. The "ordinary virtues" of the many—including the embodiment of "common sense" in a society's cultural practices—could and ought to restrain the overweening ambitions of the few. And, the privileges typically available to the few—including liberal education and leisure—were to benefit those less fortunate and elevate the potential debasement of the many. The prospects for a successful "mixing" of the classes rested on a political order dedicated to stability, not churning change; continuity, not "progress"; and balance, not the ascendancy of one class over the other.

The Mixed Constitution in the Classical Tradition

Within the classical tradition there was disagreement. Some thinkers—beginning with Aristotle—argued that "the many" and "the few" should be blended into an entirely new form, a "middling" class that exemplified political moderation. A later defense of "mixed constitution," often associated first with Polybius and later with Machiavelli, argued that the classes would always be distinct, and the aim was not a "blending," but a balancing of distinct forces.

Thus, there were two senses of mixing when speaking of "mixed constitution." One form of mixing occurs when the ingredients blend completely together, forming a new substance in which the ingredients are no longer distinguishable. The other form of mixing leaves the various elements still distinguishable, if tossed together in an appetizing new blend. For the first, we might conjure the image of a smoothie in which a mix of various ingredients are no longer separable or distinct. Reflecting the second, a tossed salad still leaves the various constitutive elements distinct if nevertheless combined.

The first great articulator of the ideal of the "mixed constitution" was Aristotle, who argued that a well-blended political order—what he called "polity"—must be more like a bread dough or a smoothie, though in the messy world of reality, it will likely be lumpy and not as smooth as the recipe might ideally call for. In the most fortunate circumstances, however, a well-mixed regime would be so completely blended that the distinct classes would be barely discernible, and instead a "middling" class would emerge, one marked by moderation and internal harmony.

Aristotle argued that polity can only emerge through an artful mixture of oligarchy and democracy—or, the wealthy few and the many poor. If mixed well, he argued, observers of such a regime would be able at the same time to claim that it is *both* a democracy and an oligarchy, but also *neither*. It becomes something altogether new, neither rule for or by the benefit of the few nor of the many. Moreover, he wrote, "it should be preserved through itself"—that is, its citizens should seek to perpetuate the mixed form not because each side is merely biding its time until it can dominate the other side, but because "none of the parts of the city generally would wish to have another regime."[1]

Far from seeking to institute a mere arrangement of "checks and balances," however, Aristotle went further, insisting that such institutional practices would—it might be hoped—eventually deeply shape the ethos of "polity," giving rise to a wholly new and distinct regime rather than simply leaving intact the distinct and mistrustful elements of each. Polity shapes the souls of the citizenry, in particular, by drawing them away from the self-interested constitutive components of oligarchy and democracy, and cultivating instead a disposition of trust, concern for common good, and even "an element of affection." This is achieved, Aristotle wrote, by a weakening of the conditions that lead either to oligarchy or democracy—namely, the concentration of wealth, on the one hand, or widespread poverty, on the other—and instead through cultivation of a dominant "middling" element in the society.

Aristotle recognized that extremes of wealth and poverty give rise to a host of vices (as extremes are just as likely to do within the individual soul). The wealthy are likely to become "arrogant and base," accustomed to having their way. Because their wealth and position leads to a belief in their own self-sufficiency and often induces deference in those around them, they neither wish to be ruled, nor do they "know how to be ruled." This unruly disposition is cultivated from the youngest age, a corruption of luxury and indulgence. They are marked by contempt toward those who do not share their wealth and advantages.

The poor, in turn, are likely to be malicious and base in petty ways. They are consumed by envy and resentment. Aristotle suggested that when it comes to rule, they are "too humble." While they might seek domination were they given the opportunity, Aristotle's critique of their excess humility points to the likely consequences of constant subjugation and humiliation by the few, which can lead the *demos* to internalize a lack of worth, resulting in an underestimation in their abilities and capacities. They combine too little confidence with too much hostility in relation to the wealthy, leading to a toxic combination that makes them at once unlikely to ascend to good and decent rule, but when given the chance, likely to rule capriciously and out of resentment and vengeance.

Polity involves the cultivation of citizens who transcend the constitutive elements of "the many and the few," of democracy and oligarchy. Driven neither by arrogance and contemptuous wealth, nor the resentment and envy of poverty, a dominant "middling" element is marked by a readiness "to obey reason," and, by extension, to be law abiding. Those of great wealth and poverty are challenged to "obey reason," given their self-interest instead to obey only their own advantage. A polity is dominated by people who are, generally speaking, "equal and similar," and thus more capable of extending their interests beyond themselves to the swath of citizens who share similar prospects and experience. Because this regime minimizes both resentments and contempt, relations between citizens are marked by "affection" and harmony, a willingness to consider the good of others that is not too distinct from the benefits to oneself. Aristotle stressed that this regime ceases to be composed of the two elements, but becomes its own distinct, "mixed" regime. Thus, class-based factions are absent in a well-blended polity; rather, absent the few wealthy and the many poor, the citizenry in such cities "most particularly preserve themselves" as a middling class.[2] "Polity" must become a wholly new regime, not just a combination of two distinct regimes. If achieved, its citizens seek to "preserve it themselves"—they value and treasure the distinct regime of which they are a part and share with fellow citizens—rather than bide their time waiting for the opportunity to change the regime for their own distinct class advantage.

HOWEVER, there is another sense of "mixing" within the classical tradition that held that such blending was impossible, and, instead, argued that the main elements of any regime would remain distinct and opposed. Polybius, a second-century Hellenic historian of Rome, believed that the Roman example offered a different model: a form of mixing that leaves intact and identifiable the classes that compose it. Rome was more akin to a salad in which the different vegetables are still identifiable and distinct, but their artful combination produces a superior taste than when eaten separately. Polybius believed that the course of history proved that this latter form of mixing was more successful and practicable.

Polybius famously argued that all good regimes eventually decay into their opposite: the good monarchy is eventually succeeded by a tyranny; a noble aristocracy is corrupted by money, becoming an oligarchy; and a virtuous democracy devolves into a self-serving form of mob rule. Polybius concludes that all good regimes contain the seeds of their own self-destruction, as rust destroys iron or cancer overwhelms healthy cells. In his view, these corrosions are internal to the regimes, not due to contingent external circumstances such as invasion or natural disaster. The cycle of regimes is inevitable, in his view, because, subject to their own logic, nothing can arrest the internal decay of each good regime. All regimes in their "pure" form are doomed to decay and decomposition.

However, Polybius praised Rome for fashioning a solution that forestalled this internal decay, one first discovered by the art and prudence of one of Sparta's founders, Lycurgus. Lycurgus "bundled together all the merits and distinctive characteristics of the best systems of government, in order to prevent any of them growing beyond the point where it would degenerate into its congenital vice."[3] By designing a *mixed constitution* that would give official powers to each regime type within a single government, the virtues of kingship, aristocracy, and democracy could be preserved, while the descent of each into its vicious form could be prevented. Lycurgus first, and later the Romans, "wanted the potency of each system to be counteracted by the others, so that nowhere would any of them tip the scales or outweigh the others for any length of time; [they] wanted the system to last forever, maintained in a high degree of balance and equilibrium by the principle of reciprocity."[4] What Lycurgus designed by reason, the Romans adopted through experience and constant adjustment. The benefits of kingship were manifested in the unitary rule of the emperor, but the tendency of the monarch to become overbearing and tyrannical was restrained by the political power of the common citizens. They in turn were ennobled by the aristocracy—gathered in the Senate—who in turn were balanced by the other elements of the government. With each distinct political form governing for the common good, the greatest beneficiary would be the entire people, especially undergirding the values and mores that were central to democracy. The characteristic feature of democracy, in the view of Polybius, is not majority rule (a feature that it shared with mob rule), but, rather, a form of governance that "retains the traditional values of piety toward the gods, care of parents, respect for elders, and obedience to the laws."[5]

Polybius commended a form of mixing that retained the distinct contours and qualities of each form of government—recommending the "salad" form of mixing over a blend of ingredients. "The common good" is best secured by inclusion of each ruling form within a single government—the one, the few, and the many. Such a government is thus able to protect and enhance the respective advantages endemic to each class of society—the unitary and decisive rule of one; the wisdom and prudence of the few; the common sense and conservative virtues of the populace that, if artfully combined, would prevent each class's devolution into its antithesis. In the view of Polybius, political and social balance is the aim, and once achieved, it should become the main object of the people *beyond their interests as a class* to sustain this balance and prevent the ascendancy of one regime not only at the expense of the others, but to prevent the descent into the decay of regimes and ultimately barbarism.

THE DISTINCT, if related, arguments by Aristotle and Polybius were wed in the High Middle Ages by Thomas Aquinas, who deeply admired both thinkers. Like most classical thinkers, Aquinas echoed the likes of Plato and Aristotle, who favored monarchy *in theory*; however, in everyday practice, he favored a form of mixed constitution that was fundamentally a conservative mixing of the classes. Like Polybius, he viewed "the people" as forming the base of a moral order, and elites responsible for protecting and deepening the core virtues of "the many" embedded in a culture of common sense. A "mixing" came about as the result of a leadership class that saw its primary role as the defender of bottom-up custom as the ground condition for human flourishing, rather than— as in the case of modern liberalism—as the class responsible for its uprooting and dismantling in the name of progress and liberation.

While Aquinas was generally of the view that law must be the intentional promulgation of legislation born of rational and conscious deliberation—the result of the "reason and will of the legislator"—he also recognized that there can be a functional equivalent of law that emanates in a different manner from the community at large. Aquinas pointed to the emergence of "repeated actions" in a community that can "reveal internal motives of the will and concepts of the reason"—what he called "custom." Custom can act in place of law, or as another form of law altogether: "Custom has the power of law, it abolishes law, and it acts as the interpreter of law."[6]

Custom can arise in two ways. In a free community—a community ruled at large by the people—custom arises from "the consent of the whole community which is demonstrated by its customary observation." Aware of the limitations of the explicit and codified form of law one finds in a juridical regime, Aquinas commended widely accepted norms that govern in place of law. Because of their widespread acceptance, custom is "worth more than the authority of the ruler who does not have the power to make the law except as the representative of the people." Because "the whole people" make customary law, it has far greater force and is more readily observed than the rule by one or a few people. And because custom develops over a long period of time—Aquinas noted—it can undergo alteration through generalized assent over time, and as a result, such gradually altered custom is far more likely to have more legitimacy and acceptance. Notice that through "custom" we arrive at a preliberal conception of "consent"—the consent of a community to govern itself through the slow accumulation and sedimentation of norms and practices over time. Such "consent" is, at its core, fundamentally distinct from the individualistic, deracinated, and rationalistic theory of consent found in the liberal social contract tradition.

The second form of rule by custom is more consonant with governance by elites, so long as they are respectful of the dominant role of custom, and do not seek its disruption or dismantling. Aquinas argued that rule by custom can be extensive even where there are rulers appointed or selected to make law, inasmuch as rulers can tacitly assent to the governance of custom simply by tolerating its existence. "If the community does not have the right to make its own laws to abrogate a law made by a superior authority, a custom which becomes established acquires the force of law if it is tolerated by those whose responsibility it is to make law for the community, since in this way they seem to approve what custom has established."[7]

If, according to Aquinas, "democracy" in its pure form tends to internal division, and hence results in an inferior kind of regime, Aquinas here describes a form of self-governance that is effectively democratic and can coexist extensively with rule by various elites—whether a monarch or aristocracy. Such elites, he further suggests, would be wise to "tolerate" beneficial existing customs that function as law, at least insofar as for Aquinas, a true law is "nothing else than an ordination of reason for the common good promulgated by the one who is in charge of the community."[8] Aquinas thus describes the formation of a virtuous mixed regime in which "the many" are apt to govern themselves in accordance with good custom that functions as law, while selecting leaders who are apt to "tolerate" good custom in accordance with the common good. The "mixed constitution" by Aquinas's telling is a beneficial symbiotic relationship between the many and the few, in which the many largely develop the capacity to govern themselves in their daily affairs through the development of "custom," while an elite—acceptable and even chosen by the many—governs with considerable deference to the settled customs of the people.

The Modern Mixed Constitution

Aquinas anticipated the idea of a "mixed constitution" that would be articulated by conservative thinkers in later centuries. Conservatism as a self-conscious modern political theory was born when a different kind of elite emerged: progressive elites. Liberalism justified the emergence of an elite whose primary self-assigned role was to prevent the masses from forestalling progress, either as revolutionaries who would be tempted to interfere in a capitalist economy, or as progressives who sought the overturning of traditional culture. This new elite sought to circumvent the inclination of the *demos* to preserve a way of life—balance, order, and continuity that were the necessary preconditions for a mixed constitution—in the name of progress, liberation, and innovation. The economic revolution of capitalism and thereafter the social and political upheaval of the French Revolution were the watershed world historical events that at once gave birth to a new elite of the anti-culture, as well as a self-conscious conservatism that, perhaps for the first time, fully recognized that a bottom-up culture needed explicit and self-conscious defense by a cultured elite that previously had not recognized the extent to which it was—or should be—aligned with the broad popular sentiments of the people.

Both the revolutionary movements of anti-culture, as well as conservatism's defense of culture, rested upon an essential role played by elites who laid claim to the support of "the people." Revolutionary movements—whether the French Revolution, Marxist-inspired revolutions, or contemporary activism by activist progressive groups such as Antifa—all claim to speak in the name of "the people" against an elite that seeks to oppress and circumvent the popular will. At the same time, historically, Marxist strains sought to deny their reliance upon elites, while conservatism was frank in its call for an alignment of the few and the many. The explicit call for elites has been used as evidence by the left in long-standing and strident critiques of the elitism of conservatives. Conservatives have been generally unwilling to make explicit the claim that such an alignment is necessary for support of the stability and support for "the many," the "commoners" who rely upon elite support for a "common sense" that undergirds a way of life.

A dominant narrative among left intellectuals—particularly those influenced by currents of Marxism, but that has seeped from academe into the popular mind—is that conservatism is the ideology of the elite, aligned with those who seek to preserve the wealth, status, and power of the upper classes against the egalitarian longings of the people. This narrative has gained widespread purchase in the wider intellectual world and has been successfully advanced as a main condemnation of conservatism in an age committed to egalitarianism. Conservatism, it is alleged, was born in reaction against the efforts of ordinary people to gain some degree of political influence, economic justice, and social dignity against the brutal and inhumane oppression of the aristocratic classes. By the telling of one of these chroniclers of this inegalitarian ideology—Corey Robin, in his book *The Reactionary Mind*—"conservatism is the theoretical voice of this animus against the agency of the subordinate classes. It provides the most consistent and profound argument as to why the lower orders should not be allowed to exercise their independent will, why they should not be allowed to govern themselves or the polity. Submission is their first duty, and agency the prerogative of the elite."[9] Per Robin, conservatism is the default ideology of those who seek to *conserve* the status and privileges of the elite.

Marxist-tinged thinkers like Robin regard early conservatism's alignment with the old aristocracy as damning. Pointing to nascent conservatism's alignment with the aristocracy, in the view of such critics it has sufficed to dismiss conservative philosophy as inegalitarian, all the while overlooking Marxism's unswerving embrace of a revolutionary ruling elite that was supposedly only necessary until political conditions have ripened. Conservatism's historically explicit support of an aristocratic element in society is damning, while the ineluctable presence of a Marxist revolutionary vanguard is dismissed as a temporary and accidental feature of an otherwise egalitarian philosophy.

The premise of this charge is patently false and misleading. The proper debate between Marxists and conservatives is not over which approach is genuinely egalitarian (since neither is), but to what popular end an elite will inevitably govern. Marxism justifies a revolutionary elite that will give way to a classless society, albeit only after the transformation and even outright elimination of nearly all existing institutions—not only economic, but social, including family, schools, churches, and the civil order. Incipient conservatism's defense of the *ancien régime* was—at its most insightful and prophetic—not an obtuse, reactionary call to defend the existing elite or a call to oppress the people, but a recognition that a self-consciously *conservative* elite was needed to protect the people against the destabilizaing threat of a new capitalist oligarchy and a class of social revolutionaries that were emerging at the same time. At its origins, conservatism arose in defense of the way of life of ordinary people against the destabilizing ambitions of progressivism in both its economic and social guises.

Historically, this meant a defense of the old aristocracy against the two most dangerous forms of progressive elitism. The first and most obvious threat for the authors who articulated the earliest modern arguments of conservatism was the revolutionaries seeking to overturn the entire existing order—the revolutionaries in France or those inspired by them. While architects of the French Revolution claimed in speeches and pamphlets that a revolution would result in a truly egalitarian political and social outcome (much like Marx and later Marxists), early conservatives recognized that the most radical and destabilizing element in a revolutionary movement was led by a small cadre of elites who were, in fact, hostile to the interests and ways of life of ordinary people. Thinkers like Edmund Burke recognized that the decimation of a long-standing way of life in the name of a wholesale reordering would fall heaviest and most punitively on the very working-class people on whose behalf the revolutionaries claimed to act.

The second group of progressive elites that posed a threat to a conservative society, and required resistance by a countervailing conservative elite, was the rising business class—not arising from the turmoil of the French Revolution, but the staid and otherwise settled way of life in a nation such as England. It was this latter elite that was perhaps even more dangerous to an otherwise traditional society, given that its progressivism was shrouded in the mantle of conservative values, and arose from the heart of a stable society such as Britain (or the United States).

If Marx could sound like Burke in his criticism of the dislocating effects of modern progress, Burke sounded like Marx in his condemnation of the rising class of wealthy capitalists whose main aim was personal enrichment while subverting the settled ways of life of ordinary people. Echoing Marx and Engels's recognition that a new order would displace all ancient settlements, Burke lamented the replacement of a nation of "men of honor and cavaliers" *not* with revolutionaries—much as he condemned them—but "sophisters, economists, and calculators."[10] Burke viewed this less obviously revolutionary class aligned ultimately with the spirit of modern social progressivism, seeking to uproot and transform settled folkways in the name of advancing economic and social progress. Burke's was a broadside that not only excoriated the social upheavals effected by the French revolutionaries and (by extension) commended by Marx, but the continual economic and social instability prized by modern liberal economic philosophy and practice. Against a new class of elites—mainly, an alliance between ideological progressive theorists and a rising financial oligarchy—Burke urged protection of the stability, tradition, and social continuities vital for the flourishing of ordinary people.

Burke condemned the progressive spirit that was producing a new economic oligarchy. Recognizing even then the predilection of modern oligarchs to *liquefy* property, transforming property (in all its forms) into readily tradable assets, he offered a prescient warning about how such a new monied oligarchy would divorce economic activity from place, history, and culture. This new oligarchy, he argued, sought to transform the nation into "one great playtable" populated entirely by "gamesters." Not satisfied to take risk on their own, rather, risk would be socialized, with the aim of making "speculation as extensive as life; to mix it with all its concerns and to divert the whole of the hopes and fears of the people from their usual channels into the impulses, passions, and superstitions of those who live on chances."[11] The result, Burke anticipated—almost prophesying the 2008 economic catastrophe wrought by "gamesters"—was punitive consequences on the steady habits of more rural, less sophisticated, working-class people:

> The truly melancholy part of the policy of systematically mak-
> ing a nation of gamesters is this, that though all are forced to
> play, few can understand the game; and fewer still are in a condi-
> tion to avail themselves of the knowledge. *The many must be the*
> *dupes of the few* who conduct the machine of these speculations.
> What effect it must have on the country people is visible. The
> townsman [i.e., urbanites] can calculate from day to day, [but]
> not so the inhabitant of the country. . . . The whole of the power
> obtained by this revolution will settle in the towns among the
> burghers and the monied directors who lead them. The landed
> gentleman, the yeoman, and the peasant have, none of them,
> habits or inclinations or experience which can lead them to any
> share in this the sole source of power.[12]

As Burke discerned, a revolutionary age would be driven not simply by episodic political spasms of disruptive revolutionary fervor, but
would be fed above all by the steady transformations wrought on the
political and social order through economic arrangements that would
favor the urban and global over the rural and local. The same aims
pervaded both the anti-capitalist Marxists and the basic interests of a
financier class: a revolutionary establishment, an elite culture dominated by the interests of a society of the constantly unsettled, favoring
those best able to negotiate intentional economic and social instability.

The necessity of developing and backing an elite *for* the people and
against a progressive elite was taken up by Burke's nineteenth-century
heir, Benjamin Disraeli. While Burke is often regarded as the "father of
conservatism," he did not, in fact, describe himself *as* a conservative, or
even develop a political philosophy explicitly under the title of conservatism. His writings against the French Revolution were written as a

self-identified liberal, though a liberalism of a very different dispensation than the philosophical liberalism that developed through the eighteenth and nineteenth centuries. For Burke, to be a liberal was to be connected to the classical tradition of liberty as interpreted and commended largely through the living legacy of Christianity—namely, the liberty of self-rule, self-command, and self-sacrifice. Writing in a pre-ideological age, to be liberal was simply to partake in the civilized inheritance of the Christian West.

By contrast, Disraeli was among the first clear-eyed critics of liberalism in its modern, ideological incarnation, and explicitly proposed and described a substantive conservatism as liberalism's rightful opponent. Drawing on Burke's main lines of critique of the revolutionary disposition, which by the mid-nineteenth century had crystalized into an identifiable ideology of liberalism, Disraeli outlined a self-conscious conservative alternative that was more than merely a slower form of liberalism, but a genuinely distinct political philosophy to that of liberalism.

Disraeli perceived deep philosophic, social, and economic trends that were already transforming the English political landscape, and alternatively addressed them both in political speeches on behalf of the Tories, as well as through imaginative literature in the "Young England" novels—in particular, *Sybil, or The Two Nations*. At base, he perceived a growing power in the modern world that aligned philosophical radicalism and a new form of commerce that combined large-scale production with powerful financial institutions aimed at fragmenting the institutions of organic society and replacing them with an increasingly centralized government. These interests—broadly, in his view, "liberal"—were directly hostile to three main entities: the working class, the aristocracy, and the Church, along with the institutional forms in which those orders of society were embedded and embodied. Disraeli saw the need both for a philosophical and political realignment: where the Whigs had historically been the party of the people, and the Tories, the party of the aristocracy, instead he proposed a form of "Tory democracy"—one-nation conservatism that combined the shared dedication of the working class and the aristocracy in a nation defined by cultural continuity, economic stability, the thick presence of relationships through a web of organic, mediating institutions.

Disraeli's conservatism was housed and preserved above all by the working class, which he regarded as the natural home of ordinary virtue and common sense. He was explicit in connecting the language of conservatism with the working class, rather—in contrast to the historic alignment of the Tory Party—with the aristocracy. In his Crystal Palace speech, he declared: "When I say 'Conservative,' I use the word in its purest and loftiest sense. I mean that the people of England, and especially the working classes of England, are proud of belonging to a great country."[13] The main institutions of British society were, in Disraeli's view, distillations of working-class experience and values. In the words of one Disraeli scholar, he recognized that "the working-class stream is but a large tributary of the main national river." To extend the image, the main currents of this national river originated in and were renewed by the values of the working class, and those waters, in turn, fed the main British institutions beyond the working class—particularly the aristocracy and the Church. To the extent that the river was healthy and regularly fed, all British institutions were effectively the creation of the people—not by the theoretical consent of liberalism, but the actual grounded practices of a people in places and over time and safeguarded by the institutions of the powerful.

In his commentary on the dangerous revolutionary progressivism of the Whigs, Disraeli advanced a Burkean idea of national origins at odds with liberal "state of nature" theory, arguing that a nation's institutions and practices were the living embodiment of the collective activity of previous generations. Disraeli argued that "the blended influences of nature and fortune" form the national character. Institutions and practices are built from the bottom up, through time and experience, but shaped by both nature and particular circumstance ("fortune"). This character is largely unexamined, and, in many ways, most healthy when it is simply lived and not "theorized." Echoing Burke, too much theory is likely to introduce a radical and even violent discontent with inherited institutions, but some degree of reflection and reform is inevitable and desirable. In particular, as he argued in his sustained examination of the English Constitution, there are

> great crises in the fortunes of an ancient people which impel them to examine the nature of the institutions which have *gradually* sprung up among them. In this great national review, duly and wisely separating the essential character of their history from that which is purely adventitious, they discover certain principles of ancestral conduct, which they acknowledge as the causes that these institutions have flourished and descended to them; and in their future career, and all changes, reforms, and alterations, that they may deem expedient, they resolve that these principles shall be their guides and instructors.[14]

Discerning these essential principles is the "greatest amount of theory that ever enters into those political institutions." It becomes the role of the philosophical statesman—generally a member of the "elite"—to articulate these principles that are discerned and understood to be drawn from the broad practice and institutions of the people. The effort to displace or overturn those institutions—even if undertaken in the name of the people—is effectively to commit a form of national suicide by poisoning the wellspring of the nation. Any effort to impose new institutions from above is the very opposite of constituting a nation, but a false and unjust imposition of raw power by an illegitimate elite.

What Disraeli observed already in the nineteenth century was that the two forces of modern liberalism—the economic libertarian and social revolutionary wings—were combining as a single party, a progressive

Whig Party. Disraeli perceived by the nineteenth century that the Whigs were becoming a revolutionary party, in particular, aligning those of a liberal philosophical bent ("dissenters") with the monied interests of London ("utilitarians"). He observed that these two seemingly opposite forces combined to advance the destruction of mediating institutions of church, estate, guild, and local power, and ultimately had its aim at the nation itself: "The Whigs are an anti-national party. In order to accomplish their object of establishing an oligarchical republic, and of concentrating the government of the State in the hands of a few great families, the Whigs are compelled to declare war against all those great national institutions, the power and influence of which . . . make us a nation."[15] Disraeli perceived that the Whig Party was at once the party of individualistic laissez-faire and a deracinated socialism that rejected the basic forms of human sociality, seeking to disaggregate the organic institutions of British society into a pot of "liberated," loosely connected individual actors who could then be used as a deracinated labor pool by a financier class who had no real loyalty to the British nation or its traditions. He viewed this party as embodying the ethos of liberalism, a "disintegrating" force based upon "cosmopolitan, rational, commercial, utilitarian and Jacobin" commitments.[16]

Disraeli viewed these two seeming opposites—what came in the United States to be regarded as "conservative" (libertarian) and "liberal" (progressive)—as in fact working in tandem to destroy the very institutional forms and traditional bases that supported the working class. Disraeli offered an alternative to these equally destructive forces especially in his thinly fictionalized novel of social commentary, Sybil— particularly through the character of Gerard, a stout member of the working class. Gerard yearns for a restoration of the effective dominion by the lower classes of British society, reflected in its main institutions of guild, township, and church. The Church, especially, was a democratic and democratizing institution, open and caring equally for all members, regardless of rank. More importantly, the ethos of the Church pervaded British society, emphasizing the social and communal nature of society, rejecting an image of society based on competition and individual achievement (or failure), and emphasizing beauty and the transcendent over the utilitarian and banal. The working classes in some senses were to direct the governance by the elites charged with rule, forced from below to govern out of a dedication to preserve and fortify the traditional rhythms and institutions that connected the ordinary and the elite, the inherited traditions, and bottom-up decencies of the common people. Those in the working classes seek the provisions necessary for physical, moral, and spiritual flourishing, and rely especially on an aristocracy, motivated out of "noblesse oblige," to afford "access to the humanizing arts of civilization."[17] Gerard reflects Disraeli's belief that the working classes were not instinctively, nor in principle, a revolutionary class. They were, rather, deeply *conservative*, seeking more to preserve and pass on a heritage than to disrupt and overthrow traditions, and relied especially upon an elite that would protect them from other aspirants to political, social, and economic rule whose aim was to damage and even destroy the traditional and organic society that they viewed as an obstacle to progress.

For this reason, Disraeli sought to redefine the Tory Party as the party not only of a certain traditional set of elites, but one whose traditionalism aligned with the deepest commitments and needs of the working classes. It was a certain vision of the aristocracy who *protected* England's long-standing institutions—ones built by the contributions of countless generations of ordinary people—that Disraeli believed could stand in alignment with the larger mass of society that had not been traditionally part of the Tory Party. Disraeli described the Tory Party— traditionally, the party of "the few"—to be "the really democratic party of England."[18] The Tory Party would heal the divide now widening in England, forging instead "one nation." To achieve this end, Disraeli understood that the Tory Party must become explicitly committed to policy reforms that were beneficial to and supportive of the working classes, especially as they faced hardships from the costs of "progress." These included social welfare policies as well as greater openness to suffrage. But more fundamentally, "Tory democracy" adopted many of the positions associated with an older form of British socialism—a position described by scholar Tony Judge as "Tory socialism." Eschewing the radicalism of Marxism, Tory socialism—and Disraeli's "Tory democracy"—instead defended traditional British culture, valued and even idealized the inheritance of the past, favored the pastoral and craft traditions of a more traditional economy, commended "common sense" and everyday wisdom over a fetishization of expertise in the service of forms of progress destructive of traditional ways of life, and emphasized the alignment of the aristocracy and the people against the rise of progressive philosophies and political movements.[19] Through a traditionalist alignment that was also open to an expansive use of state power to improve and support the lives of the working class, Disraeli believed that the Tory Party would unite England into "one nation," because the party would draw support from the elements of "the many" and "the few." "The rest of the nation—that is to say, nine-tenths of the people of England—formed the Tory party, the landed proprietors and peasantry of the kingdom, headed by a spirited and popular Church, and looking to the kingly power in the abstract, though not to the reigning King, as their only protection from an impending oligarchy."[20]

In the American tradition, there was no aristocracy that might serve as the natural class to resist the innovators and elevate the masses, but functional equivalents have long been noted. The professional classes were regarded by many early commentators as bearing this "conservative" responsibility. Perhaps most notably, Alexis de Tocqueville regarded lawyers as playing the role of conservator and the link between an aristocratic and democratic ethos within an otherwise democratic society. Law—as understood, studied, and practiced in Tocqueville's time—fostered a traditionalist mindset and cultivated a strong link between the guiding spirit of the past and its continuity into the future.

Describing this cultivated disposition of lawyers, Tocqueville wrote that "men who have made the laws their special study have drawn from their work the habits of order, a certain taste for forms, a sort of instinctive love for the regular sequence of ideas, which naturally render them strongly opposed to the revolutionary spirit and unreflective passions of democracy."[21] Concerned that the masses could be drawn into the "revolutionary spirit" of a progressive class, Tocqueville praised this professional class for its "superstitious respect for what is old . . . , their taste for forms . . . , [and] their habit of proceeding slowly."[22]

Tocqueville might well have drawn out these similar elements in various professions that would have exhibited many similar features at the time—clergy, medical, professorial, even local business leaders. While Tocqueville claimed to be skeptical of the idea of a truly "mixed constitution"—at one point describing it as a "chimera"—in his praise for the role played by the professions such as lawyers, he pointed to the way that key features of a mixed constitution could nevertheless even be manifest in an otherwise democratic regime. He described lawyers as "a natural liason" between "the people" and "the aristocracy," regarding these custodians of the legal tradition as "the sole aristocratic element that can be *mixed* without effort into the natural elements of democracy and be combined in a happy and lasting manner with them."[23] As the profession likely to "occupy most public offices," lawyers would act as a "lone counterweight" to what Tocqueville feared might be more revolutionary or innovative temptations within democratic societies.[24]

Such professions as a kind of "American aristocracy" can be fruitfully contrasted to the other likely aristocracy that Tocqueville believed would eventually arise on American soil—an "industrial" aristocracy, or what we would today point to as an oligarchic, commercial, managerial class. With remarkable foresight, Tocqueville prophesied the rise of an economic class that would live and think wholly apart from the working class. Rather than living among the working class like those of the professions whom he hoped would form the leadership class of a modern form of "mixed constitution," this "new" aristocracy instead would enjoy the fruits of its status while commending "public charity" to the workers. Tocqueville contrasted the noblesse oblige that at least reigned in theory in "territorial aristocracy," which, he stated, "was obliged by law or believed itself to be obliged by mores to come to the aid of its servants and to relieve their miseries." By contrast, the "manufacturing aristocracy that we see rising before our eyes is one of the hardest that has appeared on earth"—not because of its oppressiveness and cruelty, but precisely because of its separation and indifference. Tocqueville feared that the functional equivalent of an "aristocracy" comprised of the professions, effectively forming the leadership of a de facto mixed constitution, would be replaced in a distinctly "unmixed" constitution by a new, managerial aristocracy that separated itself from the working class and farmed out its concerns to the ministerial functions of the state. He rightly suspected that this would lead to a hardening of both classes toward each other, and a politics that could no longer be called, in a real sense, a "democracy."

Conclusion

What has passed as "conservatism" in the United States for the past half century is today exposed as a movement that was never capable of, nor fundamentally committed to, conservation in any fundamental sense. All along, it was a species of "liberalism" that rejected the core tenets of an original conservatism, originally a common-good tradition that predated the progressive revolutions. In response to the rise of liberalism, a common-good conservatism instead stressed the priority of culture, the wisdom of the people, and the necessity of a "mixed constitution" that especially gave pride of place to preserving the commonplace traditions of a polity. The political shocks of the past several years have been, to a considerable extent, not only an expected repudiation of the revolutionary social projects of progressive liberalism, but a bottom-up rejection of a false "conservatism" bankrolled by oligarchs that was all along a form of liberalism. Instead, around the world there has been a rise of popular and populist movements aimed at jettisoning the liberal priorities of the ruling class in both its "conservative" *and* "progressive" forms. A fundamental realignment has taken place in which the contest at hand will be decided when either the elites are reformed or replaced, or the people are bridled and broken. Common-good conservatism today vocally seeks the former.

Yet, to constitute a political and social order worth conserving, something revolutionary must first take place: the priority of the liberal progressive agenda must be displaced for one that seeks stability, order, and continuity. In order to reset the political conditions in which conservation can be a suitable aim, the current ruling order must be fundamentally changed. The prospects for a renewal of culture, the ascendancy of common sense, and a reimagined form of a mixed constitution rest upon the success of a confrontational stance of the people toward the elites—namely, the effort to force the vanguards of progress to work instead on behalf of the aims of ordinary people in preserving stability and continuity. In order to conserve a social order, there must first be fundamental upheaval of its current revolutionary form. The project at hand is the combination of two seeming opposites—a better aristocracy brought about by a muscular populism, and then, in turn, an elevation of the people by a better aristocracy. What is needed, for want of a better term, is a new combination of two long-standing opponents: "aristopopulism."

PART III

WHAT IS TO
BE DONE?

6

Aristopopulism

No tyranny lasts forever. Despotic regimes can persist for a time, always too long and against reason, but all despotisms eventually fall due to some combination of corruption and internal or external opposition, and often all of the above. While the current rise of a "soft," pervasive, and invasive progressive tyranny seems genuinely new and virtually insurmountable, recent events have shown it to be susceptible to that oldest form of resistance: an opposing political force. In response to classical liberal, progressive liberal, and Marxist ideologies increasingly combining as a single power elite, its opposite has arisen in a nascent political form, largely percolating from the bottom up in the discontents of a recalcitrant working class. Arising outside of the official corridors of power, this largely unguided movement has been indifferent to the scornful disdain of both right and left liberals. While spurred by populist rejection of progressivism, nevertheless it has arisen without elite guidance from "Conservatism, Inc."—numerous think tanks in Washington, DC, the official keepers of political party orthodoxy, the countless programs that have sought to shape young conservative elites to embrace the "fusionism" that defined top-down conservatism for a generation. The outlines of a "common-good conservatism" is a new political force that has surfaced to contend with the anti-cultural mandarins, the gentry liberals, and the laptop class. The rise of this unplanned populist opposition to elite rule marks the return of a political force that is predicted in classical theory: the mixed constitution, a fruitful mixing of "the many" and "the few."

This movement from below is untutored and ill led. Its nominal champion in the United States was a deeply flawed narcissist who at once appealed to the intuitions of the populace, but without offering clarifying articulation of their grievances and transforming their resentments into sustained policy and the development of a capable leadership class. While the political galvanization of the working class may yet wax or wane, what is needful for the genuine advance of the alternative of a "mixed constitution" is the conscious and intentional development of a new elite. Where necessary, those who currently occupy positions of economic, cultural, and political power must be constrained and disciplined by the assertion of popular power. However, merely limiting the power elite is insufficient. Instead, the creation of a new elite is essential—not just the "meritocrats" whose claim to rule is based upon credentialing at institutions that shroud their status in the thin veil of egalitarianism, but self-conscious *aristoi* who understand that their main role and purpose in the social order is to secure the foundational goods that make possible human flourishing for ordinary people: the central goods of family, community, good work, an equitable social safety net supportive of these goods, constraints upon corporate power, a culture that preserves and encourages order and continuity, and support for religious belief and institutions.

Thus, a new elite can only arise with the support of insistent political power exerted by an increasingly multiracial, multiethnic working-class party. Only such a new elite, in turn, can begin to use political power to alter, transform, or uproot an otherwise hostile anti-culture that is today dominated by the progressives on both the right and the left within modern liberalism. While political power is necessary to begin the process of cultural transformation, only through the full development of a distinct and new elite, attuned to the requirements of the common good, can a virtuous cycle be created that will reinforce the mutually improving relation of the many and the few.

What is needed is a mixing of the high and the low, the few and the many, in which the few consciously take on the role of *aristoi*—a class of people who, through supporting and elevating the common good that undergirds human flourishing, are worthy of emulation and, in turn, elevates the lives, aspirations, and vision of ordinary people. What is needed is a political form that might be labeled "aristopopulism."

The Decline of Nobility

We live in a peculiar moment in human history, in which "elite" is a bad word, while every political figure invokes the imprimatur of "the people" as the deepest source of legitimacy. In the long history of ordinary usage in the West until very recent times, most words used to describe the upper class had positive connotations, while those used to describe the people generally carried deeply negative overtones. Think, for example, of the word "aristocracy," meaning "rule by *aristoi*"—not just "few," but "the excellent" or "the best," people of distinctively good quality. Or, consider the word "patrician," derived from the word for father (*pater*), a name sometimes conferred upon those of noble birth, such as Patrick, the patron saint of Ireland. Another signifier is the word "dignity" itself, the root of the word "dignitaries," people of worth, distinction, character.[1] In a similar vein, consider the word "nobility," derived from the Latin *nobilis* and used widely throughout Europe to describe the upper classes, meaning not only "highborn," but—as today—something "noble," which then and now means "excellence," "dignity," "grace," "greatness," as distinguished from "base," "common," or "ordinary." The terms "gentleman" and "gentlewoman" have their root in a word meaning "highborn" or "of a good family," with connotations of "courageous, valiant; fine, good, fair," according to its etymology.[2] Many of the words we use to distinguish fine from base, superior from inferior, excellent from deficient, draw on this long-standing and implicit set of high expectations and praise for those in positions of leadership and distinction in earlier societies.

By contrast, the words used to describe "the people" have more typically derogatory and critical connotations. After all, "common" is a word used to describe something "ordinary" or "not distinguished," in contrast to something "excellent." Other words used to describe "commoners" have been "plebeians," or "plebes," "mob" (or its Greek original, *okhlos* as in "ochlocracy," or "rule by the mob"), "peasants," "multitude," "crowd," and "mass." Even the somewhat neutral term that I've used in these pages, "the people," shares a common root with the word on everyone's lips today, "populism" (from the Latin *populus*), a word with generally negative connotations, then as now.

What is striking especially today is the reversal of this long-standing set of positive and negative associations with words distinguishing the high from the low. The word "people" is regularly invoked as an almost divine entity by political leaders, especially in that almost mystical incantation of the phrase "the American people." The word "democracy" is everywhere embraced as the gold standard for political legitimacy today, in sharp contrast to the long-standing view throughout Western tradition that ranked democracy as among the worst forms of government of all the possible options from antiquity until fairly recent times, including by our Founding Fathers who explicitly argued that they were founding a republic, and not a democracy.[3]

Of course, not only has the word "democracy" seen a dramatic reversal in its fortunes—beginning already in the nineteenth century, when it went from being viewed largely in a negative light to becoming seen as the only legitimate form of government—but we have witnessed the corresponding rise of negative connotations with any word denoting

the upper class. Almost no one today—outside of a few deposed nobility in Europe—would seek to claim the designation of being an aristocrat, a member of the nobility, a "patrician." What's even more striking
is that *we do not have a positive word to describe someone of today's
upper class.* There is no positive word used by members of the upper
class to describe themselves—indeed, it is frequently observed that no
matter one's status and position in American society today, all claim
to be a part of the "middle class." The one word that is regularly used to
describe such people today is "elites," and it's not a word used *by* members of the elite to describe themselves, but rather as an implicit *critique*
and denunciation. Rather, most members of today's ruling class readily
embrace the labels of egalitarianism, and considerable energy is exercised by their most vocal leaders to root out any vestiges of "privilege"
or "elitism."

This form of politics in fact masks what is an age-old contestation
between mass and elite in which the elite is generally advantaged by
power and wealth, but called either by a portion of its own, or forced by
the populace, to act *on behalf of the common good*—in both senses, a
good that is both shared as well as especially necessary to "commoners."
The elites today, instead, veil their status—even, and especially, to
themselves—through efforts to eradicate privilege, engaging in a stupendous effort of self-deception about the nature of their position.

In earlier ages, most efforts to cultivate certain excellences among
the elite arose from a philosophic element within the elite itself. Arguably, the oldest "self-help" literature was focused on cultivating the desired virtues of the elites, recognizing that they set the tone and example
for the society as a whole. Works such as Aristotle's *Ethics* were aimed
at the education of a "gentleman" (*kaloskagathos*, literally "beautiful good
person"), the people who were expected to lead the political and social
order. During the Renaissance, a genre known as "Mirror of Princes"
was aimed at the education of the aristocratic class, often focusing on
the formation of aristocratic virtue through habituation at a very young

age and counsel on the prudent exercise of power. What is consistent within this literary tradition, in spite of many changes in emphasis and aspirational virtues over several centuries, is a singular focus upon the education of an elite qua elite, with firm awareness of its distinct and important duties and responsibilities in the order of society.

That element today—to the extent that it exists—tends to be most vocal in denunciation of "privilege" and elitism. Precisely because the main institutions in which the elite is formed are insistently organized to deny their own status, there is correspondingly no effort to ennoble the "nobility," to foster excellence among the "*aristoi*," and, in turn, efforts to ennoble the masses and elevate the polity as a whole. In an earlier age, John Adams could write without hesitation of the essential need for those with privilege and advantage to elevate their less fortunate fellow countrymen, writing in his treatise *Thoughts on Government,* "Laws for the liberal education of youth, especially of the lower class of people, are so extremely wise and useful, that, to a humane and generous mind, no expense for this purpose would be thought extravagant."[4] Today's elite instead scorns those they deem backward, an animosity that is returned in equal measure by those who are the objects of their scorn, the "populists."

Due to a combination of economic dislocation and cultural breakdown, a distinctly populist working-class party has coalesced in opposition to a party that has benefited from the libertarianism in both economic arrangements and social norms. A significant realignment is underway in the advanced postindustrial nations, with formerly left-leaning native working-class citizens aligning against an educated, credentialed elite, largely in the industries that have flourished in an increasingly virtual, global economy, and drawing broader electoral support from recent immigrants.[5]

There is no better proof of the extent of this realignment than postmortems of the 2020 US election. The electorate was divided increasingly between a dominantly credentialed professional class, on the one hand, and an increasingly multiracial, multiethnic working class, on the other. One particularly revealing study grouped 2020 presidential election *donations* by profession—not merely voters, but those dedicated enough to open their wallets. A striking contrast emerged. Those largely engaged in trades, small business, or caring for children at home didn't merely vote for, but donated money to, incumbent President Donald Trump. These donors were largely noncollege credentialed, hourly or self-employed, private-sector rank-and-file union members, and generally working class. Those supporting the eventual winner of the election, President Joe Biden, were dominated by members of the credentialed professional class—with most more likely to be salaried and working at home during COVID-tide. In a separate graph, the specific companies or organizations that showed the largest percentage of donations to Joe Biden were employees at the largest technology companies (Google, Apple, Facebook), universities (particularly elite universities such as Harvard, Columbia, and the University of Chicago), and public-sector unions (for teachers, employees of the federal government). Very few employees of large organizations donated predominantly to Donald Trump, but among them were the US Marines and the New York City Police Department. By and large, Trump donors included people likely to be self-employed or wage workers, such as carpenters, contractors, truck drivers, electricians, and small business owners. Notably, the demographic with the highest percentage of donations to Trump, relative to Biden, was homemakers.[6]

The divide was professional, geographic, educational, and reputational. Those more likely to be in the "professions" that relied on a globalized economic system supported Biden; those likely to be in the trades supported Trump. Traditionally "masculine" professions donated more to Trump, along with stay-at-home moms, while more female-dominated professions such as teachers and nurses donated to Biden. There was a divide reflecting levels of religious observance, with Trump voters more likely to be religious, and Biden's supporters more likely to identify as secular.[7] But above all, those who populate and control the main cultural institutions of American society donated (and presumably voted) in the interest of the professional class, while those who exercise little power in the cultural sphere donated (and presumably voted) for Trump.

This realignment along class lines increasingly moves the West away from its effort to obscure such distinctions by dividing the polity between proponents of Lockean economic progress and Millian social progress, and instead toward one in which the division is between the party of progress and the party of conservatism. While the various members of the party of progress aspire to a return to the divide that debated means over ends—such as market vs. state as the best means of achieving the same liberal end of equal individual liberty—it is far more likely that the growing class divide will come to define and reorder Western politics to an altered form in which the shared progressivism of liberalism will become a *party* rather than a *system*. As such, the liberal contest that pitted an economic elite against a progressive elite will fade as those two coalesce into one party, and taking its place will be a divide that will more closely resemble the political division described by all ancient political philosophers as inescapable and fundamental: the few against the many, or *oligarchy* vs. *demos*. In such a condition, the foreseeable future is one in which the mass and elite remain locked in a prolonged adversarial contest.

The American constitutional order was not actually designed with this classical model in mind. It represented the Founders' belief in a "new science of politics," specifically, a system in which a designated elite would govern with an aim to advancing an ideal of progress while rendering tractable any recalcitrant popular resistance. While the constitutional design was originally created to allow the ascendance of an economic elite while keeping at bay the potential inegalitarian discontents of the economically less successful, constitutional and political developments since the Progressive Era were especially aimed to give greater dominance to an educated and credentialed elite that would order the nation toward moral progress achieved by an emphasis on social liberation. Strikingly, today the resistance to the elite is directed at *both* these elements—financial and social elites, economic and cultural libertarianism. It opposes simultaneously the "openness" of libertarian economics and the "openness" of libertarian social policy. While America was not designed to be a classically "mixed constitution," conditions today dictate that the nation learn anew the lessons of classical political philosophy if it will avoid an outright civil war, whether hot or cold.

However, is a "mixed constitution" even possible? I have suggested throughout that classical theory is superior to modern practice, but perhaps that is finally because modern theory recognized what ancient theory did not: no regime can be "mixed," or divided against itself. "A house divided against itself cannot stand," Lincoln famously said, arguing that finally the United States must be all one thing or all another—slave or free. While the divide today is not so morally clear as the choice in the mid-nineteenth century, the nation appears just as riven and irreconcilable. Can one have a nation in which half the nation is fundamentally opposed to the other—a progressive, wealthier, and more powerful elite against a less powerful, less wealthy, but potentially more numerous party of conservatism?

Given the trajectory of contemporary Western politics, two options appear most likely: either domination of elites over the working classes, manipulated through complete control of the main institutions of society and even outright suppression of opposing views through control of mainstream media, educational institutions, the bureaucracy, and social media corporations; or, less likely, a decisive uprising from below, likely led by a demagogue, creating a dictatorship of the proletariat in ways that Marx did not anticipate or intend. Either of these prospects, in fact, follows the predictions of classical theory: a deeply divided regime is likely to give rise to tyranny of one part over another part, or anarchy for all.

However, classical theory suggests a third option: while difficult, nevertheless not only is a further alternative possible, but essential if tyranny is to be avoided. The genuinely "mixed constitution" becomes a "blending" of the various parts, no longer discernible as internally divided because it has achieved an internal harmony. That harmony must come about by aligning the sympathies and interests of the powerful few to the needs and interests of ordinary citizens to live in a stable and balanced order. To become blended, there must first be mixing.

In this sense, Tocqueville is actually in agreement with the classical tradition: one political form will come to predominate. A "chimera" is not possible—the melding of different animals into a single body.[8] Such a creature arises from feverish imaginations, or, if attempted in reality, would quickly perish. Yet, as Tocqueville himself argued throughout *Democracy in America*, the best outcome is a polity that is united through a sympathetic relationship between the elites and the many, the great and the ordinary. Tocqueville thus does not envision that an elite will disappear, even in a democracy; rather, one of his predominant concerns is whether the elite that will inevitably exist within a democracy will support and ennoble, or—developing deep mutual hostility—will instead degrade the lives of ordinary citizens. A well-mixed regime is no longer a "chimera"—the mythical beast made of many parts—but one thing composed of sympathetic and compatible elements. The elite must govern for the benefit of the many, while the many must restrain the dangerous temptations of the elite.

Tocqueville's warning applies not only to those who believe that one of today's two contesting parties should simply dominate the other, but to fruitful contemporary arguments that we should aim at achieving a kind of "mixed constitution" that leaves intact the two parties, and instead aims at a productive stalemate. This is, in effect, the suggestion of Michael Lind in his otherwise superb study *The New Class War*—an outcome he calls "democratic pluralism."[9] Such pluralism, in his view, echoes the teachings of the Founding Fathers, seeking to foster a relatively equal power differential between the elite and the many, and thereby allowing even the less powerful and wealthy populace to extract concessions from the powerful. For Lind, the thriving conditions of the 1950s working class—achieved through the power of unions and the robust social institutions of the lower middle class, such as churches and civic associations—is a model that should be emulated today. Yet, while I would not dispute this aim, I think Lind finally misunderstands the dynamics of that era, which were more Tocquevillian than Madisonian.

Lind asserts that the managerial elite has a vested self-interest in protecting its position indefinitely. Only *fear* will make this elite face political reality, and force it once again to concede some wealth, power, and status to the lower and working classes. Fear of losing their positions to populist replacements, Lind believes, is the only plausible motivation that could force members of today's ruling class to change course on a number of policy fronts, such as: limiting low-skill immigration, narrowing the economic divide, and expressing grudging respect for the traditional and religious beliefs of the working class. His greatest worry is a prolonged battle in which the elites refuse to cede some power, prosperity, and position, leading either to outright "illiberal liberalism"—in an intensification of what we are already witnessing in their treatment toward the working class and religious believers—or the rise of a demagogic populism that takes America down the route of many nations in Central and South America. His book is aimed as an appeal to his fellow elites to compromise now, or bear the lion's share of responsibility for losing the republic.

Lind is correct that fear is a powerful motivator, but I am skeptical that fear will suffice in this case.[10] The ruling class of every age has a long historical record of successfully co-opting populist uprisings, and while some are occasionally successful, the record suggests oligarchs have a good reason to wager on maintaining power at whatever cost. In the American tradition, the subversion of populism has succeeded more through co-option or patient outlasting of intense but brief bursts of populist anger and resentment, rather than outright violent suppression (though the history of violent oppression of organized labor should not be forgotten). America's earliest populist uprising led to the Constitutional Convention, and a new political settlement that its opponents predicted would lead to a centralized government, an economic oligarchy, and would leave ordinary citizens feeling relatively politically impotent and voiceless. The eponymous Populist movement of the late nineteenth and early twentieth centuries, while politically potent for the span of a decade, was eventually bled of its reformist energy by the more technocratic, upper-class, and elitist Progressive Era movement. And, in a similar trend, the working-class gains of the 1950s—due to the unique circumstance of total military mobilization and the existential threat faced by liberalism—were largely disassembled within the span of thirty years, many through the machinations of so-called "conservatives" who assumed that label to shroud their libertarianism. Lind's belief that fear will motivate today's woke capitalists to provide anything more than flimsy Band-Aids to the working class seems belied by the evidence.

Rather, by Lind's own telling, the high-water mark of the 1950s was not merely the result of concessions from an otherwise neoliberal ruling class; rather, *the ethos of the ruling class itself was broadly in line with the values and ethos of a broad working and middle class*. It wasn't merely the power of labor unions, local politicians, and religious congregations that forced the managerial elite to respect their demands; rather, a more pervasive influence of the values embodied in what Lind describes as the organizations of "guild, ward, and congregation" reflected a very different governing philosophy than that informing the self-congratulatory individualistic meritocratic calculus of today's managerial elite. The sorts of communal organizations that drew on, and cultivated, broadly corporatist and even Catholic values of solidarity and subsidiarity were not merely restricted to dominantly Catholic working classes but informed the ethos of mass and elite alike. There was an alignment of values between corporations, small business, and Main Street. Hollywood produced and lionized such films as *The Song of Bernadette, Boys Town*, and *It's a Wonderful Life*. Religious figures like Fulton Sheen, Billy Graham, and Reinhold Niebuhr were widely admired, regardless of class. The ruling class were not secretly neoliberals who grudgingly made concessions to the rubes in flyover country—they *were* "Midwestern" in their broader ethos, themselves steeped in the mid-century values of guild, ward, and congregation that had been advanced and fortified by earlier waves of Catholic immigrants.

Lind finally does not draw the correct conclusion from his own analysis. What's needed is not "democratic pluralism" in which the ruling class remains a neoliberal, managerial elite who, purely out of fear, grudgingly, if only temporarily, concedes some wealth and status to its inferiors. Instead, the entrenched conditions of a dominant economic and cultural elite require a fundamental *displacement* of the ruling class ethos by a common-good conservatism, one that directs both economic goals and social values toward broadly shared material and social capital that will prove supportive especially of stability and security in economic, family, and community life. We need not libertarian overlords who buy off the working class with schemes for universal basic income or free internet in favelas;[11] not a federal government that doles out occasional stimulus checks while a deeply inegalitarian economy proceeds undisturbed; and not credentialed secularists who grudgingly grant some shrinking private space to religious believers. Rather, of paramount importance today is the development of a ruling class that is itself informed by the very values that Lind believes were once regnant *as the price of admission* to elite status itself. Only the fear of *not conforming* to the regnant ethos will sufficiently move and shape elites— just as it does today to an elite that enforces a progressivist worldview, one that has proved so damaging to the prospects of flourishing for ordinary people.

This means, contra Lind, what is not needed is the creation of "the

functional equivalent" of guild, ward, and congregation to which the
working class belongs: what is needed is for all of these forms, and their
dominant ethos of solidarity and subsidiarity, to guide and inspire the
ruling elite as well. Lind too quickly dismisses the idea that a revival of
the working class through a revival of older forms, such as union, ward,
and church, is a bridge too far. Yet the decline of these organizational
forms has been intentionally advanced by an opposing individualist,
materialist, and secular ethos embraced by today's managerial elite.[12] If
these institutions declined due to sustained efforts by the managerial
elite, their renewal lies in part in the displacement of that elite with a
different one informed by a common-good conservative ethos. The power
sought is not merely to *balance* the current elite, but to *replace* it. If *fear*
is to have a salutary effect, those who seek to remain in the ruling class
must be forced to adopt a fundamentally different ethos. In the end, there
is no "functional equivalent" of solidarity and subsidiarity; only a leadership *and* working class steeped in such values will restore the republic.

What is first needed is a "mixing" that shatters the blindered con-
sensus of the elite, a mixing that must begin with the raw assertion of
political power by a new generation of political actors inspired by an
ethos of common-good conservatism. In order to achieve this end, control and effective application of political power will have to be directed
especially at changing or at least circumventing current cultural as well
as economic institutions from which progressive parties exercise their
considerable power. Otherwise, those institutions will be utilized to
circumvent and obstruct the only avenue to redress available to the
"many": demotic power. The aim should not be to achieve "balance" or
a form of "democratic pluralism" that imagines a successful regime
comprised of checks and balances, but rather, the creation of a new elite
that is aligned with the values and needs of ordinary working people.

While Aristotelian "blending" should be the aim, Lind commends
a necessary means to that further end. These means, as well as the com-

mendation of *realpolitik*, were originally detailed by that "evil" genius of practical political theorizing, Niccolò Machiavelli. Like the classical thinkers he otherwise criticized, Machiavelli believed that the clash between these two main elements of society—the *grandi* and *popolo* (or, nobility and the plebes)—was inevitable and unavoidable. Machiavelli held the view that it was, in fact, the very dissensus and clash between the two classes—the "elite" and the populace—that had provided the condition of liberty that in turn fueled Rome's rise from a republican city-state to a world-straddling empire. Machiavelli excoriated critics (and, implicitly, older authorities like Aristotle and Aquinas) for their disapproval of the discord and division that was a characteristic feature of Roman political life. In fact, he viewed such discord as a sign of Rome's political health, and, in particular, evidence of a vital resistance among *the populace* to the greater ability of the "nobility" to suppress the popular party. Machiavelli dismissed the "attacks" that "criticize[d] the clashes between the nobility and the populace," which in his view were "the primary factor making for Rome's continuing freedom."[13] This form of discord was evidence of the vitality of the populace to gain concessions from the elites that not only ended up resisting oppression and protecting the freedom of the populace, but ultimately protecting Roman freedom and extending Roman power as a whole. In a description that was doubtless written to invoke laughter, yet is likely to strike us as remarkably contemporary, he described some of these forms of resistance as follows:

> If someone were to argue the methods employed were extralegal and almost bestial—the people in a mob shouting abuse at the senate, the senate replying in kind, mobs running through the streets, shops boarded up, the entire populace of Rome leaving the city—I would reply such things only frighten those who read about them.

Machiavelli goes on to point out concessions that the people were able to extract from the elite, either through demonstration or by refusing to serve in the military. He concludes, "The demands of a free people are rarely harmful to the cause of liberty, for they are a response either to oppression or to the prospect of oppression."[14]

In resisting this new manifestation of an ancient form of tyranny, we can valuably turn to those ancient lessons that today have new resonance and can be brought creatively up to date. While one main aim of populism of the left is the redistribution of wealth—particularly in its Marxist variant—such efforts have proved evanescent to the end of shaping a very different ruling ethos. More often than not, such efforts have led to extensive damage to the broader economic order while leaving in place the institutions and attitudes that divide the elite from the people. What is needed, rather, is not an economics that purportedly seeks the equalization of outcome through the actual or effective elimination of private property, but an economic order embedded within a broader context of the common good that especially seeks conditions for the flourishing of people of all classes, particularly a balancing of change and order that allows for strong families and encourages strong social and civic forms. This will require the development of national economic policies that will displace the primacy of economic wealth creation for a small number of elites and replace it with a concern for the *national distribution of productive work, the expectation of a family-supportive wage for at least one member of a family, and the redistribution of social capital.* Such policies will view with deep suspicion the egalitarian claims of today's elites as nothing more than forms of class self-interest, particularly as an effort to retain exclusive possession of the relative social health that sustains their oligarchic status. This does not preclude efforts to create an economy grounded in solidarity and aiming toward greater equality, but such material approaches will prove insufficient to the task if progressive elites continue to advance a project that undermines the social conditions that are essential for the flourishing of the foundational social institutions of society: family, neighborhood, civil associations, and religious institutions. To revise a famous mantra: *It's the economy **and** the social order, stupid.*

The current political power of populism should be directed at the creation of a *mixed constitution*, breaking up the monopoly not only of economic power, but the social power that today reserves social well-being only to those with sufficient status and wealth. It should not require wealth to achieve social stability, nor should broad social instability be the acceptable consequence of concentrated economic prosperity. Rather, a stable and healthy civic society can afford prospects for flourishing even for those in average economic circumstances. What is needed is the application of **Machiavellian means to achieve Aristotelian ends**—the use of powerful political resistance by the populace against the natural advantages of the elite to create a mixed constitution *not* ultimately of the sort imagined by Machiavelli, but in which genuine common good is the result. The aim should not be a mixing of hostile elements, but a genuine blending of the classes in which the elites, under pressure from the people, actually take on features of *aristoi* and nobility—excellence, virtue, magnanimity, and a concern for the common good—and by means of which the people are elevated as a result.

Mixed Up (and Down)

Rather than thinking in a piecemeal fashion, a fuller program is needed to secure a "mixed constitution." As Tocqueville understood, this mixing cannot merely be focused upon reforms of official mechanisms of government, but must pervade society more widely. While working toward a genuine mixed government is essential, more important is that "mixing" occur throughout the social order. To the extent that elites govern especially through the main cultural institutions, those must be internally transformed ultimately toward the end of blending them with the needs and sentiments of the people. Such efforts to "mix" should be willing to alter the way that the professional classes (including, but not limited to, Tocqueville's focus on those in the law profession) view their work, the locus of political activity to more local levels, efforts to moralize the economy and social order alike, and pursue a healthy combination of what Tocqueville described as "the spirit of religion and the spirit of liberty." While political mixing should certainly be pursued, a far more fundamental effort at "mixing" the classes should be undertaken.

In pursuing "Machiavellian means to Aristotelian ends," the exercise of political power to increase the voice, status, prestige, and resources of the *popolo* should be unstinting. A main impetus should be the "mixing" of the classes, with a particular focus on putting elites into greater contact with, and developing sympathies for, the values and commitments of "the many." But these efforts should be understood as necessary, but not sufficient, to the further goal of "blending" the classes, fostering a deep and sympathetic alliance between the many and the few, the working and laptop classes. Initial efforts to this end should be focused on decreasing the power and influence of progressivism— whether in the form of right or left liberalism—in the main institutions of the West, and in turn, elevating the power and status of those concerns and commitments that are currently underrepresented in those domains.

Various ways of increasing the "mixing" of ordinary and elite in our political lives should be considered. On the political front, we could turn to some lessons of the original "populists," the anti-federalists, who feared that the Constitution's design would lead to the rule of an oligarchy concentrated in the nation's capital. They insisted that the people be given a stronger presence and voice in the national government, particularly by ensuring relative proximity between representatives and the represented. They called for small districts and potentially many representatives in the House, and James Madison, fearing that the Constitution would be scuttled by their demands, introduced an amendment along with those we count as the "Bill of Rights" that would limit the size of congressional districts to 50,000 people—in contrast to an average of 800,000 people living in districts today. The Congressional Apportionment Amendment passed the First Congress and was approved by eleven states without a deadline, meaning that it would need twenty-seven more states for ratification. Passage of this amendment would require an increase of approximately 5,500 representatives, for a House of about 6,000. A main effect of such a major change would be to amplify the voices of ordinary citizens among their representatives and help repair the divide that grows between the capital and its citizens.

Of course, such an exponential growth would be radical and difficult to digest (not to mention the challenge of gathering that number of people in any chamber in Washington, DC), but a substantial growth of "the People's House" well short of that proposal would be both more feasible and palatable. One recommendation, proffered twenty years ago by George Will, was to raise the number of representatives in the House to 1,000. Such an increase would ensure a more "representative" House of Representatives, and would significantly lessen the distance between representative and constituents. A major advantage, Will acknowledged, would be the possibility of a return of more "retail" politics, lessening the influence of money and media that is a source of bipartisan (as well as civic) aggravation.

> Candidates could campaign as candidates did in the pre-broadcasting era, with more retail than wholesale politicking, door to door, meeting by meeting. Hence there would be less need for money, most of which now buys television time. So enlarging the House can be justified in terms of the goal that nowadays trumps all others among "progressive" thinkers—campaign finance reform.[15]

Such an expansion would have the further advantage of increasing the numbers of people who are able to participate in the nation's governance, while decreasing the need for either wealth or fame as a requirement for office. Expansion could increase the number of "regular people" who might hold office, and decrease the presence of a professional political class. A relatively large House, and small districts, was seen as a desideratum of previously mentioned anti-federalist Melancton Smith, who, in his notable engagements with Alexander Hamilton during the New York ratification debate, stated his hope that the House would not be the stronghold of "speculative men"—an older term for "Anywhere" people—hoping instead for a House composed of people extensively informed by "local knowledge": a common and shared stockpile of accumulated wisdom that is derived from the lived experience of people in the places they lived and knew and loved. Smith stated:

> The idea that naturally suggests itself to our minds, when we speak of representatives, is that they resemble those they represent; they should be a true picture of the people; possess the knowledge of their circumstances and their wants; sympathize in all their distresses, and be disposed to seek their true interests. The knowledge necessary for the representatives of a free people, not only comprehends extensive political and commercial information, such as is acquired by men of refined education, who have leisure to attain to high degrees of improvement, but it should also comprehend that kind of acquaintance with the *common concerns* and occupations of the people, which men of the middling class of life are in general much better competent to, than those of a superior class. To understand the true commercial interests of a country, not only requires just ideas of the general commerce of the world, but also, and *principally*, a knowledge of the productions of your own country and their value, what your soil is capable of producing, the nature of your manufactures . . . ,

[and] more than an acquaintance with the abstruse parts of the system of finance.[16]

In this same spirit, we might consider additional ways to "mix" the classes within the federal government suggested by the later populists of the late nineteenth century. Of particular concern was not just an increase in overall representation, but what an earlier generation might have called representation of "estates"—important institutions and professions. The populists recognized that the wealthy and prominent actors in an increasingly financialized and industrial American economy would gain access to corridors of power with relative ease. Those in less wealthy or influential professions—but still signally important, such as farmers—would be disadvantaged. In order to forestall a de facto oligarchy, an earlier generation of populists recommended ways to gain representation of various estates. At the time of the creation of the Federal Reserve, for instance, populist legislators inspired by William Jennings Bryan's political success called for the inclusion of a farmer, a wage earner, and a small businessman on the Federal Reserve Board, suspecting that the Fed composed entirely of bankers would naturally favor the financiers.[17] In a different context, German companies practice a form of representation of "estates" through the legally required participation of employees in *Betriebsrat*—"workers' councils"— in corporate and business decisions. More than simply strengthening labor unions—itself a worthy undertaking—such an arrangement officially lodges representation of workers within the business organization, rather than as an oppositional force that must attempt to exert influence from outside the institution. Greater representation of *individuals* will almost always redound to the wealthy and influential; representation of "estates," in both the public and commercial domains, is more likely to achieve the ends of "mixing."

A further, if even more radical, way of mixing would be to "break up" Washington, DC, itself. As Ross Douthat has written, "We should treat liberal cities the way liberals treat corporate monopolies—not as growth-enhancing assets, but as trusts that concentrate wealth and power and conspire against the public good. And instead of trying to make them a little more egalitarian with looser zoning rules and more affordable housing, we should make like Teddy Roosevelt and try to break them up."[18] It is obscene that the nation's capital has become the center of such wealth, with the nation's largest concentration of what Charles Murray calls "Super Zips," where those with a combination of elite education and prosperity congregate.[19] If there was a good reason to have a geographic concentration of government departments and agencies at the time of the expansion of the federal government, before not only the advent of the telephone, but of the widespread adoption of online meetings during the COVID pandemic, the only reason today is the continuing self-interest of a wealthy and powerful bipartisan elite that perpetuates itself increasingly at the expense of the rest of the country (even counties farther flung, to where those who cannot afford housing must commute every day). Across the nation there are many affordable if struggling cities with beautiful, if deteriorating, buildings that would greatly benefit from the redistribution of jobs, an educated workforce, and a morale boost. Better still, those who circulate only with other denizens of DC would now work alongside people from other walks of life and would unavoidably encounter those with very different life circumstances. This is the kind of "mixing" that is needed for a renewal of "mixed constitution."

It is also high time to revisit the question of national service. An earlier generation regarded military service as a requirement for good citizenship, but the last president to serve in the military, George H. W. Bush—indeed, one who enlisted before he was legally of age—and the ethos of his generation have passed away. The infantry today is composed increasingly of people from parts of the country that are never encountered by those living in "Super Zips." Indeed, fewer Americans today than at any time personally know someone serving in the military, either through family acquaintances, or community connections. According to a 2011 Pew survey, only 33 percent of people eighteen to twenty-nine have had a family member serving in the military, as compared with nearly 80 percent among those age fifty to sixty-four.[20] Given contemporary trends, in which only 1 percent of the population now serves in the military, a widening military-civilian divide has likely only increased in the intervening decade.[21]

Here again, long-standing republican theory—echoed by the antifederalists at the time of the American founding—offers a cautionary note about such a divide. Republican theorists consistently warned that a divide between those who would decide *whether to fight*, and those who would be *required to fight*, was a mortal threat to any republic. Machiavelli warned against the reliance upon mercenaries who fought for reasons of financial gain or necessity, urging instead the overwhelming presence of citizen armies in which the broadest representation of the nation was present in the armed forces.[22] Critics of the proposed American Constitution warned against the perils of a standing army, particularly the temptation of political leaders to engage in wars that were desired by a political class—whether for personal glory, cynical political reasons, or imperial temptations—who would suffer no consequences in the prosecution of such wars.[23] More recently still, some called for the reintroduction of mandatory national military service in the lead-up to the war in Iraq, rightly suspecting that the eagerness of the ruling class to engage in war in the Middle East was unbalanced by concern for the lives of their own children.[24] Echoing this long tradition, military historian Andrew Bacevich has argued: "As Americans forfeit personal direct responsibility for contributing to the nation's defense—abandoning the tradition of the citizen-soldier—then the state gains ownership of the military. The army becomes Washington's army, not our army. And Washington has demonstrated a penchant for using the army recklessly."[25]

It may be, as our generals would quickly tell us, that there is no great need or demand for a large conscript army, but it would be a matter of political will to insist that it is in the civic interest that more Americans engage in military service, reviving ancient claims that a standing army is always a threat to the self-government of a republic. Still, differential forms of service could easily be instituted, with arguably greater need for a large civilian army to address the extensive need for repairs to our infrastructure and an even greater need for repair to our civic culture, especially through the mingling of people from a variety of walks of life.[26] A service requirement should be compulsory for all Americans—especially if we were to move to greater social benefits in areas of health care and education. During a time when young people are burdened with unconscionable levels of debt, a service requirement would be one just avenue to debt forgiveness, or a way of gaining a stake that could be devoted to education or a first home. Not only should there be an accompanying requirement to contribute to the commonweal in exchange for such benefits, but a universal requirement of a year's service to the nation would afford the invaluable benefit of mandating opportunities for interaction with people outside one's bubble.

Such forms of mixing should be a major priority in rethinking the role of elite universities in America today. These places are well-tuned sifting machines, separating economic wheat from chaff, and perpetuating a class divide that they purport to condemn. Already some especially wealthy institutions have had taxes imposed on endowments (proportionate to the numbers of undergraduate students), but this is a blunt instrument that does not adequately alter their behavior. President Trump's relatively fleeting and unfocused efforts at withholding federal funding to institutions that do not ensure free speech, or that train students in ideologically tainted critical race theory, were also examples of Machiavellian means, but these efforts, too, were largely symbolic impositions that left intact the structures of the meritocracy. Instead, both taxes on endowments and threats to federal funding should be used as inducements to wealthy and elite institutions to pursue genuine socioeconomic variety in order to foster *genuine* diversity of the student body at main campuses, as well as opening satellite campuses in less prosperous locations, attracting (at significantly reduced cost) local students who might well both desire a Harvard degree and not have the means or inclination to move to Cambridge (either before or after graduation). Also, rather than simply forgiving student debt (which perversely leaves in place bad incentives at these institutions), educational institutions should be required to assume a significant degree of responsibility for the indebtedness of students where those burdens are extensive and worsening. Public funding of public schools should be increased, albeit tied to expectations that faculty and administrators at public institutions respect the social and political commitments of the broader public that funds these institutions. Greater influence and oversight by elected political leaders over public educational institutions to ensure their commitment to the common good is essential—if necessary, including opposing faculty and administrative resistance—for instance, by the appointment of more activist trustees dedicated to fostering a "mixed constitution."

Further, creative ways of encouraging graduates from elite institutions to pursue atypical livelihoods should be explored. One possibility would be to provide incentives to the wealthiest institutions to repay or forgive loans of those students who pursue careers outside the areas of finance, consulting, and high-powered law firms, instead pursuing lower-paid vocations as teachers, soldiers, public servants in local and regional settings, religious vocations, and so forth. Even years spent as small-town professionals outside the corridors of power might be encouraged. Today these institutions are using both direct federal funds and indirect state and federal tax advantages to perpetuate an oligarchy, while shrouding these results with claims of woke equality. They should be forced through creative means into participation in a new regime of "mixed government."

But more importantly, the relative importance and centrality of these institutions should decrease in modern American society. Colleges are now engaged in what has been described as the "overproduction of elites," an over-credentialed and underemployed generation saddled with extensive debt and justified resentment.[27] Whatever commendation liberal education possessed for John Adams has long been eclipsed by the role of liberal arts colleges in advancing a narrow progressive ideology that shrouds oligarchic status maintenance while such institutions work assiduously to produce and sustain an elite. A vast number of students would benefit from more strenuous secondary education, steeped in the liberal arts for reasons commended by John Adams, and then directed at more focused vocational preparation than is currently available in the typical collegiate or university setting. A better model would be that of the German education system, which does not automatically privilege attendance at an academic university, and instead provides extensive options for various forms of vocational preparation. Apprenticeships and training in trades in a variety of professions is the norm.

University education could be substantially reduced, particularly for the eighteen-to-twenty-two-year-old demographic, and the public largesse now expended in expectation that most high school graduates will enroll in college in order to enter the professional class could instead be redirected to equally advantage other vocational options, as well as opening university education to an older population that is less likely to view it as a "hoop" and a subsidized four-year landlocked cruise excursion. Vocational schools or tracks ought to be supplemented by required introductory courses in a university-level general education, keeping open a potential track to university education for those who are genuinely inspired by and drawn to these studies, and redirecting the oversupply of PhDs from a shrinking collegiate job market into contact with the working class. Requirements in civic education at more vocational institutions would correct the potential for narrowness that can accompany a focus on work. Movement toward a genuine "mixed constitution" would seek to end the default norm of college education as synonymous with professional success, and with it, a significant redirection of public funds going toward support of a higher education industry that has increasingly become a highly partisan and ideological program at odds with the requirements of supporting a genuinely mixed constitution.

A great deal more expenditure and approbation should be expended on education in trades. Many parts of the country are experiencing a shortage in skilled trade workers. As much of the built environment of the previous century begins to decay, there is a growing need for skilled masons, carpenters, plumbers, electricians, and a host of trades. The elimination of "shop class" from high schools across the country signaled a form of official disapprobation; this trend should be reversed, and the study of trades should be reintroduced in secondary schools.[28] Public support for people studying the trades should be comparable to both financial and adulatory support that has long existed for university educations. At the same time, university students should be required to take at least a "trade" course—an introductory course in how to repair various systems in a typical household, for instance. My experience over the past quarter century in higher education suggests that a decreasing number of students have had any real encounter with "how things work," a consequence of members of the professional class losing touch with such skills that were prevalent in an earlier generation, and typically handed down from parents or grandparents to children. Today's universities are centers of "gnostic" indoctrination, or the near-complete disassociation of mind-work from the work of hands and the physical laws of reality. Even a passing acquaintance with the work of electricians, plumbers, farmers, and carpenters could help correct the dominant ethos that all of reality is manipulable and human nature itself is malleable.

Similar efforts should be undertaken to break up or limit the power of monopolistic economic organizations, reviving the long-standing populist suspicion toward and fear of the disfiguring effects of concentrated economic power. Such efforts have the potential of drawing support from corporate critics on both the right and the left, and revitalizing the trust-busting tradition that was a legacy of the populist and progressive traditions alike. The recent economic threats and political interference in states and localities such as Indiana, Arizona, Arkansas, and North Carolina should not be brooked. Any economic institution with sufficient power to bring financial ruin upon a sovereign political entity should be severely curtailed in the name of the common good. This should be true also of those semiprivate institutions, such as the NCAA, which use their privileged positions, accorded significant legal protections, to circumvent the political will of "Somewhere" people. Political leaders whose position is owed to such people should dispel any nostalgic views about free enterprise, instead recognizing that such economic institutions are seeking to shape a social order that is amenable to an oligarchic ruling class. A Machiavellian assertion of popular tumult should be directed at either preventing such abuses of financial power, or dismantling such institutions.

Strenuous efforts to encourage and support manufacturing industries should once again be a central and vigorous role of the federal government. Alexander Hamilton rightly regarded a strong manufacturing base as a basic feature of national security, stability, and prosperity, a view that has been forgotten especially by today's libertarian cheerleaders of free-market globalism who claim to revere "the Founders." Hamilton emphasized especially the role played by manufacturing in achieving national independence, and the corresponding freedom from the debasement and servitude that inevitably accompany economic reliance upon foreign powers. He also stressed the necessity of developing a middle-class workforce essential to a self-governing society, with financially secure and independent workers serving as a microcosm of the same independence necessary at the national level.[29] A society of producers was preferred to a society of consumers—the very reverse of today's economic ordering, in which consumption, debt, and waste are prized as main economic activities of many Americans.

Domestic manufacturing in certain sectors should simply be mandated. Various shortages at the start of the COVID pandemic, and continuing with supply chain shortages for several years after the pandemic, reveal that national security hangs in the balance. A secure supply of medicines, basic building supplies, food, and energy are essential. These kinds of manufactured goods, like military equipment, cannot be outsourced without compromising national security. No nation can be secure without the basic provision of these goods, and national policy should mandate that domestic sources of these and other basic goods always be readily available, even by blocking or at least minimizing their importation from other nations.

Hamilton called for the imposition of tariffs to secure necessary advantages against more developed foreign industries, a policy that was recently brought back to prominence under the presidency of Donald Trump. Tariffs, however, are generally crude instruments, often used as much or more for domestic political advantage than true enhancements to national competitiveness. Where necessary, tariffs can prevent dumping and counteract advantages that foreign manufacturers receive from public funding. However, they should generally be a policy of last resort, focused especially on protecting national manufacture of essential goods such as pharmaceuticals and basic materials. Instead, America (and any nation) should seek to improve its competitiveness and productivity by supporting several vital sectors that in turn are vital to a vibrant manufacturing base: infrastructure, manufacturing and R&D innovation, and related forms of education.[30] In each case, the use of public funds and support can enhance the position of private actors, countering similar forms of industrial support that exist in nearly every other advanced nation.

Debates over immigration should be reframed as yet another way that the elite class perpetuates its position, suppressing the income of

working classes while ensuring an affordable service class, the new
peasantry who replace yesteryear's indentured servant class.[31] Rather
than attacking immigrants, however—which is too often rightly perceived as cast in racist overtones—the efforts should be directed at
those who employ illegal immigrants, a tactic not unlike that of the
pro-life movement that focuses not on the despair of pregnant women,
but the greed of those who would profit from their misfortune. High-
profile arrests and prosecutions of employers who break the law should
become regular features of national reporting, and would act as a powerful deterrent that would in turn have far greater impact than any wall
is likely to have. Reminders should be given that such efforts to restrict
illegal immigration in the effort to support the working class were the
positions of renowned civil rights leaders such as former Notre Dame
president Fr. Theodore Hesburgh. As head of the Select Commission on
Immigration and Refugee Policy that was convened by President Jimmy
Carter in the late 1970s, Hesburgh viewed restrictions to illegal immigration as a means of reducing the "pernicious effects" of competition
"from this source of inexpensive labor," and as a means of combatting
generalized "lawlessness" perpetrated by those who flouted immigration laws, the effects of both of which were more likely to be felt by
members of the working class.[32]

Renewed efforts to enforce a moral media should be pursued. Here,
Charles Murray's observation that elites do not "preach" what they practice should be emphasized. Programming that lionizes various forms of
transgression and libertinism—sexual, drugs, and mockery of religious
belief—should be denounced for perpetuating the class advantage of
the elite, a form of propaganda that seeks to suppress the life prospects
of the lower working class for whom "transgression" is not the safe play
of sophomores on a college campus, but the difference between life and
death. Pornography should be extensively controlled and even banned
for obvious reasons: it is degrading and corrupting to both participants
and viewers, and inescapably involves exploitation especially of poor

women.[33] Where necessary, further forms of legislation that promote public morality, and forbid its intentional corruption, should be considered. Such legislation was long regarded as an essential feature for the inculcation of civic virtue required among a republican citizenry—and efforts to develop jurisprudence and judges who will respect the original "police powers" of states and even, where possible, the nation should be encouraged.[34] Those with a megaphone should not only emphasize the immorality of a large swath of contemporary popular culture, but its elitism, an implicit effort to destroy the lives of the less fortunate. To do so, of course, is to point out its degradation to the moral character of citizens, but in a way that ought to shame and correct rather than embolden the shameless.

Many other efforts at "mixing" should be considered. A change to our electoral process, one favoring caucuses over primaries, would shift power from opinion makers in the media and the sheer force of money in advertising to the living rooms of citizens, who should be afforded the opportunity to exercise political self-government. Efforts to impose the actual costs associated with suburbs and commuting, and the massive costs of a transportation system that favors placelessness, should be more directly borne by those who would live as "Anywhere" people.

Following the counsel of Tim Carney in his book *Alienated America*, one of the best ways to ensure the "redistribution of social capital" is strengthening the institutions of civil society. There needs to be a more frank assessment of the role of both concentrated political and economic power in the destruction of social institutions whose benefits— a flourishing family and community life—ought to be more equally available to every citizen in our nation. A common-good conservatism, moreover, rejects the right-liberal stance that a healthy civil society can result both from encouragement and the shrinking of government. Government, both local and national, can serve as a counterweight to the destructive forces of a destabilizing economic order. A focus on new policies in which the public realm fosters and supports a healthy civil society should become a conservative priority.[35] "Localism" is easily destroyed in a globalized system but can flourish if protected under an umbrella of public policy devoted to breaking up concentrations of economic power.

Public efforts to support and shore up marriage and family must be a foremost commitment. A Cabinet-level position, whether in the Cabinet or an equivalent to the national security advisor, should be a priority of a future administration that aims to develop a common-good conservatism at the heart of a "mixed constitution." Policies rewarding marriage and family formation should be given pride of place.[36] A "family czar" should look not only to promising proposals and examples in the United States, but adapt comparable efforts abroad, such as those undertaken by Hungary's Ministry of Family Affairs. This ministry has pursued an array of creative policies, under the rubric "Family Protection Action Plan," that seek to increase family formation and birth rates in Hungary, including paid leave policies for parents and grandparents, financial incentives for families producing three or more children—including a generous grant for families with multiple children—and even relief from all future income taxes for working mothers of four children or more. Families with children are extended substantial support for housing and other costs.[37] Over 6 percent of Hungary's GDP is now devoted to policies that support family formation, amid efforts more broadly to support a distinct Hungarian culture. While Hungary predictably is the object of condemnation from Western progressive elites, it has charted a distinct path from that of progressive liberal democracies whose future looks more likely to be that of internal cold civil wars to movement toward a genuinely "mixed constitution."

Most importantly, aristopopulism will advance in the Western nations through forthright acknowledgment and renewal of the Christian roots of our civilization. The emaciated liberalism that marks today's elite—valuing the deracinated freedom of the individual and the purported merit of economically successful lives—has led to governance by a deeply corrupt oligarchic class. The legacy of Christianity called for service and sacrifice by the advantaged on behalf of the poor and forgotten—moreover, it understood such actions were the truest acts of nobility and generosity. Public acknowledgment and celebration of these Christian roots are essential to the creation of an ethos of genuine service by elites on behalf of those who do not share their advantages. Right-liberal and left-liberal progressives effectively combine to undermine the waning presence of this Christian ethos that, according to authors like Lind, once guided a more solidaristic economic and social order as recently as the 1950s. "Christian democracy" was thought by many leading intellectuals and political figures in the post–World War II era to be the necessary corrective to the cruel left and right ideologies that dominated the world at the time. That hope has largely been abandoned, in both Europe and the United States, crowded out by the ideology of liberalism and its devotion to economic inequality and social libertinism. The revival of forthright and strenuous efforts to reinstitute the ethos and the kinds of policies once pursued by Christian Democrats is vital to efforts to achieve "Aristotelian ends."

Recently, a number of thinkers have pointed in the direction of such a revival, calling for the revitalization of a public Christian culture. Journalist Sohrab Ahmari, theologian C. C. Pecknold, and political theorist Gladden Pappin have argued that only a Christian culture can recharge the West's potential for law and culture that undergird flourishing for ordinary people who are otherwise drowned in the overwhelming tides of liberal "progress." In an essay published in the journal *The American Conservative*, they wrote:

Christian nations take care of the sick and the poor, preserve life from conception until natural death, incarnate their faith in holidays and festivals, and inspire public life with hope for eternity. Because of that, traditional Christianity stands to regain importance whenever and wherever liberalism falters.

This Christianity remains latent but palpable, a vestigial
structure whose importance cannot be overlooked. . . . Like the
quiet country shrines still visited by the faithful, these vestigial
practices could become functional parts of Christian politics
once again.[38]

Such a politics infused with the West's Christian inheritance will
combine religious and working-class calls for days of rest; holidays (a
word meaning "holy days") that allow families to gather, free of the
distractions and demands of commerce; public opportunities for prayers
of hope, comfort, and mourning; public support for schools and chari-
ties that care for the young and the sick and the frail not out of lucre,
but inspired by Christian charity; and a revitalization of our public
spaces to reflect a deeper belief that we are called to erect imitations of
the beauty that awaits us in another Kingdom.

These and other broad policy proposals are no doubt subject to the
manifold criticisms of unintended consequences but would shift fundamental priorities and corrupt arrangements. Many, some, or few may
ultimately prove both feasible and likely to advance the aims of forming a new elite, while others that are yet to be recommended might prove
to be wildly successful in the aim of fostering a common-good conservatism. Most important is that policies in this spirit be developed, encouraged, and pursued in an effort to foster a different kind of elite, one
aligned with the requirements and needs of the working classes. Political leaders seeking to use the power of the state to foster a different
kind of elite should cease thinking within the worn-out ruts of liberal
ideology—one that is generally content with the fiction that all citizens
can eventually become members of the laptop class while abandoning
all semblance of cultural inheritance. Instead, creative and experimental efforts to foster a new, distinct, genuinely *noble* elite should be a
main aim of a successor political form to the decaying progressivism of
an exhausted liberalism.

The task of a renewed political movement seeking to repair and move beyond the divide of our nation and globe ought to pose real threats to the continued advantages of the current elite. But the deeper aim ought not to be its destruction—for, as we know from history, those who replace the elites simply become the new elites, and are often harsher and more brutal. Rather, using Machiavellian means to Aristotelian ends, efforts aimed at genuine forms of "mixing" should be undertaken with the aim that today's elites—for lack of a better word, the oligarchs—instead become (again, for lack of a better word), or are replaced by, genuine aristocrats. Such "aristocrats" are commended not in that contemporary, negative meaning of a word describing a person possessing a superior position who has not earned or deserved that state, but in the classical sense: someone of virtue, excellence, and, above all, who regards that status as a kind of gift and obligation to be put in the service of those of less advantage and power—in other words, the common good. Today, with the elite adopting the banner of "democracy" and egalitarianism as cover for the further advancement of their status, it is safe to conclude that an ennobling of our elite will not come about from goodwill, but rather through the force of a threat from the *popolo*. In days yet to come, it might be hoped, through a kind of Aristotelian habituation in virtue, a genuine *aristoi* might arise, ironically through the efforts of an energized, forceful, and demanding populace. In turn, such *aristoi* ought to work to improve the lives, prospects, and fate of the people, cultivating in turn the kind of people who themselves take on the qualities of genuine *aristoi*. Through a kind of genuine mixing of the excellences possible to a noble nobility, and the decent hopes of a grounded people of common sense demanding better from those with advantages, we might actually come to witness a kind of regime change—the flowering of a mixed constitution, a kind of "aristopopulism" that might deserve the name Republic.

7

Toward Integration

If "Machiavellian means" may be necessary to disrupt the credentialing monopoly, the promotion of anti-culture, and geographic separation of the ruling class from those who are falling behind, the more fundamental aim must be "Aristotelian ends." As Aristotle envisioned, the aim of a "mixed regime" is not the "checks and balances" between the classes, but their eventual melding into an entirely different regime— what he called "polity," or, simply, a "constitution." More than "mixing-as-*balancing*," what is ultimately needful is "mixing-as-*blending*." For this to occur, a successor regime must eschew liberalism's core value of *separation*, and instead seek a deeper and more fundamental and pervasive form of *integration*.

The ideal of "integration" has been variously defined over the decades, including racial, economic, and the creation of new transnational identities. While the word is well worn, a new situation requires a new way of thinking about the political possibilities of "integration." To overcome the *dis*integration that is so central to liberalism, what is needed is a pervasive form of *postliberal integration*.

The integration needed is less subject specific than previous forms (such as aspirations to economic or racial integration) aimed instead at the overcoming of the *dis*integration of most forms of relationality that is a major aim and realization of the liberal order. From the mundane—the *dis*integration of how we live, passing our lives in wholly separate spheres of commerce, schooling, domesticity, and the religious; to the political—seeking to reintegrate the aims and ends of the leadership class with ordinary people; to the ontological—overcoming the narrow ideals of progress that animate human beings in favor of the shared goal of *flourishing*—the alternative to a liberal order rests far less on systemic political arrangements, and more on a different way of understanding the human creature in relation to other humans and with the world and cosmos. Ideals and ends of integration must confront and defeat liberal *dis*integration.

The Problem of Disintegration

The French political philosopher Pierre Manent has stressed that the most "distinctive" trait of liberal democracy is its "organization of separations."[1] He regards both the success and the perils of liberal democracy as arising from its tendency to generate an increasing number of "separations" in every domain of life. Among those separations he lists as most distinctive and pervasive are these six:

1. Separation of professions; or division of labor
2. Separation of powers
3. Separation of church and state
4. Separation of civil society and the state
5. Separation between represented and representative
6. Separation of facts and values, or science and life[2]

The foundational "separation" of liberal democracy is the "division of labor," famously described by Adam Smith as the subdivision of work into increasingly specific and discrete activities. This "separation" gives rise to greater productivity as each worker is responsible for one distinct part of the production, though it limits each worker's knowledge about the full nature of the product as well as shrinks the interactions among workers. While its impact in the economic sphere is celebrated and well known, Manent rightly notes that this form of separation is far more extensive and implicates many more aspects of life than merely the economic domain.

Manent argues that these and countless other forms of separation are hallmarks of the liberal order: "These separations *must* be put into effect, and thereafter they *must* be preserved. Why? Because these separations are necessary for liberty. Better yet, they define liberty as the moderns understand it. Modern liberty is founded on an organization of separations."[3] A main separation that has been the subject of this book is that between the ethos of the ruling class and those it governs. This separation has both been required for, and been worsened by, the "progress" that today has led liberalism to a loss of legitimacy in the eyes of the governed, and an increasing imposition by the ruling class of liberal policies and ends to advance its advantages while rendering tractable the governed. Its solution lies not simply in the political imposition of "Machiavellian means" aimed at "mixing," but overcoming the very basis of the "organization of separations" toward the end of a more pervasive "organization of integration." In the remaining pages, I will address how the potential "integration" that combats "the organization of separations" would begin to move us to a time "after liberalism." In particular, I will sketch out aspirations toward "integration" in several critical spheres that currently reflect societal "*dis*integration":

1. Overcoming "Meritocracy"
2. Combatting Racism
3. Moving Beyond Progress
4. Situating the Nation
5. Integrating Religion

Overcoming "Meritocracy"

Perhaps the most fundamental "separation" that defines liberalism is the distinction between winner and loser, or, to echo Locke's words, the "industrious and rational" in distinction to the "quarrelsome and contentious." The liberal economic and social order rests on winnowing those who flourish under its unbounded anti-culture from those who either lack the requisite economic skills or refuse to be caught up in the "race to the top," or both. A number of recent authors have explored the political, social, and economic pathologies that have accompanied the increasingly stark divide between those who win and lose the meritocratic sweepstakes, noting in particular that the political tumultuousness and instability of recent years arises as a direct consequence of the growing domination of meritocrats as a ruling class. In his important book *The Tyranny of Merit*, Harvard political theorist Michael Sandel has diagnosed some of the deepest sources of today's political discontents arising from the "toxic brew of hubris and resentment," inevitable consequences that result from the pervasive belief in "self-making."[4]

Under meritocracy, the belief that one's status and position has been wholly earned and deserved becomes widespread, leading to internalization of self-congratulation among the successful for their achievements and corresponding condescension toward the unfortunate, while those who fail to make the cut simultaneously are likely to blame themselves as well as develop deep reservoirs of resentment toward the successful. The divide between society's winners and losers comes to be seen as rational and justified. Larry Summers—an economic advisor to Barack Obama as well as former president of Harvard University—expressed the inevitable inequality of a meritocracy as an accurate if somewhat regrettable measure of justifiable personal worth: "One of the challenges in our society is that the truth is kind of a disequalizer. One of the reasons that inequality has probably gone up in our society is that people are being treated closer to the way that they're supposed to be treated."[5]

Sandel concludes his study by suggesting that one way to redress especially the self-congratulatory ethos that directly arises from meritocratic achievement would be to introduce an element of chance and luck into the mix—specifically, a "lottery of the qualified." Under such a scheme, admission to the top-tier "sorting machines" of the meritocracy—Harvard, Yale, Princeton, etc.—would be the result of both selectivity and randomness. Once applicants had been determined to be qualified, any further selection would be the result of a purely randomized lottery. A main result, Sandel argues, would be to "deflate meritocratic hubris, by making clear what is true in any case, that those who land on top do not make it on their own but owe their good fortune to family circumstance and native gifts that are morally akin to the luck of the draw."[6]

Yet, under this slightly altered meritocratic arrangement, the greater likelihood is that the winners would continue to have ample cause to congratulate themselves. The introduction of more obvious forms of randomness would be as minimally influential as current forms of luck; instead, what would continue to exert the greatest influence in the minds of both "winners" and "losers" is the fact that those who rise to the top were among "the qualified." The "organization of separations" would remain intact, and under that regime, the tendency to self-congratulation (and self-blame) would continue to dominate. Sandel—like so many of those who command the meritocratic heights—accepts the fundamental legitimacy of a deeper "organization of separations."

Liberalism typically seeks to keep intact the separation between "merit" and equality. Classical liberals stress the necessity of merit, while pressing for true equality of opportunity. Progressive liberals, like John Rawls, seek to close the economic gap between winners and losers while nevertheless keeping intact the system of merit. All of these proposals are forms of "*dis*integration": keeping separate what rather needs to be joined.

The "meritocratic" system established by liberalism is especially susceptible to the *political* divisions that arise from the "organization of separations." The purpose of the political order is to separate the wheat from the chaff—Jefferson's "natural aristocracy"—encouraging those with prized abilities to pursue their own success while relying upon impersonal mechanisms of the market or the state to afford some secondary benefits to those who are not similarly blessed. The battle among elites in the liberal order is fought over which depersonalized mechanism is the best means of benefiting the unfortunate while the successful are liberated from any actual obligations to their fellow citizens. "Classical" and "progressive" liberalism are two sides of the same coin, and eventually, those who are ill served by *both* depersonalized mechanisms will turn against the partisans of the false divide. That is one main feature of our contemporary political tumult: a reaction against both guises of the meritocracy.

The conclusion by some is that the American tradition was established explicitly to reject any notion of solidarity: we were conceived as a nation of self-making, striving individuals. Sandel, among others, notes that the more individualistic and achievement-based ethos of the American meritocracy contributes to a significant extent to the relative weakness of American social welfare and an economic safety net. While the sense of solidarity has waxed and waned during American history, it could well be argued that America's deepest ethos was born of the Lockean belief in individual self-fashioning and the resulting earned status and position of individuals in American society and economic order. At its base, belief in the legitimacy of rewards accrued from individual striving constitutes a main feature of "the American Dream."

By contrast, postliberal integration would take the following form: inequality based upon differences in talent, interest, and achievement is not a marker of individual "merit," but, rather, a sign of our deeper solidarity, a window into our mutual need and insufficiency. Inequality is a window into our deeper equality, demanding not the flattening of our differences, but recognition of our mutual obligations.

One way of exemplifying the difference is to underscore how the two worldviews differ in regard to the relationship of difference and commonality. Classical liberalism sees unity in a secondary relationship to our differences: as stated in the Declaration of Independence, in order to secure our individual rights, we establish something common—our nation. Thus, that which is *common* (the nation) serves our *differences* (our rights). What we share in common supports, and even accelerates, an ever more pervasive system of inequality.

By contrast, there is a competing conception of the American order that predates this understanding, and has exercised countervailing influence. By this alternate understanding, our differences "serve" (or direct us toward) our commonality. What appears private, individual, and "mine" is actually understood to be more fundamentally in the domain of the public, common, and "ours."

Notwithstanding the unstinting efforts of "right liberals" to define America exclusively in Lockean, individualistic terms, this latter conception of how to understand our differences was articulated especially through the Christian tradition that was carried to these shores by European settlers and coexisted with and tempered liberalism until recent American history. Confronting the same challenge of how to reconcile difference to commonality, Christianity approached the challenge through an opposite perspective to that of the liberal: the Christian is called to understand natural differences in light of a deeper unity. This is the insistent appeal of St. Paul in 1 Corinthians 12–13, a call upon the squabbling Christians of Corinth to understand that their gifts were bestowed not for the glory of any particular person or class of people, but for the benefit and flourishing of the body of the people as a whole.

For the body does not consist of one member but of many. If
the foot should say, "Because I am not a hand, I do not belong
to the body," that would not make it any less a part of the body.
And if the ear should say, "Because I am not an eye, I do not
belong to the body," that would not make it any less a part of
the body. . . . But as it is, God arranged the organs in the body,
each one of them, as he chose. . . . As it is, there are many parts,
yet one body. The eye cannot say to the hand, "I have no need of
you," nor again the head to the feet, "I have no need of you." On
the contrary, the parts of the body which seem to be weaker are
indispensable.[7]

Keenly aware of how the diversity of gifts was dividing the community of Corinth—as it tends to divide all human communities that lack
a strong ethos of solidarity—Paul sought to call to mind an *integrated*
understanding of how different gifts were bestowed not to the individual glory or benefit of any particular individual, but instead for the
benefit of the whole community. "That there may be no discord in the
body, but that the members may have the same care for one another. If
one member suffers, all suffer together; if one member is honored, all
rejoice together."[8]

America was settled in this tradition before it was America. The
Puritan John Winthrop echoed this teaching in his oft-quoted but
seldom-read sermon aboard the ship *Arbella*: "A Model of Christian
Charity." From this sermon is drawn the inspiring phrase "we shall be
as a city on a hill"—a line that has been invoked by countless political
figures, though almost always to ends completely opposite to those intended by Winthrop. It was Ronald Reagan who so often and reverently
invoked that phrase, but without conveying or perhaps even knowing its
original context: the new colony should be a model of "charity" based
in shared obligations, duties, and care toward all of the members of the
community.

Winthrop began his speech with the observation that people have in all times and places been born or placed into low and high stations. This pervasive and even permanent differentiation, however, was not permitted and ordained for the purpose of the degradation of the former and glory of the latter—as "meritocracy" encourages its winners to believe—but for the greater glory of God, expressed in particular through a predominant understanding that one's talents are gifts bestowed to individuals so that they might in turn be contributions for the benefit of the whole community. Rather than fragmented individuals who consider themselves owners of their own talents and its rewards, rather, we are all stewards of gifts that are intended for the benefit of one's fellows. Winthrop stressed that the "fact of difference" should be understood to reveal a deeper unity.

Echoing Paul's passages in Corinthians (as well as "the counsel of Micah" of the Old Testament), Winthrop limns an image of community in which the various forms of diversity are offered as common gifts as a means to greater unity:

> We must be knit together in this work as one man. We must entertain each other in brotherly affection; we must be willing to abridge ourselves of our superfluities, for the supply of others' necessities; we must uphold a familiar commerce together in all meekness, gentleness, patience, and liberality. We must delight in each other, make others' conditions our own, rejoice together, mourn together, labor and suffer together: always having before our eyes our commission and community in the work, our community as members of the same body.[9]

For Winthrop—in profound contrast to Reagan's later condemnation of the solidaristic dimension of government and his elevation of individual liberty—the political order was duly constituted as a necessary tutor in requisite public-spiritedness, especially with a focus on restraining the temptations of the high, mighty, and wealthy to unjustly and selfishly benefit from their gifts. Under "a due form of government," he stated, "the care of the public must oversway all private respects by which not only conscience but mere civil policy doth bind us; for it is a true rule that particular estates cannot subsist in the ruin of the public."[10] While public-spiritedness was rightly to be encouraged in the private, familial, and civil spheres, it required as well the force of law, particularly to restrain the self-serving temptations of the strong and direct them to support of the weak in their communities. Law directed to fostering solidarity thereby reinforced the greater majesty and priority of the public over the private. If the new colony was successful in this effort, the "city upon a hill" would deserve the admiring gaze of the world. This was the original aspiration of the aspirational exceptionalism of the first European settlers—before there was an America.

This ethos coexisted with, and often combatted against, the privatism and *dis*integration of liberalism, yet in recent years especially lost ground to these forces. Still, this nonliberal understanding of the *public* responsibility entailed by the very fact of our *differences* is not only an *American* tradition, but one that arrived here before the founding of a liberal nation, and which has its deepest roots in the premodern inheritance originating in Christian wellsprings.

This nonliberal tradition of public-spiritedness and communal responsibility was noted and even lauded by Tocqueville as the source of the active civic engagement and social equality manifested in the "spirit of the township" in the New England states that he visited. The citizens of New England, he wrote, are habituated to self-government through a mutual and ongoing participation in public life that cultivates "a taste for order," "the harmony of powers," "the forms without which freedom proceeds only through revolutions," and "the nature of his duties as well as the extent of his rights."[11] More than a utilitarian venue where policy is pursued, the constant reminder of the mutual public obligations of strong and weak alike constituted a form of ongoing education: "The institutions of a township are to freedom what primary schools are to science; they put it within reach of the people; they make them taste its peaceful employ and habituate them to making use of it."[12] While aboard the *Arbella*, Winthrop acknowledged the permanence of distinct classes; nevertheless, what struck Tocqueville about life in the New England townships was a pervasive experience of equality: "In New England, division of ranks does not even exist in memory; there is, therefore, no portion of the township that is tempted to oppress the other."[13]

The pattern of civic life in the township was established by pervasive acceptance of what Tocqueville describes earlier as a "beautiful definition of freedom" that was articulated by one of New England's Puritan founders. Contrasting what the Puritans held to be a "corrupt" version of liberty, which held that people should do as they "list" ("wish"), Tocqueville's Puritan source offered instead a "beautiful definition of freedom": "There is a civil, a moral, a federal *liberty*, which is the proper end and object of *authority*; it is a *liberty* for that only which is *just* and *good*; for this *liberty* you are to stand with the hazard of your very *lives*."[14] The source of this "beautiful definition of freedom"? John Winthrop.

This older and foundational understanding of liberty arising from the shared duties and call to a contribution of various gifts to one's community remains in our collective DNA. While liberals relentlessly claim that the essence of America is an understanding of liberty entailing the freedom of individuals to "do as they list"—whether in the economic or social domains—Tocqueville noted that any prospect for the flourishing of democracy in America rested on a premodern understanding of liberty, one that predated the arrival of its corrupt liberal form not only historically, but even arriving first on the shores of America. There is no deeper American corrective to the disintegrating form of liberty that exacerbates our divisions than the predecessor understanding of liberty that would obligate the strong to the weak and encourage every citizen to understand their gifts in light of our public weal.

Today, a renewal of this "beautiful definition" would entail the integration of a working-class ethos of social solidarity, family, community, church, and nation, with the supportive requisite virtues of those blessed by privilege. Rather than winners and losers in the meritocracy, a more generalized pursuit of flourishing can be made widely available to a people, no matter their station in life. This requires special duties and responsibilities on the part of the elites—those who must "abridge themselves of their superfluities"—and whose main pursuit must become not individual self-fashioning and achievement, but support for a social, economic, and political order that supports the flourishing of all.

Combatting Racism

During the pandemic year of 2020, America renewed a wrenching and necessary self-examination of its legacy of racial inequality. Emotions have run exceedingly high amid a backdrop of disease, death, lockdowns, economic crisis, political violence, and profound partisan division. The prospects of achieving sufficient national solidarity and goodwill over the long-standing and pervasive fact of racism—while ever more pressing—nevertheless in this historical moment seems inauspicious. But even more challenging is the obdurate fact that the issue of racism has remained trapped in the dominant paradigm of "separations," tracking with the same logic as the social disintegrating forces in economics, education, social life, and family life.

Ironically, a long-dominant approach to racial inequality was labeled as "integration." One of its most inspiring articulations is found in an oft-quoted passage in Martin Luther King's "I Have a Dream" speech, delivered on August 28, 1963, from the steps of the Lincoln Memorial. King eloquently declared, "I have a dream that my four children will one day live in a nation where they will not be judged by the color of their skin but by the content of their character." In this dream of "integration," differences of race melt away, and only the natural distinctions of merit—"the content of one's character"—remain. King linked this call to the phrases of the Declaration of Independence and, by extension, its roots in Lockean philosophy. To this day, King's evocation of a color-blind meritocratic society remains a powerful attraction to classical liberals, and is invoked not only on behalf of equal opportunity for blacks, but also by groups who today experience unjust exclusion from open access to the meritocracy, such as Hispanics and Asian Americans.

If this was a goal, a profound political disagreement over means has persisted to the current day. While classical liberals have typically held that meritocratic criteria should apply in a wholly race-blind manner, progressive liberals have insisted that a color-blind approach to inclusion unjustly assumes a relatively comparable starting point in the race of life. Because of historic injustices that have collectively penalized African Americans—a legacy of slavery, Jim Crow, and ongoing forms of both explicit and implicit racism—a degree of equalization needs to be achieved through preferential admissions, hiring, and other forms of affirmative action. Implicitly, the end remains the same: a world in which there will eventually be rough equality of opportunity for all the races, in which meritocratic criteria can be applied in a wholly color-blind manner. This was the stated hope, for instance, of Justice Sandra Day O'Connor, who supported some forms of preferential admission to historically disadvantaged groups, but only as a temporary measure that, she hoped, would no longer be necessary with enough passage of time. In her majority opinion in *Grutter v. Bollinger* (2003), she wrote that "race-conscious admissions policies must be limited in time," predicting that "twenty-five years from now, the use of racial preferences will no longer be necessary to further the interest approved today."[15]

Yet, such aspiration to "integration" seeks universal, equal inclusion in the "organization of separations," into a social order of *dis*integration. A reigning presumption has been that *inclusion* in America is achieved especially through an ever-perfected sifting of the talented from the below average, with the benefits of progress advanced by meritocratic winners indirectly benefiting those who are outside the charmed circle. In place of separation by race, the implicit aim was the universal racial inclusion that would be achieved by separating individuals by talent and achievement.

Recently, that aim has been challenged from an anti-liberal left, grounded in arguments of "critical race theory." Rather than seeing racism as a temporary *departure* from liberal aims and norms, critical race theory holds that the very basis of the Western liberal order is deeply, pervasively, and systemically racist. Definitions of "excellence," "achievement," and "merit" are informed by the assumptions of white descendants of Europeans, ones that are fundamentally designed permanently to hold nonwhites in a subservient position. Forms of enacted "whiteness" are discovered in the treatment of all nonwhites, women and transgendered, nonheterosexuals, non-Christians. According to a theory called "intersectionality," all nonwhite, nonmale, nonheterosexual, non-Christian peoples are comparably maltreated and aligned in their resistance to the oppressiveness of dominant white European civilization. At every turn, its proponents denounce "white privilege."[16]

This theory proposes a different form of "separation": white from black, men from nonmen, nonheterosexuals from heterosexuals, Christians from non-Christians. The implicit claim is that only the effective elimination of whiteness—if not wholesale extirpation, the replacement of whites in elite positions and institutions by those of "intersectional" identities, and, presumably, those of unacceptable identity who approve and applaud antiracism (i.e., progressive whites)—will give rise to a genuinely just society. These theories originated first in various "iden-

tity" disciplines on university campuses—black studies, women's studies, gay studies, etc.—they have now become increasingly mainstream
in the operations of corporations, bureaucracies, and a host of major
organizations. The presumption seems to be that the only true path to
human reconciliation is through the effective elimination of the sole
oppressor class in existence—white, heterosexual Christian men (and
anyone sympathizing with them). It is not accidental that this theory
acknowledges influences of Marxist theory, which—like Marxism—
identifies an oppressor class that must be overthrown by an uprising of
an oppressed class, after which there is a vaguely sketched utopian future in which old divisions have been overcome and a perfected solidarity is achieved.

Yet this vision has been thoroughly pervaded with the liberationist
ethos of progressive liberalism, particularly a vision of liberation from
all traditionalist norms, the overthrowing of custom as a main conduit
of tyranny, and a pervasive ethos of sexual liberation. With only the
slightest alteration, this new articulation of a progressivist Marxism identifies the great barrier to liberation as racism, rather than merely capitalism (indeed, capitalism is increasingly defined as one form of racism). It is
a new iteration of a revolutionary vision that stands to advantage especially the intellectual and professional classes. "Intersectionality" proposes
the equation of the experience of African Americans with all oppressed
groups—women, gays, transsexuals, Muslims—that, together, will overthrow the dominant class and introduce a new dawn in human history.

Yet even beneath the umbrella of "intersectionality," this imagined
future seems no less likely to usher in a utopian future than its Marxist
precursor. Already, the various groups within the intersectional fold
jockey for position in the future dominance over their current allies,
arguing over which marginalized group is most oppressed.

Given the likely continued positioning for victimhood status among
identity groups, it appears unlikely that there will be a quick and easy

conclusion for who counts as *most* or *especially* oppressed—particularly
as plum positions available for installation of approved identities decrease. The likely outcome of successful implementation of "critical
race theory" will not only lead to marginalization of whatever identity
is deemed inherently unjust, but a growing effort to define various "intersectional" identities as *more* or *less* oppressed than others. An intensification of the "organization of separations" is inevitable.

Rarely mentioned in rarified academic circles is that this theory
has arisen with remarkable coincidence with the worsening circumstances of white working-class Americans and members of the native
working class throughout the Western world. Over roughly the time
frame examined by Charles Murray—1960–2000, when, around the
1990s, the fortunes of well-credentialed white Americans began to significantly diverge from the fortunes of less-educated white Americans—
once-dominant hopes and efforts for "integration" began a decades-long
loss of traction in favor of arguments for the *inherent* and *systemic* racism of all white people. That is, *just as the conditions for working-class
solidarity across racial lines became increasingly possible*, the ruling
class changed the narrative. As the system of meritocratic sorting became more politically tenuous, losing support and legitimacy particularly among the working class *regardless of race*, the institutions charged
with maintenance of the "organization of separations" moved from a
narrative of racial affirmative action to charges of *systemic racism*, regardless of one's economic and social status. Wealthy, well-educated
blacks were to be understood to be as oppressed as those in the black
working class, while those in the declining white working class enjoyed
"privilege." The titanic effort to make this the new, dominant narrative
about race in America (and, increasingly, across the Western world) reflected a deep, vested interest of the ruling class in maintaining its position by dividing the shared condition of the working class between
a "privileged" and "oppressed" class drawn along racial lines. Michael

Lind has perceptively identified this international trend, and, by implication, the growing attractiveness of "critical race theory": "The pattern of politics in today's Western democracies is best described as a struggle with three sides—the overclass and two segments of a divided working class. Working-class immigrants and some native minority group members whose personal conditions are improving compete with many members of the native working class, mostly but not exclusively white, who find their economic status, political power, and cultural dignity under threat from below as well as from above. *The only winners are a third group: the mostly native, mostly white overclass elites who benefit from the division of the working class.*"[17]

Thus, we have witnessed three dominant proposals for improvement of the condition especially of African Americans, all reflecting a progressivist slant that keeps intact the current elite structures of modern liberal orders: 1. "integration" through inclusion in the meritocracy (classical liberal); 2. "integration" through inclusion in the meritocracy through preferences and affirmative action (progressive liberal); and 3. a proposal to replace the current ruling class that, it turns out, in fact strengthens the position of the current ruling class by adopting a revolutionary project that damages the life prospects of the working class it claims to defend (Marxist). All of these approaches propose to keep intact the "organization of separations," in particular, holding at bay the efforts of "the many" to restrain the tyrannical impulses of "the few," even as they are branded as the inegalitarians. The outcome is already visible as a not-so-cold civil war.

A different tack would seek "integration" first through a realignment in pursuit of common interests of a multiracial, multiethnic working class, a more confrontational form of multiracial "aristopopulism" that seeks to constrain elite power while "mixing" the classes, and then a deeper integration of the ennobling ethe of both classes to foster a new ruling and governing ethos. Only through a more genuine aspiration of

"integration" aligning the activities of society's elites with the requirements of flourishing for ordinary citizens is there any prospect of overcoming the worsening racial divide in the United States.

Arguments for the integration of a working-class ethos with the
ruling virtues of the elite are quickly accused of—and dismissed for—
racism. The accusation of racism is especially powerful, and, once lev-
eled, puts the accused in a position of permanent defensiveness. The
defender of "traditional culture" is immediately accused of wanting to
preserve the order that advantaged a white upper class, a patina of cultural conservatism shrouding a deeper and more pervasive racism.
This accusation is powerful because it has often been true, particularly
invoked to defend the practices of "Jim Crow"—both legal and informal practices of racism that for too long marred America's history.
Claims that the plight of the underclass is just as evident in the social
declines of large numbers of the white working class, as reflected in the
statistics amassed by Charles Murray, are plausibly characterized as
concern for the downtrodden only when it comes to the effect on the
white population, and deemed likely to result in responses that benefit
only white Americans. It is arguably one of the great tragedies of the
American tradition not only that slavery and racism marred its history,
but that defenses of traditional institutions and practices too often were
bound up with defenses of racial injustice. Today, the very power of that
accusation is now extended to accusations of those who defend such
institutions as family defined as a man and woman; the desirability of
children born in conjugal marriage; orthodox biblical religious beliefs;
and against those who seek limitations on sexual licentiousness, such as
pornography.

However, the same arguments that are marshaled to improve and
promote the conditions of the working class in relation to today's elites
apply just as thoroughly to redressing the sins of racism as the declining fortunes of the broader white working class. A main consequence of
the enslavement of Africans was the generational destruction of the same

long-standing cultural forms—family, communal forms of solidarity, religion—that are today being decimated in a less direct but extensive way among people of *every race* living within advanced liberal society. The direct destruction of the slave's family bond—in the wholly legal and brutal separation of husband and wife, parents and children—continues to impact the African American community to this day. While African slaves came to embrace Christianity—indeed, developed deep and distinct forms of gospel spirituality, often centered on the Old Testament themes of bondage, deliverance, and emancipation—those cultural practices have declined precipitously over the past several decades, tracking with similar declines in the religiosity of nearly every other race and denomination.[18]

Today, the focus of liberals is upon political and economic approaches to equal justice, particularly focused on policing and the possibility of reparations. There can be no gainsaying that equal justice of law and economic stability are basic requirements for racial and broader social justice. But, today, largely unsaid and increasingly unsayable is that even if legal inequalities and unequal access to economic opportunities could be largely eliminated, such approaches would not fundamentally redress the disadvantages arising from the multigenerational devastation arising from familial and social decay. A generation ago, it was more common and acceptable for thinkers on both the political right and left to raise cultural questions and explore ways that the public order could support cultural improvements in seeking to redress persistent racism. In particular, the difficulties faced by black families was a theme discussed by prominent liberals (of a more centrist sort) such as Daniel Patrick Moynihan, and conservatives like Nathan Glazer.[19] Today, those arguments are condemned as insufficient at best, racist at worst.

More recent interventions into these waters were offered by then senator and presidential nominee Barack Obama, who, notably during a campaign speech on Father's Day in 2008, encouraged black fathers to be present for their children: "Too many fathers are MIA, too many

fathers are AWOL, missing from too many lives and too many homes. . . .
And the foundations of our families are weaker because of it."[20] It was a
theme he repeated several times during his presidency, including during
a commencement address at HBCU Morehouse College in 2013. And, it
was on the occasion of these and similar speeches that progressive liberal intelligentsia criticized President Obama perhaps more harshly
than at any other moment of his presidency. Ta-Nehisi Coates was severe in his judgment, charging that President Obama was "singularly
the scold of 'black America.'"[21] More recently still, academic critics
have folded their criticisms of Obama into general critiques of traditional norms. In a 2020 essay, Gabby Yearwood of the Department of
Anthropology of the University of Pittsburgh criticized Obama's 2008
speech in these terms: "He over-privileges the nuclear family as the
standard, as well as the heterosexual privilege that only men are fathers
and they can only be so in a state-recognized marriage."[22] As President
Obama prepared to leave office in 2017, Mychal Denzel Smith devoted
a *Washington Post* column to criticizing this one aspect of his presidency, noting that the president had downplayed, if not entirely ignored,
institutionalized and systemic racism.[23] A recurring theme throughout
these and other critiques insisted that calls to personal and communal
responsibility are largely obviated by the systemic nature of racism, rendering those who make them effectively racist in their avoidance of addressing the institutional sources of cultural devastation. Those who
make them are "scolds," blaming the victims.

A distinct narrative has begun to dominate the mainstream liberal
discourse on the scourge of racism. On the one hand, it is insisted that
the source of racism against African Americans is *systemic*, and can
only be redressed by system-wide changes, including massive efforts to
increase inclusion in elite institutions and shift resources to the descendants of slaves in the form of reparations. However, the white working
class, increasingly hostile to the meritocratic class that (among other
things) advances these views, are accused of the personal moral failing

of racism. They should be excluded from exercising any significant voice in American public life, treated as people who have failed in the economic and social sweepstakes that can be won by those who try. They are the bitter and resentful, and their political responses are driven mainly by recidivist racism. Though the conditions of working-class blacks and whites increasingly resemble each other, in one case—that of African Americans—the cause is *systemic*, a condition over which its victims exercise little agency; in the other—the white working class—their plight is a *moral failure* (racism) for which merely *purported* victims are personally culpable.

This dominant narrative seems well designed with one object in mind: reinforcing the structures that sift economic and social winners from losers. Since the woeful conditions of African Americans are systemic, the system can largely be adjusted to advance "diversity and inclusion" initiatives. But because the white working class is irredeemably racist, the breakdowns of social and economic conditions can largely be waved off as personal failures.[24] In both cases, liberal elites are justified in ignoring or even condemning any efforts to support, reinforce, or create in new forms the social (and even economic) conditions for the flourishing of ordinary, working-class people *of any and all races*. The fact that liberal elites in every Western nation have adopted slogans and arguments from racial movement activism suggests that the issue affords a powerful means of maintaining existing class structures, even in places where the distinct historical race dynamics of America are wholly absent (such as Black Lives Matter protests throughout Europe during the summer of 2020).

Further, by using charges of racism and other intersectional "-isms" to stain efforts to support the conditions for social flourishing for people of all and any race and background—calling especially for state-based remediation of racial injustice, but disdain and dismissiveness toward the downward mobility of the white working class—a political benefit redounds to the governing elite by dividing the racially diverse working class on the basis of race, and short-circuiting discernment of the deeper similarities and common sources of their plights. A beneficial political result is the formation of an alliance of upper-class educated (dominantly) white professionals and a large percentage of the African American electorate that is often more traditional, religious, socially conservative, and rooted. While rarely acknowledged by the ruling class, the growing similarity of the situation and concerns of white and black working classes was obvious enough to be brought into entertaining relief in a 2016 *Saturday Night Live* sketch titled "Black Jeopardy." The sketch comically portrayed the deeper class similarities between working-class African Americans and a character played by a disheveled Tom Hanks wearing a red "MAGA" baseball hat and speaking with a Southern drawl. The competitors begin the contest assuming that they have nothing in common, but increasingly realize that similarities arising from their downward mobility and lower-class status are more fundamental than racial differences.

Once we recognize that there may be a class interest in perpetuating the racial divide, a question from a different perspective arises: What if the deteriorating conditions of working classes of all races are systemic in a different form, namely, the result of the "organization of separations" required by a liberal order? What if the challenging conditions for the working classes—"the many"—are directly the consequence of a liberalism that systemically destroys the ecology for the flourishing in the social and cultural spheres, contributing in turn to the destruction of stability and order in the economic realm? The very *systemic* nature of the undermining of social forms that contribute to human flourishing leads as well to demonizing charges against more "traditional" forms of life—charges that are now increasingly shrouded in the mantle of "racism," even as such defenses ought to be embraced by a multiethnic working class. Liberalism as the most pervasive "system" thus creates a deep incentive to wholly attribute the deep economic and social disadvantages suffered by African Americans to "systemic racism" rather than "systemic liberalism" and thus exclude considerations of the deeper interaction between economic and social mores. At the same time, "systemic liberalism" in turn attributes to the white working class the base and personal motive of racism that arises from its particular social mores, the elimination of which requires systemic focus. In both cases, arguments for strengthening, maintaining, and fostering robust traditional cultural practices within a moralized economic order, toward the joint end of cultivating human flourishing, are nonstarters for both classical and progressive liberals—the first in the name of economic liberty, the second in the name of personal liberation.

Much less noticed in Martin Luther King's "I Have a Dream" speech are several sentences that eschewed the more liberal "dream" of the equal opportunity to become individually unequal, and rather that intentionally appealed back to a more classical, Christian, and Pauline form of solidarity.

> This is our hope. This is the faith that I go back to the South with. With this faith, we will be able to hew out of the mountain of despair a stone of hope. With this faith we will be able to transform the jangling discords of our nation into a beautiful symphony of brotherhood. With this faith we will be able to work together, to pray together, to struggle together, to go to jail together, to stand up for freedom together, knowing that we will be free one day.

These phrases are rarely, if ever, noted for their direct echo of Winthrop's call to solidarity in "A Model of Christian Charity"—almost word for word. The next sentences put these evocations expressly into the context of the "other" American founding, its primary documents not of Lockean descent, but biblical: "This will be the day when all of God's children will be able to sing with new meaning: 'My country, 'tis of thee, sweet land of liberty, of thee I sing. Land where my fathers died, land of the pilgrims' pride, from every mountainside, let freedom ring.'" While King's message has often been read as an endorsement of the "organization of separations," he saw more deeply still that the ultimate aim must be a deeper "integration." Today's dominant approaches to the racial divide will only engender new and deepening divisions. America's "other" founding offers a different path, one that King himself recognized and commended, even if most of his admirers, then and now, did not recognize his deeper teaching.

Moving Beyond Progress

The demise of "mixed constitution" theory resulted from the rise and eventual dominance of the philosophy of *progress*. The aspiration for "mixed constitution" rests on an ideal of relative stability and balance, undergirded by a social order that is wary of upsetting the hard-won equilibrium of otherwise divisive forces in society. The philosophy of progress inevitably unleashes these divisions in a particularly destabilizing form, leading inevitably and directly to the civilization-threatening political enmity that exists throughout the Western world today.

Liberalism was the modernist political philosophy that at once embraced the Enlightenment faith in progress and rejected the long-standing endorsement of "mixed" constitutions. Classical liberalism stressed the paramount goal of economic progress, the aim of which John Locke described as "indolency of the body"—material comforts such as "the possession of outward things, such as money, lands, houses, furniture, and the like," which, it was hoped, would eclipse spiritual, cultural, or transcendent aspirations. Progressive liberalism retained classical liberalism's endorsement of material comfort, but added a belief in *moral* progress that accompanied humanity's material advance. As Richard Rorty described modern, liberal democratic humanity, because of both material and moral advance, "they have more being."[25]

The separation of the progressed from the recidivist became an essential feature of the modern liberal regime: progress can only advance
by recognizing, distinguishing, and promoting the elements of society
that most ensure the forward progress of history. The ascendant elite is
selected for its *distinction from* the perceived backward elements of society, and not for any exemplary virtue that should be widely shared
and emulated. The ruling class and those who must be ruled come to be
perceived as different classes of humans, a foreboding that haunts some
of our popular imagination in such fictive renderings as *Gattaca, Ely-
sium,* or Margaret Atwood's less famous but superior dystopia *Oryx
and Crake.* Liberals differ over who should be ascendant, but agree that
the masses must be restrained from interfering with the trajectory of
progress. Classical liberals point to the increase in wealth and material
comfort as the aims of modern society; progressive liberals point to an
"arc" of history that bends toward enlightened forms of social justice—
especially racial equality and sexual liberation. Progress is at once the
desired outcome, but also the inevitable trajectory of human civilization. A fundamental division is introduced into society that gives rise to
a foundational partisan divide: those on the side of progress, and those
who stand against the faith in a better future. Today's politics reflect the
growing divide between the party of progress and those who stand on
"the wrong side of history." This division is inevitable and only worsens, with the ruling class claiming ever more dictatorial power over the
backward in the name of an ideology of progress.

Our current political divisions thus arise from a deeper separation:
the fragmentation of time. The ideology of progress—one that underlies
the modern political philosophy of liberalism and neo-Marxism—
asserts that time is divided between an era of darkness and light, and that
portions of humanity make their home on one side of the divide or the
other. Modern political philosophy was reconstituted as a battle between
those either advancing or in tune with progress, on the one hand, and
the recalcitrant remnant who either refuse to catch up, resist progress,

or, worse, actively fight to preserve a present (or past) that is morally indefensible. The regimes arising from the political philosophies of modernity thus pit an enlightened ruling class against a backward, unprogressed element in the population. In practice, this results in the elimination of a "mixed constitution" in favor of a ruling class that governs in the name of progress, visibly and measurably at the expense of the flourishing of the large swath of the population that is—justifiably, in the view of the elite—"left behind."

At an elemental level, a "mixed constitution" must propose an integration of *time*, above all by replacing the ideology of *progress* with the lived experience of *continuity*. Where the ideal of progress necessarily generates a division between past, present, and future, above all by fostering a dismissiveness toward the past, discontent with the present, and optimism toward the future, a politics of *continuity* weaves together past, present, and future in a relationship of mutual influence and correction. The integration of time forefronts the importance of memory toward the past, gratitude in the present, and a wary cautiousness toward unintended consequences resulting from an overly optimistic view of the future. A politics of continuity eschews nostalgia, which too often can be an inversion of progressivism, locating an ideal in the past instead of the future; yet, at the same time, it fosters appreciation toward inheritance and the achievements of the past, recognizing that we are all shaped by our times, by their assumptions, and by the inescapable imperfection and frailties of humanity.

Our experience of time must negotiate between two equally dangerous proclivities, both ably captured by the bioethicist William May. Responding to an invitation to reflect on Nathaniel Hawthorne's story "The Birthmark"—which portrays the efforts of a scientist to eliminate a small blemish on his wife's face, leading to her simultaneous perfection and demise—May contrasted the imperatives of "transformation" and "acceptance."[26] Describing the two impulses as especially visible in the relation of parents toward children, May notes that it is at once a deeply interpersonal tension as well as one that defines the very nature of a society more broadly. The impulse of transformation results in encouragement—sometimes overbearing, but always necessary—for the child to improve herself, to strive to realize her inherent potential, talents, and gifts. If such encouragement is deficient, the child will likely fall far short of her potential; if excessive, the pressure and unrealistic expectations can overwhelm, disillusion, and devolve into resentment and disappointment.

The second impulse—acceptance—is expressed as love for the child as she is, a gift that does not require some fundamental change to be the object of love and acceptance. If such acceptance is deficient, any child will despair for absence of unconditional love; if excessive, the result is likely to be a kind of quiescence that can too easily shade into indifference. Just as both must be present in the parent's relation to the child, so too must this be our human relationship to our place in time, in our society, in our tradition: an imperfect and always challenging negotiation and relationship between the impulse to transform and accept. The modern world has embraced the imperative of *transformation* at the expense of the *acceptance*, and—just as the transformative impulse can destroy the child—it has imperiled the prospect for our civilization.

A political, social, and economic order based upon *progress* necessarily embraces *transformation* at the expense of *acceptance*. Such a society measures achievement by rate of change and evident achievements of science, technology, and economic prosperity. But—as the writer Wendell Berry often notes—it loses the ability to "subtract," to recognize how what it counts as achievements also generate mounting losses. In our time, those losses—whether in the form of fair and decent economic prospects; social stability; family and communal membership and belonging; and the prospect of passing on a legacy to the next generation, whether material or memorial—fall far more heavily upon the lower classes of our society. Because they are not sufficiently "progressed," their worsening condition is generally, if *sotto voce*, regarded as justly deserved.

These unequal costs of progress were explored a generation ago with particular force by intellectual historian Christopher Lasch. Lasch also turned to Hawthorne as a source of skepticism toward the modern and American ideology of progress, entitling the final book published during his lifetime *The True and Only Heaven: Progress and Its Critics*. The title was drawn from a passage in Hawthorne's allegorical story "The Celestial Railroad," a skeptical retelling of Bunyan's *Pilgrim's Progress* for a time when already Americans were beginning to think of their nation as ushering in the Kingdom of Heaven. Those on the "celestial railroad" were inclined to believe that the city of "Vanity Fair"— our present world—was "the True and Only Heaven," leading people to abandon their striving for "the Celestial City." In his magisterial account of the American (and British) development of faith in progress, Lasch struck upon a valuable contrast that highlighted how belief in progress fragmented time, and instead proposed a different set of dispositions that might move toward the reconnection of past, present, and future.

Lasch contrasted the characteristic beliefs of a society arrayed around faith in progress, and hence experiencing time as fragmented and disconnected, in place of a society for which time was continuous and related. In a progressive society, most people were likely to see the future through the lens of optimism; those who opposed the progressive view were nevertheless just as likely to experience a fragmented time, and instead were given over to nostalgia, placing the best times in the past rather than the future. For the optimist, there is an unjustified faith in the predictable outworking of history, and hence a kind of moral lassitude, an incapacity to sacrifice in the present out of reliance on history's work on our behalf, and, perhaps above all, an inability to see the costs of purported progress. On the other hand, the nostalgic sees the past "outside of time, frozen in unchanging perfection."[27] Both are unrealistic utopians, willfully ignoring the limitations that all times impose upon all people.

Each exists in a hostile relationship toward one element of time. For the nostalgic, the future is one of inevitable corruption and decline. The only recourse is a restoration of the past—an impossibility in any place and time. Permanent discontent, bitterness, and regret are their lot. The progressive optimist regards the past as a record of benighted backwardness. The past is a time of darkness that is better not remembered. Indeed, the contemporary undertaking to erase the past—most visible in the destruction of monuments and the erasure of names of buildings, but more subtly in the way that the past is taught today as a record of injustice that has been overcome by the children of light—makes us strangers to our forebears and to the constitutive elements that compose the whole of what we are today.

Both lack the opposite dispositions that mark those who experience the continuity of time: hope and memory. Lasch perceptively differentiated hope from optimism—echoing a long theological tradition that identified hope as one of the three Christian virtues—noting that hope expected justice based on a "deep-seated trust in life." This trust arose not from an expectation of future improvement so much as "confidence . . . in the past," in which "the experience of order and contentment was so intense that subsequent disillusionments cannot dislodge it." Hope is based in a melding of realism and idealism that is laced through all human time, properly experienced, one in which "trust is never completely misplaced, even though it is never completely justified."[28]

For Lasch, it was the fragmentation of time that led to the deep and inescapable divide between the classes. The elites—powerfully condemned in his prophetic essay "The Revolt of the Elites"—regard ordinary people as backward, too enmeshed in the past and present, not sufficiently advanced through the trajectory of history. This withering dismissiveness led, in turn, to some envy but, even more, resentment by the lower classes toward the putative leaders of society. Only a society in which all classes and people in different walks of life were informed by the disposition of *hope without optimism* and *memory without nostalgia* might expect to achieve what Lasch described as the "spiritual discipline against resentment," to which might as well be added the *spiritual discipline against condescension*.[29] Echoing Winthrop, Lasch called for the capacity to see ourselves bound together in a shared condition of limited and imperfectible humanity.[30] Lasch wrote admiringly about populism as the antidote to the liberal tendency toward fragmentation, intuiting the ideal of mixed constitution in which a proud and accomplished working class sets a tone for the vigor and decencies of a society. He stressed the need for a producer economy over one dedicated to consumption, tapping a long British and American tradition that stressed virtues of craft, thrift, the discipline of work, and a preference for local economy within a national system of over-extended supply lines that left a people dependent on those who might wish them ill. Yet, he praised "interdependence" of a tactile, interpersonal sort, the tutoring of mutual need that Winthrop also believed was at the heart of the mutual work of a community.

Rejection of the modern ideology of "progress" does not entail rejection of reform and improvement. But the reintegration of time—the weaving together of past, present, and future—introduces a missing element of humility from considerations of progress. An ideological belief in progress is marked both by unwarranted optimism about the future and self-satisfaction about the superiority of the present against the past. The dogmatic faith in progress—one shared by all the dominant political parties, and even defining the political outlook of the classical liberal stance that is widely labeled "conservative"—is dispositionally incapable of recognizing unintended consequences. Further, progressivism as an ideology is incapable of discerning how accumulating "costs" of progress can easily be redescribed as at least a mixed legacy, if not outright failures. The blinders necessitated by ideological commitment to progress render us socially and politically incapable of deliberation about social changes that can be, and ought to be, legitimately debated—particularly to the extent that their impact will disproportionately result in dislocation and instability for the lower classes. The ideology of progress tends especially to benefit the contemporary leadership class who are generally insulated from the deleterious consequences of "progress." Further, the fealty to the orthodoxy of progress insulates this class from critique and challenge, encouraging a self-confident belief in their presence on the "right side of history," while fostering contempt toward challenges from people deemed backward and "clinging" to antiquated beliefs and practices.

Many of the economic, social, and political challenges we face today arise from the very success of "progress." To name only a few, some of our most significant civilizational challenges arise from past achievements considered as unambiguous milestones in human progress. Challenges such as climate change; soil exhaustion and erosion; species extinction; the depletion of natural resources; hypoxic zones; and massive areas of oceanic pollution arise directly from industrial progress. Meanwhile, on the social and political side, breakdown in family stability, deaths of despair and a recent reduction in years of life expectancy, declining levels of participation in civic institutions, increased loneliness, waning experience of friendship, the domination of wealth and money in our electoral system, and the rise of divisive and even internecine forms of political partisanship can be traced to aspects of social and technological "progress." Under the ideology of progress, we tend to treat each of these challenges as discrete problems that suddenly confront humanity as if out of nowhere—often requiring new advances and applications of progress to "solve." We are constantly seeking to repair the damage caused by our blind adherence to progress without being able to balance the costs in our ledger.

The main parties of the right and left exhibit particular pathologies of this faith. The party of the left decries the consequences of industrial and economic "progress," particularly environmental degradation. The party of the right laments the outcome of social "progress," particularly the breakdown of familial and civic life. Yet, they laud the respective

consequence of progress that the other condemns, seeing in their results a desired outcome of progress. Neither recognizes how the two
kinds of "progress" proceed together and become mutually reinforcing,
with economic progress undermining family and social stability, and
social instability a helpmeet to economic individualism that in turn
feeds short-term considerations about the environment. In the main,
each in turn proposes *more progress* as the best means of redressing the
deleterious consequences of past progress. Technological fixes are the
main path to reducing environmental degradation; while an education
in the hot new careers is the answer to declining social capital.

Human society will always change, but change driven by the ideology of progress renders us supine to unintended consequences and
leads inevitably to overestimation of purported benefits. We don temporal blinkers that force us to confront the accumulating costs of progress in fragmentary and reactive ways. Our capacity to deliberate together
over the less obvious but often severe costs of changes, and a presump-
tive effort to protect the most vulnerable from ongoing transformations,
would result from the *integration of time.* Only through such integration
can there in fact be a political community, and not merely a collection
of individuals seeking their individual, personal ends. By connecting
the present to past and past to future, we repair the narrow social contract of liberalism to include "those who are living, those who are dead,
and those who are to be born." Only through a repair of time can we
move toward a repair of the nation.

Situating the Nation

Praise for the nation today is seen almost exclusively as a hallmark of
conservatism. Supporters of Donald Trump identify as nationalists, an
identification regarded by the legions of Trump opponents as disposi-
tive proof of its malevolence. A number of prominent conservatives

have written works in defense of a strong identification with the nation, including Israeli political philosopher Yoram Hazony's much-discussed book *The Virtue of Nationalism*; *National Review* editor Rich Lowry's *The Case for Nationalism*; and *First Things* editor R. R. Reno's *Return of the Strong Gods*.[31] Current forms of political populism are powerfully associated with strong assertions of national sovereignty, whether an emphasis upon limiting immigration, increasing childbirth rates of the native population, or resisting the characteristic globalist tendencies of international organizations such as the European Union or the United Nations.

In the heat generated by contemporary divides, it is unsurprising that the liberal origins and progressive commitments to nationalism have been altogether forgotten or suppressed by the various parties. The nation—born of the effort to settle the so-called wars of religion, notably through the resolution achieved by the Peace of Westphalia— was considered to be the means of resolving the long-standing tension within Christendom between the sovereignty of the Church and the sovereignty of the secular ruler. What had previously been at least *in principle*, and to varying degrees *in fact*, a supranational Christian order under which various political governors acted as the political arm of Christendom was displaced by the unitary sovereignty of a national political ruler, one of whose main powers was to declare the religious belief within the boundaries of his own political territory. As determined at the Peace of Augsburg in 1555, "*cuius regio eius religio*": "Whose realm, their religion."

The architects of liberalism were explicit that the nation required absolute sovereignty of the political ruler. Undiluted sovereignty entailed the power to command public conformity to the national religion—and, thus, the power to command any perceived disruptive sect or community within the national boundaries—as well as the resistance to any transnational claim to sovereignty, particularly the threat of papal claims upon Catholic citizens. Even as the liberal order eventually abandoned its initial insistence upon an official civil religion, the basic principle of national sovereignty over religion remained. As historian Brad Gregory has noted, arguments for liberal toleration—such as those found in Locke's "Letter Concerning Toleration"—even while allowing for diverse religious expression and belief, nevertheless established the same principle as the national "civil religion" demanded by Hobbes—or early Locke, for that matter.[32] In both cases, the political sovereign was ultimately responsible, and wielded sole authority, to determine acceptable and unacceptable forms of religious practice and expression. Even today, religious believers of liberal democracies implicitly recognize this liberal principle of exclusive *national* sovereignty over religious belief when they appeal to the nation's political and court systems for recognition of rights of religious liberty.

Thus, the nation represented a *unification* of belief (even if in the form of belief in liberal toleration) within national boundaries, but *fragmentation* of belief between nations. Citizens were expected to become more liberal, and more devoted to the liberal nation, to the exclusion of other loyalties both smaller and larger than the nation. Over the intervening half millennium, the nation would achieve political prominence through two prongs: solidifying internal cohesion while denying any claims to external sovereignty. This effort is often told as the story of blood and persecution, both in the form of militarized nationalism that sought to establish national boundaries and identity, as well as the internal effort to achieve domestic cohesion. But the effort to solidify the status of the nation was also achieved perhaps most effectively and lastingly through the transference of loyalties, at once away from any more local form of identification (cultural, tribal, local, or regional), as well as away from any potential transnational identification that could pose a threat to the claim of exclusive national sovereignty (especially in the case of Catholics, a religion that Locke explicitly denied toleration because of its "supra-national" dimension). "Nationalism," as a primary and defining form of membership and identity, was originally a key aspect of the liberal political project.

For all the differences between "classical" and "progressive" liberalism, liberalism's architects deeply shared the aspiration to create and strengthen national sovereignty that would prove to be a new unifying force, thereby replacing the imperial structures of Christendom in the West. Once liberalism abandoned its initial effort of achieving national cohesion through an established religion (although remnants of national religious establishments persist in some European nations), internal cohesion was instead achieved through less direct methods. War and commerce proved the most effective tools in this effort, breaking down the onetime solidarity of subnational communities as well as effectively limiting transnational religious or ethnic allegiances. National military mobilization and the required mobility of a national economy combined to effect a powerful transference of allegiances to the nation. Today, modern Americans are no more likely to identify primarily as citizens of their respective states—much less their localities—than American Catholics are to view the Pope as their rightful sovereign.[33]

The rise of nationalism in the United States was especially pronounced during the Progressive Era, during which the likes of Woodrow Wilson and Theodore Roosevelt rose to prominence. The embrace and rise of nationalism in America was not the project of "conservatives," but promoted especially by the self-described progressive liberals. This project was particularly aimed at the weakening of more local and regional forms of identity and identification that had been a hallmark of the American political experience, not uncoincidentally gaining prominence in the decades after the Civil War. Theodore Roosevelt—whose name is today often invoked as a guiding light of a new "national conservatism"—stated in his important 1910 speech "The New Nationalism" that "the New Nationalism puts the national need before sectional or personal advantage." This is a refrain that was found throughout the writings of the progressives, the need to move the loyalties and identities of Americans from their local places and people to a more abstract devotion to the nation and its ideals. Indeed, historian Daniel Immerwahr notes that it was during this exact historical period when the word "America" began to be used as a self-description, replacing what had been the main name for the nation: the United States, followed by the grammatically correct plural "are," not the singular "is."[34] This transference was to an increasingly abstract entity of the nation, now thought of as embodying an "idea" or a providential destiny. Allegiance moved from the more concrete to the more theoretical—local to national— while also from less universal to the more "particular," particularly in how the nation began to occupy the devotional space once held by religion.

This two-pronged move toward abstraction and particularism was especially present in thinkers during the Progressive Era, who were at once suspicious of local particularisms and transnational universalism. Such thinkers were especially suspicious of the more immediate and, in their view, limiting and parochial identities of people as members of towns, communities, states, and regions. In this regard, they were at least to this extent inheritors of the views of at least some of our Founding Fathers, especially Alexander Hamilton (whose name was often positively invoked by progressives), who was explicit in *The Federalist Papers* about his hopes that people would ultimately transfer their allegiance from their localities and states to the nation, and identify far more with the political entity that made it possible for them to enjoy their natural rights.[35] Progressives such as Herbert Croly, in his 1909 book, *The Promise of American Life*, were explicit in this praise and embrace of Hamilton's vision of a more uniform America.[36]

At the same time, the nation would come to embody quasi-religious aspirations, "containing" the transcendent within the national boundary and making it an object of simultaneous religious and political devotions. The realization of the American nation would lead, Croly hoped, to a more enlightened consciousness, an actual evolution of human nature, toward a perfected humanity that would be brought about by the new nationalism.[37] Influenced by Auguste Comte, Croly envisioned the replacement of old sectarian faiths with a national "Religion of Humanity" whose first churches would be through a new and purified form of national identity.[38] It was around this same time, in 1892, that the Christian socialist Francis Bellamy published "The Pledge of Allegiance," with the hope and aim of aligning people's loyalties and commitments to the nation and away from the parochial identities that had previously defined the identity of the citizens of the United States, and instead inaugurated the new "creed" of a new national church.[39]

The aspiration for a kind of civic-religious devotion necessarily required, and led inevitably to, the weakening of an array of subnational civic associations and practices in which most people practiced "the arts of association," as described by Tocqueville. In order to see oneself primarily as a member of the new national order, other affiliations had to recede in centrality and importance, replaced instead by an increasingly fungible identity of individual self. The trajectory from a perception of oneself as a subject of God, to one's identity as membership in a nation, and finally to one's essence as *self* has been documented by a number of prominent thinkers—among them historian Andrew Delbanco and political theorist Jean Bethke Elshtain—who stressed how the requirement for a national identity weakened the local, civil, and religious forms of attachment as it expanded one's view of "self" and accelerated the tendency toward individualism.[40] The first trajectory of liberalism was toward a kind of national solidarity that required the weakening of local forms of attachment, and that tended in turn to strong assertions of national superiority. It was not uncoincidental that the rise of progressive nationalism coincided with the spread of nationalist imperialism—with America's imperialist foray coming at the height of progressive nationalism—the belief that one's political form and beliefs were superior and ought to be enforced elsewhere.

This limiting, "chauvinistic" form of nationalism has led to its repudiation by the heirs of the progressive tradition—though for reasons entirely consistent with liberalism, which came to reject as too confining the national container it once embraced. One can discern the course of this trajectory in the changing motto of Princeton University, the institution that has played an outsize role in initiating the American nation in its gradual movement toward globalism. James Madison—"the Father of the Constitution," and Princeton graduate—and Woodrow Wilson, later a president of Princeton, represent the figures at the peaks of classical and progressive liberalism, both of whom saw the American nation as the container of progress. As if underlining the Madisonian roots of America, Princeton's unofficial motto was introduced in 1896 by Woodrow Wilson as: "In the Nation's Service." The university and its graduates were to see their highest calling to be in the service of the consolidated nation. A century later this unofficial motto was subsequently augmented by a later president, Harold Shapiro, to read: "Princeton in the Nation's Service and in the Service of all Nations." The nation was increasingly too confining, its devotions too narrow. More recently still, it was altered again in 2016 by Princeton president Christopher Eisgruber to its current incarnation: "In the Nation's Service and the Service of Humanity." Identification as a member of any nation was finally too confining: one's service needed to be unbounded by any national identification, and one wonders whether "humanity" will eventually be too confining as well.

Because of its abstraction, particularly its detachment from concrete identities in specific locations, the nationalist impulse ultimately required transcending the bonds of the nation. Today's progressives regard nationalism with horror, not because they have abandoned its logic, but because they have now gravitated to its next logical form: an identification with a globalized liberal humanity. The nation itself is now seen as too particularistic, requiring the same disintegrating logic of yesterday's nationalism. Yesterday's liberal nationalism is today's progressive globalism, requiring the same soft and hard mechanisms of disaffiliation that are evinced in the pervasive individualism, disengagement, and even loneliness of modern peoples. The ultimate logic is a globalized *dis*integration, the weakening and outright elimination of all cultural, geographic, traditional forms of membership in favor of what Pico Iyer has deftly called "the global soul."[41]

Unsurprisingly, it is today's "conservatives" who have risen to defend the nation as the proper object of their devotions. In the wake of severely weakened, if altogether nonexistent, local and cultural identities, the largely abstract form of the modern nation appears to today's conservatives as the only "particularistic" identity that still plausibly remains as a membership that resists the individualism of the liberated self, on the one hand, and the deracinated "global soul" on the other. Having successfully eliminated the plausibility of identities that are simultaneously both *local* and *transnational*, a truncated conservatism finds itself taking up the banner of yesterday's liberals. It is especially in light of the recent efforts of today's progressives—the heirs of the nationalism of Wilson, Roosevelt, and Croly—to transcend the nation, to aspire to membership in a cosmopolis—that it seems natural for conservatives to rally around the ideal of the national community. But such conservatives seem altogether unaware that they today occupy the space recently vacated by progressives.

Liberalism today proposes a globalized form of *dis*integration, a false universalism that dismantles all embodied and situated forms of human membership. It must be opposed not by assuming the previous stage of this process and simply embracing "national conservatism"—which, uncoincidentally, carries with it its historical lineage of liberalism—but through *a new form of integration of local, national, and international.*

Practices of membership and belonging are learned first in the smallest society: the family. In ideal settings, communities are an assemblage of families, mutually concerned with the upbringing and formation of the next generation, providing the private, social, and public spaces for their children. Hillary Clinton was not wrong to embrace the mantra "It takes a village." The problem with her understanding of that appeal lay in the progressivist ideology that has always in fact been hostile to the authoritative claims of the village.

Yet, such membership always does, can, and should point outward as well. We prepare young people for life beyond the village not by shutting out the world, but by preparing our young to bring the values and truths learned in their families and communities into the nation and the wider world—and, we hope, infusing those places with an ethos of care and commitment that transcends generations. As Pope Francis has written in his commentary on this layered experience of "membership" that spans the local and the transnational, "Just as there can be no dialogue with 'others' without a sense of our own identity, so there can be no openness between peoples except on the basis of love for one's own land, one's own people, one's own cultural roots. I cannot truly encounter another unless I stand on firm foundations, for it is on the basis of these that I can accept the gift the other brings and in turn offer an authentic gift of my own."[42]

As Francis acknowledges, an openness to a wider sphere beyond our local circumstance is itself a *part* of that identity, and to the extent it is experienced as a form of exclusion, our loyalties and identities too easily become stunted and deformed. Similarly, liberalism's hostility to these kinds of local identities has had the effect of creating its own deformations—the barren wasteland of globalist homogeneity. The ideal of membership in a more universal human kinship does not mean, Francis writes, a world that is "bland, uniform, and standardized based on a single prevailing cultural model, for this will ultimately lead to the loss of a rich palette of shades and colors, and result in utter monotony."[43] The deforming "universalism" of globalism is ultimately hostile to all particular cultures, whether local or national. Instead, just as a nation ought to be conceived as a "community of communities," the whole of humanity should be understood as a "community of nations," with the word "international" (which retains the notion of particular nations that are in relationship with each other) replacing the ideological label "global" (which suggests the erasure of the particular). The first recognizes the distinctiveness of nations, and, by implication, the uniqueness of the local places that form nations; the second reflects an effort to efface the distinctiveness of smaller societies ranging from the family to massive human forms such as nations. "Nationalism" as a *liberal project* was initially the first step of this effort of effacement, and should be rejected both by embracing, fostering, and protecting not only the nation but that which is both smaller and larger than the nation.

Integrating Religion

What can replace the *dis*integrating logic of liberalism? The ultimate aspiration of liberal "globalism" seeks to erect a universal umbrella over the ethos of effectual indifference. Its underlying assumption is that there is no objective "Good" to which humans can agree in any time and in any place, so the only defensible political form is one in which every individual pursues his, her, or xir's idea of individual good, and the global cosmopolitan order ensures the backdrop of sufficient peace and prosperity leaving everyone largely undisturbed. In theory, most elites today regard this vision as both potentially imminent and truly utopian. In practice—as the argument of this book has sought to lay out—the result is a deeply destabilizing outcome of winners and losers in which our purported "nonjudgmentalism"—our indifference—becomes a subtle justification to blame the unsuccessful.

The only genuine alternative to liberalism's commitment to a world of *globalized indifference* is one of *common good* that is secured with the assistance and support of our shared common order—the political order.

Of course, the first response of the liberal is to claim there *is no such thing* as the common good, since the liberal assumption is that any public good is merely whatever consensual agreement arises from autonomous individuals. There can be no determining in advance what constitutes "the common good," since public opinion on this question changes. Liberalism is a denial that there can be any objective good for humans that is not simply the aggregation of individual opinion. Liberalism claims that any justification based upon "the common good" is ultimately nothing more than a preference disguised as a universal ideal.

However, what we instead see arise is not a regime of toleration, nonjudgment, and "agreement to disagree," but the inevitable appearance of a new ordering principle that takes on all the features of a religion. What is often called the rise of "wokeism," or "illiberal liberalism," is, unavoidably, the result of the elimination of considerations of an objective "good" from political life. What takes the place of a public order toward the *good* becomes the concerted effort to eliminate every last vestige of any claim to an objective good. Instead, the political order becomes devoted—with white-hot fervor—to the eradication of any law, custom, or tradition that has as its premise that there are objective conditions of *good* that require public support. Instead, the whole of the social, economic, political, and even metaphysical order must be refounded on the basis that individual *preference* must always prevail. Anyone who resists this commitment must eventually be forced to conform, whether through the force of opinion, "private" power of employment and other regulations, or, ultimately, the force of law.

Ironically, this totalitarian undertaking that we witness unfolding daily and even constantly accelerating is the consequence of the most fateful and fundamental "separation": the so-called separation of church and state. As countless studies of this claim underscore, this "separation" was never complete, and can never be complete, since every political order rests on certain theological assumptions. The unseen theological foundations of liberalism were originally Christian: the dignity of every human life; the supreme value of a liberty as a choice for what is *good*; a constitution of limited government that prevents both tyranny and anarchy but establishes and protects a society in good order, peace, and abundance.

Liberalism's logic, premised on the complete liberation of the individual from any limiting claims of an objective good, eventually turns on these inherited commitments, and in their name becomes the *opposite* and yet *fulfillment* of what liberalism claims to be. The "dignity" of every life is sacrificed on the altar of the rule of the strong (economically or socially) over the weak; liberty is defined not as self-government, but a liberation from constraint to do as I wish; and in the name of tearing down every vestige of an antecedent order, the liberal state and social order becomes totalizing.

Many today believe that liberalism can be restored to its "better" form simply by recombining certain preliberal, often religious commitments in the form of leavening private and civil institutions. "Right" liberals wish (as they say) to retain the classical liberal "baby" while tossing out the illiberal "bathwater," urging a renewal of liberal nations by means of strengthening civic and private institutions while leaving intact the basic principle that the *good* must be a matter of *private* or subpolitical civic concern.[44] The very liberal indifferentism that led to the evisceration of the institutions that are supposed to save us— whether by the forces of the market, its absorption through a pervasive anti-culture, or enforcement through the power of law—is to be retained, while claiming that a civil society that restrains the worst effects of our public indifference can ensure that all will be well. In other words, they propose to retain the basic liberal principle that has led to the baby being submerged in a corrosive bath of acid, and then suggest that the baby will be fine if we dump out the acid just before all its life functions have ceased.

There is no avoiding questions of the *good*. Common-good conservatism is not an effort to *preserve* a now-superseded version of liberalism that is based in a self-deceptive nostalgia for a largely theoretical, not-yet-achieved form of liberalism. It is instead an aspiration to move *beyond* the failed project of liberalism as it now exists on the ground, and must unavoidably embrace a new effort to articulate and foster a *common good*. But rather than beginning with high-level debates over the nature of the *good*—ones attractive to academic philosophers who largely enjoy conditions of *private* flourishing—it instead begins with inquiring about, and properly understanding, what is *common*.

I've previously underscored that the word "common" has two equally dominant meanings, and that the two meanings contained in the same word are not merely coincidental. To be "common" means that which is *shared* as well as that which is *ordinary*. While we can easily think of occasions where we intend only *one* of these meanings when using the word "common," in its deepest and most essential form, the word contains these *two* meanings because they are connected by reality itself. To be *shared* in the most extensive way is to include, and to *become*, "ordinary." Contained in the word's etymological sources is this inescapable connection. The word "common" derives from the Proto-Indo-European *Ko-moin-I*, appearing later in the Latin *communis* and eventually in the French word *comun,* meaning: "common, general, free, open, public" but also "shared by all or many, *familiar, not pretentious.*"[45]

Combined with the word "good," we can see that a *common good* consists in those needs and concerns that are identified in the everyday requirements of ordinary people. The common good is the sum of the needs that arise from the bottom up, and that can be more or less supplied, encouraged, and fortified from the top down. In a good society, the goods that are "common" are daily reinforced by the habits and practices of ordinary people. Those habits and practices form the common culture, such as through the virtues of thrift, honesty, and long memory, which in turn foster gratitude and a widespread sense of mutual obligation. However, once such a common culture is weakened or destroyed, the only hope is a renewal and reinvigoration by a responsible governing class. A politics of the common good makes a good life more likely, even the default, for *commoners*.

Thus, the common good is always either served or undermined by a political order—there is no neutrality on the matter. Emphasizing this point in his indispensable book *Prayer as a Political Problem*, Jean Daniélou, SJ, wrote: "Politics ought to have the care of the common good, that is to say, the duty of creating an order in which personal fulfillment is possible, where man might be able to completely fulfill his destiny."[46]

Daniélou pointed to the duty of those charged with leading the political order not to *deprive* ordinary people of the ability both to participate in and realize the essential goods of human life. It is not enough to ensure their *freedom* to pursue such goods; rather, it is the duty of the political order to positively guide them to, and provide the conditions for the enjoyment of, the goods of human life. "Religious liberty," "academic freedom," "free markets," "checks and balances," etc. are no substitutes for piety, truth, equitable prosperity, and just government. The liberal order in its foundational form maintains that the *absence of constraint* in these and all other domains is the sufficient condition for people to attain fulfillment. The liberal sovereign treats all people equally, assuming that radically free human beings are equally capable of achieving the goods of human life. It is the liberal equivalent of the astute Anatole France quip: "The law, in its majestic equality, forbids rich and poor alike to sleep under bridges, to beg in the streets, and to steal their bread."

What we should notice is that it is *ordinary people*—the "working class," citizens in "flyover country," "the Physicals," "essential workers"— who are increasingly those who enjoy *theoretical* liberty but few of the substantive goods that are supposed to flow from their individual choices. As a political order, we have provided them "the pursuit of happiness," but deprived them of *happiness*. Indeed, a main feature of the working class is rising levels of "deaths of despair." Those who seek to advance the *common good* should attend especially to the profound ordinariness of the concept—how it can be tested especially by reference to an answer to the question "How are 'commoners' doing today?" The answer is: not good.

Even before the onset of coronavirus, reams of data attested to the economic and social devastation wrought upon less-educated, less upwardly mobile working-class people. Economic globalization had deprived many in these communities of the sources of prosperity and stability that made flourishing lives possible. Attacks on social norms of family, faith, and tradition, in addition to these economic challenges, have contributed to the breakdown of family and communal supports, leading in turn to broken lives of crime, unemployment, and deaths of despair. Elite responses to the pandemic only increased the advantages of the laptop class and the worsening conditions of the tactile class.[47]

Those in positions of power and influence have vilified and demonized these fellow citizens as backward, racist, recidivist, even too lazy to get up and move. This has been the consistent message of an elite class that transcends political categories, and it is today the hallmark of the liberal gentry that runs the major institutions of modern liberal democracies.

What elites call "populism" is a reaction by the immune system of the body politic, but it is not the cure for our political disease. The cure lies in the development of a new elite who are forthright in defending not merely the *freedom* to pursue the good—and who then shrug their shoulders when ordinary people drown amid a world without boundaries or life vests—but instead is dedicated to the promotion and construction of a society that assists ordinary fellow citizens in achieving lives of flourishing.

Daniélou provides a helpful starting point. His question was: In the pursuit of the common good—the good life that is not "extraordinary," but common, generalizable, widely achievable by most humans in a generally decent society—how do we order a society that protects and supports the life of *prayer* among ordinary people?

Daniélou posited that prayer is a central practice of a flourishing human life, one in which we are cognizant of a horizon beyond our time and place, aware of our neediness, humbled by our dependence, and called to think and pray for others. Yet, he noted that so many aspects of the modern age increasingly make a genuine life of prayer—and these attendant virtues—exceedingly difficult. Daniélou understood that encouragement to personal piety in a world of constant distraction, technological acceleration, and consumerism was not sufficient to the task. The "freedom to pray" in a world inimical to the habit of prayer was functionally equivalent to its outright deprivation.

A recent republication of Daniélou's classic book wisely chose for its cover the painting *The Angelus* by Jean-François Millet. The painting portrays what appear to be a husband and wife reciting the Angelus prayer (a prayer commemorating the Annunciation, when the angel Gabriel announces to Mary that she will bear the Messiah), likely around dusk at 6 p.m. They seem to be simple farmers, but at this moment all the farming implements and potatoes have been dropped and lie scattered at their feet as they pray together. Rising above the horizon in the distance we can discern a church tower, distant but presumably near enough that the couple can hear its bells. It is a picture of simple but profound piety, and it captures a culture that points us beyond commerce and individual desire toward a wider and transcendent horizon.

Speaking of his best-known and most popular painting, Millet would later relate:

> The idea for *The Angelus* came to me because I remembered that my grandmother, hearing the church bell ringing while we were working in the fields, always made us stop work to say the Angelus prayer for the poor departed, very religiously and with cap in hand.[48]

Millet and Daniélou both emphasize the democratic aspect of the practice of prayer in such a society: its goods are widely shared, not requiring advanced degrees at elite institutions or special language of inclusion and exclusion in order to participate and flourish. Today's church towers are overshadowed by the skyscrapers of high finance, and their bells rendered silent in preference to auto horns, the cacophony of construction, and earbuds playing noise produced by a music industry. Public goods widely available have been overwhelmed by private privations.

We can extend Daniélou's analysis to nearly every aspect of life today. We have the freedom to marry, but fewer people wed. We have the freedom to have children, but birth rates plummet. We have the freedom to practice religion, but people abandon the faiths of their fathers and mothers. We have the freedom to learn of our tradition, to partake in our culture, to pass on the teachings of the old to the young—but we give only debt to the decreasing number of children who will share the burden of supporting a growing number of elderly. In a world hostile to all these potentially "democratic" goods (and not just the freedom to enjoy them, or not), we have eviscerated their actual achievement in the name of theoretical liberty, but in reality increasing thralldom to addictions afforded by big tech, big finance, big porn, big weed, big pharma, and an impending artificial Meta world that will assuage the miseries of an increasingly unbearable world we have actually built.

Daniélou understood that flourishing required more than individual choice in a world that resembled the Wild West. Achieving the life of prayer could be made easier or nearly impossible, depending on the ambient conditions fostered by the public and social order. He lamented the loss of what had once been a "democratized" life of prayer—represented well in Millet's *The Angelus*—now replaced by a kind of elitist sequestration of leisure and contemplation:

> I might mention that monks . . . create for themselves the environment in which they can pray effectively. It is this last consideration that brings us to the heart of our problem. If monks

feel the need to create an environment in which they will find prayer possible, if they think that prayer is not possible without certain conditions of silence, solitude, and rule, what are we to say of the mass of mankind? Should prayer be the privilege of a small spiritual aristocracy, and should the bulk of the Christian people be excluded from it?[49]

Liberalism offered to humanity a false illusion of the blessings of liberty at the price of social solidity. It turns out that this promise was yet another tactic employed by an oligarchic order to strip away anything of value from the weak. Daniélou denounced the elitism that deprived ordinary people of a vital horizon of hope:

We must react against any view that makes spiritual life the privilege of a small number of individuals; for such a view betrays the essential point of a message which is not only Christian, but religious, that a life of prayer is an absolutely universal human vocation.[50]

We should similarly lament the deprivation of prospects for sound marriage, happy children, a multiplicity of siblings and cousins, multigenerational families, a cultural inheritance, the rhythms and comforts of a religious life assisted by the fortifying presence of its holy men and women, of cemeteries and the memory of the dead in our midst as reminders of what we owe and what we should pass on—of a public and political culture in which the ordinary goods were commonly found.

So, too, the fortifying forms of family, community, church, and a cultural inheritance are a "political problem" in need of political redress. The offer of mere freedom is not enough. The formative conditions in which to act well upon one's freedom make possible genuine "blessings of liberty," which paradoxically but nevertheless logically can only be supplied through the force of mutually reinforcing custom and law.

Growing evidence suggests that a social order that is publicly *indifferent* to religious belief and practice becomes especially punitive for the "commoners," or those in the most economically and socially tenuous situation in today's world. Confirming Daniélou's concerns, one recent study seeking to understand the cause of rising "deaths of despair" among working-class Americans, particularly those without a college degree, discovered a strong correlation between the decline of religious belief and practice and the rise of suicides, opiate overdoses, and alcohol-related diseases.[51] Moreover, the study discovered that these deaths were not simply correlated to *individual* loss of faith, but the public manifestation of religious indifference. Its authors found that the dramatic rise of "deaths of despair" was strongly correlated to the *public repeal of blue laws and a day of rest on the Sabbath.* The expansion of liberal indifferentism toward one of the essential goods that make for a flourishing life—the good of leisure linked to a positive encouragement to prayer—has had a disproportionate, and even deadly, effect on the least among us. Yet, both "conservative" and "progressive" liberals—the first who care about religious liberty, the second who profess to care about the poor—are silent on the question of whether our achieved public indifference is *good* for the *commons.*

It is not merely coincidence that the word "common" has so often been combined with other concepts and words that reflect the imperative to protect and support the conditions for flourishing among ordinary people: common law, common sense, common good. Promotion and protection of the common good begins with a concern for the *ordinary* and everyday, fostering especially the conditions for flourishing that do not rely upon moving out, learning to code, abandoning one's traditions, or promoting public indifference. While a concern for the *common* will entail a fundamental rethinking of the priorities that a progressive world has embraced, a simple first step would be to publicly promote and protect a life of prayer. To quote again from Daniélou: "We shall be speaking, therefore, of the prayer of man involved in social life. It is in this sense that prayer belongs not to the strictly interior life of man—with which politics has nothing to do—but to the political sphere."[52] Protecting and supporting a life of prayer, recognizing the transcendent, acknowledging the frailty and temptations of lives threatened by a madding world—all point not just to "prayer as a political problem," but politics as a place for prayer, since politics is how we together seek to realize the good that is common.

We are inexorably entering the time *after liberalism*. Liberalism has exhausted both the material and moral inheritance it could not create, and, in the course of its depletions, offered the appearance of a sound and permanent ideological order—the "end of history." History, however, has begun again with a vengeance, now driven forward by an exhausted Western civilization, an emboldened Russia, and a rising China. Many have invested titanic sums in shoring up the project of liberalism, doubling down either on progressive claims of identity politics or right-liberal hopes for a renewed "fusionism" of capitalism and privatized Christian morality.

Instead, the depths of our own tradition and living memory provide an alternative resource: the common-good conservative tradition that was developed in distinction from liberalism itself, stressing *common good* and *common sense*, *shared culture*, and a governing ideal of *mixed constitution*. The day is late, but a lighted shelter can be discerned amid the gloom. It is time to abandon the ruins we have made, seek refreshment, and then build anew.

ACKNOWLEDGMENTS

I am profoundly grateful to the Institute for Advanced Studies in Culture at the University of Virginia—and to its founder, James Davison Hunter—for its support of a sabbatical leave in 2020. As it turned out, 2020 was a year many of us were unusually often at home. My hope and plan had been to be a fellow-in-residence in Charlottesville during that year, but fate had other plans for me, and for all of us. I hope it may yet come to pass that I will have the opportunity to spend some length of time in that good company, but in the meantime, I remain grateful for the Institute's long-standing support of my work.

My thanks as well to Mary Frances Myler for invaluable editorial assistance in preparation of this manuscript.

I gratefully acknowledge R. R. Reno and *First Things* for permission to incorporate revised versions of several arguments and passages that first appeared in a number of articles and reviews in its pages.

Finally, to my fellow advocates of the *bonum commune*—Sohrab Ahmari, Gladden Pappin, Chad Pecknold, and Adrian Vermeule—my deep gratitude for our sustaining friendship. I couldn't think of a better group of comrades with whom to share a foxhole.

NOTES

CHAPTER 1: THE END OF LIBERALISM

1. Alexis de Tocqueville, *Democracy in America,* trans. Harvey C. Mansfield and Delba Winthrop (Chicago: University of Chicago Press, 2000), 280.
2. G. K. Chesterton, *Orthodoxy* (San Francisco: Ignatius Press, 1995 [1908]), 52–53.
3. Charles Murray, *Coming Apart: The State of White America, 1960–2010* (New York: Crown Forum, 2012), 144–208; W. Bradford Wilcox, "Marriage Haves and Have-Nots," *The New York Times,* July 3, 2011, https://www.nytimes.com/roomfordebate /2011/07/03/marriage-the-next-chapter/marriage-haves-and-have-nots.
4. Michael Sandel, *The Tyranny of Merit: What's Become of the Common Good?* (New York: Farrar, Straus and Giroux, 2020), 95.
5. Sandel, *The Tyranny of Merit,* 85.
6. Michael Lind, *The New Class War: Saving Democracy from the Managerial Elite* (New York: Portfolio/Penguin, 2020), 11.
7. Joel Kotkin, *The Coming of Neo-Feudalism: A Warning to the Global Middle Class* (New York: Encounter Books, 2020); Christophe Guilluy, *Twilight of the Elites: Prosperity, the Periphery, and the Future of France,* trans. Malcolm DeBevoise (New Haven: Yale University Press, 2019).
8. Kurt Schlichter, *Militant Normals: How Regular Americans Are Rebelling Against the Elite to Reclaim Our Democracy* (New York: Center Street, 2018), 58.
9. Tim Carney, *Alienated America: Why Some Places Thrive While Others Collapse* (New York: HarperCollins Publishers, 2019), 205.
10. David Goodhart, *The Road to Somewhere* (London: Penguin Books, 2017), 3.
11. Ed Pilkington, "Obama Angers Midwest Voters with Guns and Religion Remark," *The Guardian,* April 14, 2008, https://www.theguardian.com/world/2008/apr/14 /barackobama.uselections2008; Dan Merica and Sophie Tatum, "Clinton Expresses

Regret for Saying 'Half' of Trump Supporters Are 'Deplorables,'" CNN, September 12, 2016, https://www.cnn.com/2016/09/09/politics/hillary-clinton-donald-trump-basket-of-deplorables/index.html.

12. Molly Morehead, "Mitt Romney Says 47 Percent of Americans Pay No Income Tax," Politifact, September 18, 2012, https://www.politifact.com/factchecks/2012/sep/18/mitt-romney/romney-says-47-percent-americans-pay-no-income-tax/.

13. Kevin Williamson, "Chaos in the Family, Chaos in the State: The White Working Class's Dysfunction," *National Review*, March 17, 2016, https://www.nationalreview.com/2016/03/donald-trump-white-working-class-dysfunction-real-opportunity-needed-not-trump/.

14. Thomas B. Edsall, "The Closing of the Republican Mind," *The New York Times*, July 13, 2017, https://www.nytimes.com/2017/07/13/opinion/republicans-elites-trump.html.

15. Christophe Guilluy, *Twilight of the Elites*.

16. Sandel, *The Tyranny of Merit*, 81–112.

17. See, for example, Robert B. Reich, *The Work of Nations: Preparing Ourselves for 21st-Century Capitalism* (New York: Alfred A. Knopf, 1991).

CHAPTER 2: THE POWER ELITE

1. Michael Lind, *The New Class War: Saving Democracy from the Managerial Elite* (New York: Portfolio/Penguin, 2020), 1–27.

2. James Burnham, *The Managerial Revolution: What Is Happening in the World* (New York: John Day Company, 1944), 72. Thus, Burnham implicitly confirms that in a regime inspired by Locke, the primary form of "property" would be ownership of one's self—in particular, one's ability to generate value in a market system. John Locke, *Second Treatise of Government*, ed. C. B. McPherson (Indianapolis: Hackett Publishing Company, 1980), 19.

3. Burnham, *The Managerial Revolution*, 72.

4. Burnham, *The Managerial Revolution*, 123 (emphasis mine).

5. Matthew Stewart estimates that the mainstream of this managerial elite owns half of the wealth in the United States, with the remaining half mostly owned by the superrich and what remains sparsely parceled out to the bottom 9 percent. Matthew Stewart, "The 9.9 Percent is the New American Aristocracy," *The Atlantic*, June 2018.

6. See Richard Florida, *The Rise of the Creative Class: How It's Transforming Work, Leisure, Community, and Everyday Life* (New York: Basic Books, 2002), charts 4.1 and 4.2 on pp. 73 and 75. From 1900 to 1999, the "super-creative core" class rose from roughly 1 percent to 12 percent; meanwhile, the "service class" rose from approximately 17 percent to 44 percent.

7. Bill Bishop and Robert G. Cushing, *The Big Sort: Why the Clustering of Like-Minded America Is Tearing Us Apart* (Boston: Houghton Mifflin Harcourt, 2008).

8. Burnham, *The Managerial Revolution*, 126.

9. Alexis de Tocqueville, *Democracy in America*, trans. Harvey C. Mansfield and Delba Winthrop (Chicago: University of Chicago Press, 2000), 483; Christopher Lasch also notes the increasingly "depersonalized" relationship between elites and the populace in "The Revolt of the Elites," in *The Revolt of the Elites and the Betrayal of Democracy* (New York: W. W. Norton & Company, 1995), 45.

10. Ellen Terrell, "When a Quote Is Not (Exactly) a Quote: General Motors," Library of Congress, April 22, 2016, https://blogs.loc.gov/inside_adams/2016/04/when-a -quote-is-not-exactly-a-quote-general-motors/.

11. Lind, *The New Class War*, 38. Citing Robert Griffith, "Dwight Eisenhower and the Corporate Commonwealth," *American Historical Review* 87, no. 1 (February 1982): 87–122.

12. Brett Friedlander, *Chasing Moonlight: The True Story of* Field of Dreams' *Doc Graham* (Durham, NC: John F. Blair Publishers, 2009).

13. Philip Rieff, *The Triumph of the Therapeutic: Uses of Faith after Freud* (New York: Harper & Row, 1966).

14. Christophe Guilluy, "The New Citadel," in *Twilight of the Elites: Prosperity, the Periphery, and the Future of France*, trans. Malcolm DeBevoise (New Haven: Yale University Press, 2019), especially 4, 6, 9, 17, 37, and 45.

15. Robert Reich, *The Work of Nations: Preparing Ourselves for 21st-Century Capitalism* (New York: Vintage Books, 1992).

16. Lind, *The New Class War*, 122–25.

17. Monique P. Yazigi, "At Ivy Club, a Trip Back to Elitism," *The New York Times*, May 16, 1999, https://www.nytimes.com/1999/05/16/style/at-ivy-club-a-trip-back-to -elitism.html.

18. Charles Murray, *Coming Apart: The State of White America, 1960–2010* (New York: Crown Forum, 2012), 144–231.

19. According to a 2017 study by *The New York Times*, the median family income of a student from Middlebury is $244,300, and 76 percent come from the top 20 percent. While there is income mobility for Middlebury students from poor families, those who rank as poor constitute 1.3 percent of a recent Middlebury College class. "Economic Diversity and Student Outcomes at Middlebury College," *The New York Times*, 2017, https://www.nytimes.com/interactive/projects/college-mobility /middlebury-college.

20. Allison Stanger, "Prepared Testimony and Statement for the Record of Allison Stanger, Russell Leng '60 Professor of International Politics and Economics Middlebury College, at the Hearing on 'Exploring Free Speech on College Campuses' before the Senate Committee on Health, Education, Labor, and Pensions," October 26, 2017, https://www.help.senate.gov/imo/media/doc/Stanger.pdf, 1–2.

21. Valerie Strauss, "Harvard Faculty Panel Recommends Banning Fraternities, Sororities and Other Social Groups," *The Washington Post*, July 12, 2017, https://www.washingtonpost.com/news/answer-sheet/wp/2017/07/12/harvard -faculty-panel-recommends-banning-fraternities-sororities-and-other-social -groups.

22. Delano R. Franklin and Samuel W. Zwickel, "Record-Low 4.59 Percent of Applicants Accepted to Harvard Class of 2022," *The Harvard Crimson*, March 29, 2018, https://www.thecrimson.com/article/2018/3/29/harvard-regular-admissions-2022/.

23. Michael Sandel, *The Tyranny of Merit: What's Become of the Common Good?* (New York: Farrar, Straus and Giroux, 2020), 118.

24. John Stuart Mill, "On Liberty," in *On Liberty and Other Essays*, ed. John Gray (New York: Oxford University Press, 1998), 13–14 (emphasis mine).

25. The concerted intellectual effort to replace an education in objective moral values with value-neutral social science empiricism is explored by Edward A. Purcell Jr. in *The Crisis of Democratic Theory: Scientific Naturalism & the Problem of Value* (Lexington, KY: University Press of Kentucky, 1973).

26. See the "surreal reaction" to the findings of Mark Regnerus, who reported on the material and emotional disadvantages evinced by children raised by adults in same-sex romantic relationships, as retold by Christian Smith in *The Sacred Project of American Sociology* (New York: Oxford University Press, 2014), 101–14 and 157–72.

27. Wiktionary, s.v. "mispronoun," last modified August 16, 2020, 2:30, https://en.wiktionary.org/wiki/mispronoun.

28. Wiktionary, s.v., "deadname," last modified November 13, 2022, 12:22, https://en.wiktionary.org/wiki/deadname.

29. Andrew Sullivan, "We All Live on Campus Now," *New York Intelligencer*, February 9, 2018, https://nymag.com/intelligencer/2018/02/we-all-live-on-campus-now.html.

30. See remarks by Kevin Williamson cited in the previous chapter, for instance.

31. However, many thinkers such as Karl Polanyi have argued that the market order was, in fact, imposed upon recalcitrant lower classes even when it appeared merely to be the outworking of impersonal forces. Reviewing the history of the rise of capitalist markets, Polanyi pithily concluded that "laissez-faire was planned." Karl Polanyi, *The Great Transformation: The Political and Economic Origins of Our Time* (Boston: Beacon Press, 2001), 147.

32. "State Religious Freedom Restoration Acts," National Conference of State Legislatures, May 4, 2017, https://www.ncsl.org/research/civil-and-criminal-justice/state-rfra-statutes.aspx.

33. Conor Friedersdorf, "Should Christian Bakers Be Allowed to Refuse Wedding Cakes to Gays?," *The Atlantic*, February 25, 2014, https://www.theatlantic.com/politics/archive/2014/02/should-christian-bakers-be-allowed-to-refuse-wedding-cakes-to-gays/284061/.

34. Tony Cook, "RFRA Prompts Connecticut Governor to Issue Order about Travel to Indiana," *Indy Star*, March 30, 2015, https://www.indystar.com/story/news/politics/2015/03/30/rfra-prompts-connecticut-governor-issue-order-travel-indiana/70674826/.

35. "Business leaders, such as Apple CEO Tim Cook, Eli Lilly and Co. CEO John Lechleiter, and Angie's List cofounder and CEO Bill Oesterle took Indiana lawmakers to task and said RFRA would hurt their ability to recruit and retain world-class talent. Salesforce CEO Marc Benioff led Twitter opposition to the law

and threatened that the giant tech company would boycott the state. Oesterle blamed his cancellation of a planned $40 million headquarters expansion of his Indianapolis-based online ratings company on RFRA." Jeff Swiatek, "Salesforce Packed a Punch in Galvanizing RFRA Opposition," *Indy Star*, April 2, 2015, https:// www.indystar.com/story/money/2015/04/02/salesforce-packed-punch-galvanizing -rfra-opposition/70842680/; see also Dwight Adams, "RFRA: Why the 'Religious Freedom Law' Signed by Mike Pence Was So Controversial," *Indy Star*, April 25, 2018, https://www.indystar.com/story/news/2018/04/25/rfra-indiana-why-law-signed -mike-pence-so-controversial/546411002.

36. Frank Bruni, "The Sunny Side of Greed," *The New York Times*, July 1, 2015, https:// www.nytimes.com/2015/07/01/opinion/frank-bruni-the-good-among-the-greed.html.

CHAPTER 3: A GOOD THAT IS COMMON

1. Robert George and Cornel West, "Sign the Statement: Truth Seeking, Democracy, and Freedom of Thought and Expression—A Statement by Robert P. George and Cornel West," James Madison Program, March 14, 2017, https://jmp.princeton.edu /statement.

2. Anthony Adragna, "47 House Republicans Vote to Write Same-Sex Marriage into Law," *Politico*, July 19, 2022, https://www.politico.com/news/2022/07/19/house -republicans-same-sex-marriage-law-00046682.

3. Jason Brennan, *Against Democracy* (Princeton: Princeton University Press, 2016); Bryan Caplan, *The Myth of the Rational Voter: Why Democracies Choose Bad Policies* (Princeton: Princeton University Press, 2007); Damon Root, *Overruled: The Long War for Control of the U.S. Supreme Court* (New York: Palgrave Macmillan, 2014).

4. John Locke, *Second Treatise of Government,* ed. C. B. McPherson (Indianapolis: Hackett Publishing Company, 1980), 24.

5. Jonah Goldberg, *Suicide of the West: How the Rebirth of Tribalism, Populism, Nationalism, and Identity Politics Is Destroying American Democracy* (New York: Crown Forum, 2018), 7, 8, 9.

6. Goldberg states that in the course of his book, "I spell out how liberalism and capitalism created the Miracle and how the United States of America is the fruit of the Miracle." *Suicide of the West*, 11.

7. George F. Will, *Statecraft as Soulcraft: What Government Does* (New York: Simon & Schuster, 1983), 165.

8. John Stuart Mill, "On Liberty," in *On Liberty and Other Essays*, ed. John Gray (New York: Oxford University Press, 1998), 78.

9. Mill, "On Liberty," 70.

10. John Stuart Mill, "Considerations on Representative Government," in *On Liberty and Other Essays*, ed. John Gray (New York: Oxford University Press, 1998), 333–39.

11. During a debate in the House of Commons on May 31, 1866, Mill stated: "I never

meant to say that the Conservatives are generally stupid. I meant to say that stupid people are generally Conservative. I believe that is so obviously and universally admitted a principle that I hardly think any gentleman will deny it. Suppose any party, in addition to whatever share it may possess of the ability of the community, has nearly the whole of its stupidity, that party must, by the law of its constitution, be the stupidest party; and I do not see why honorable gentlemen should see that position at all offensive to them, for it ensures their being always an extremely powerful party." In *The Philosophy of John Stuart Mill: Ethical, Political, and Religious*, ed. Marshall Cohen (New York: Modern Library, 1961), xxxiii–xxxiv.

12. Mill, "On Liberty," 14–15.
13. Mill, "Considerations on Representative Government," 232.
14. Bhaskar Sunkara, *The Socialist Manifesto: The Case for Radical Politics in an Era of Extreme Inequality* (New York: Basic Books, 2019), 58–65.
15. Marx and Engels, "The Communist Manifesto," in Karl Marx, *Selected Writings*, ed. Lawrence H. Simon (Indianapolis: Hackett Publishing Company, 1994), 161.
16. Marx and Engels, "Communist Manifesto," 159.
17. Marx and Engels, "Communist Manifesto," 167.
18. Marx writes in "The Eighteenth Brumaire of Louis Bonaparte":

> The small-holding peasants form a vast mass whose members live in similar conditions, but without entering into manifold relations with each other. Their mode of production isolates them from one another instead of bringing them into mutual intercourse. . . . Every single peasant family . . . thus acquires its means of life more through exchange with nature than in intercourse with society. . . . In so far as millions of families live under economic conditions of existence that separate their mode of life, their interests and their culture from those of other classes and place them in opposition to them, they constitute a class. In so far as there is only a local connection between the small-holding peasants, and the identity of their interests begets no community, no national unity and no political organization, they do not constitute a class.

Cited in Georg Lukács, *History and Class Consciousness*, trans. Rodney Livingstone (London: The Merlin Press, 1971), 60, from "The Eighteenth Brumaire of Louis Bonaparte," in Marx and Engels, *Selected Works*, 2 vols. (London: Lawrence and Wishart, 1950), vol. 1, 302–3.

19. Cited in Harold Rosenberg, "The Pathos of the Proletariat," *Kenyon Review* 11 (Autumn 1949), 598–99. Rosenberg's essay is essential reading on the subject of the proletariat as a "character" in the drama unfolding on the stage of history.
20. Karl Marx, "Theses on Feuerbach," in Karl Marx, *Selected Writings*, 101.
21. Karl Marx, "The German Ideology," in Karl Marx, *Selected Writings*, 119.
22. Karl Marx, "The German Ideology," in *The Portable Karl Marx* (New York: Penguin Books, 1983), 179.
23. Bernard Yack, *The Longing for Total Revolution: Philosophic Sources of Social Discontent from Rousseau to Marx and Nietzsche* (Princeton: Princeton University Press, 1986).

24. Marx, "The Eighteenth Brumaire," in Karl Marx, *Selected Writings*, 191.

25. Marx, "Resolution of the General Council of the International Workingmen's Association," 1870. Cited in Harold Rosenberg, "The Proletariat and Revolution," in *Marxism: The Inner Dialogues*, ed. Michael Curtis, 2nd ed. (New York: Taylor & Francis Group, 1997), 269.

26. The phrase "professional revolutionary" was coined by Milovan Djilas to describe "the new class" of Communist elites. Milovan Djilas, *The New Class: An Analysis of the Communist System* (New York: Harcourt Brace Jovanovich, 1957), 39.

27. Andrew Collier, "Marx and Conservatism," in *Karl Marx and Contemporary Philosophy*, eds. Andrew Chitty and Martin McIvor (New York: Palgrave Macmillan, 2009), 94.

CHAPTER 4: THE WISDOM OF THE PEOPLE

1. Tom Nichols, *The Death of Expertise: The Campaign Against Knowledge and Why It Matters* (New York: Oxford University Press, 2017), 20.

2. Francis Bacon, "The New Atlantis," in *Three Early Modern Utopias*, ed. Susan Bruce (New York: Oxford University Press, 1999), 167, 177. Among those areas in which scientific mastery is encouraged and pursued are:
The prolongation of life; The restitution of youth; The retardation of age.
The altering of complexions, and fatness and leanness.
The altering of statures.
The increasing and exhalting of intellectual parts.
Making of new species.
Instruments of destruction, as of war and poison.
Impressions of air, and raising of tempests.
Natural divinations. [pp. 185–86]

3. Jason Brennan, *Against Democracy* (Princeton: Princeton University Press, 2016), 3.

4. Edward A. Purcell Jr., *The Crisis of Democratic Theory: Scientific Naturalism & the Problem of Value* (Lexington, KY: University Press of Kentucky, 1973), 95, 108.

5. John Dewey expressed this original intent of progressive social science:

   Inquiry, indeed, is a work which devolves upon experts. But their expertness is not shown in framing and executing policies, but in discovering and making known the facts upon which the former depend. They are technical experts in the sense that scientific investigators and artists manifest *expertise*.

   John Dewey, *The Public and Its Problems: An Essay in Political Inquiry*, ed. Melvin L. Rogers (Athens, OH: Swallow Press, 2016), 225.

6. One of the more striking expressions of this progressive trend was articulated by Walter J. Shepard, the 1934 president of the American Political Science Association. Shepard urged his profession to abandon its misplaced "democratic faith" in the people, and instead to devise tests to identify the ignorant and erect barriers that

would exclude them from participation in politics. Instead, an expert class should preside over the national interest, and he looked abroad to discover models for such a new arrangement. As he stated in his presidential address to his fellow political scientists, "If this survey of a possible reorganization of government suggests fascism, we have already recognized that there is a large element of fascist practice that we must appropriate." Walter J. Shepard, "Democracy in Transition," *American Political Science Review* 29 (February 1935), 18–19; see also Patrick J. Deneen, *Democratic Faith* (Princeton: Princeton University Press, 2005), ch. 1.

7. President John F. Kennedy, "Remarks to Members on the White House Conference on National Economic Issues," May 21, 1962, in *Public Papers of the Presidents of the United States* (Washington, DC: United States Government Printing Office, 1962), XXXV: 203.

8. John Dewey, *Reconstruction in Philosophy* (Boston: Beacon Press, 1948 [1920]), 28.

9. John Dewey, *Democracy and Education* (New York: The Free Press, 1944 [1916]), 53, 50.

10. In one telling passage, Dewey compares "savages" who learn to live in and with the natural world over a long period of time to a "civilized" people who effectively transform the natural world through scientific mastery in order to conform to their needs and desires. *Democracy and Education*, 47–48.

11. Aristotle, *Politics*, trans. Carnes Lord, 2nd ed. (Chicago: University of Chicago Press, 2013), 1282a, 80.

12. Edmund Burke, *Reflections on the Revolution in France,* ed. J. G. A. Pocock (Indianapolis: Hackett Publishing Company, 1987), 75, 76.

13. Burke, *Reflections on the Revolution*, 29.

14. Burke, 54.

15. Burke, 51.

16. Burke, 49.

17. Burke, 52, 51.

18. Burke, 85.

19. See Socrates's critique of craftsmen for claiming that their specialized knowledge extends beyond their expertise. "The Apology of Socrates," in *Four Texts on Socrates*, trans. Thomas G. West (Ithaca: Cornell University Press, 1998), 22d–e, 71.

20. Clark Kerr, *The Uses of the University*, 5th ed. (Cambridge, MA: Harvard University Press, 2001), 15.

21. "[The laborer] naturally loses, therefore, the habit of such exertion, and generally becomes as stupid and ignorant as it is possible for a human creature to become." Adam Smith, *An Inquiry into the Nature and Causes of the Wealth of Nations,* ed. W.B. Todd, 2 vols. (Indianapolis: Liberty Classics, 1981), vol. 2, 782.

22. Matthew Crawford, *Shop Class as Soul Craft: An Inquiry into the Value of Work* (New York: Penguin Press, 2009), 41–42; citing Keith Sward, *The Legend of Henry Ford* (New York: Rinehart, 1948), 49.

23. Wendell Berry, "The Purpose of a Coherent Community," in *The Way of Ignorance and Other Essays* (Berkeley: Shoemaker & Hoard, 2005), 77.

24. Melancton Smith, "Speech of 21 June 1788," in *The Anti-Federalist*, ed. Herbert J. Storing (Chicago: University of Chicago Press, 1985), 340 (emphasis mine).

CHAPTER 5: THE MIXED CONSTITUTION

1. Aristotle, *Politics*, trans. Carnes Lord, 2nd ed. (Chicago: University of Chicago Press, 2013), 1294b, 113.
2. Aristotle, *Politics*, 115.
3. Polybius, *The Histories*, trans. Robin Waterfield (New York: Oxford University Press, 2010), vi.10, 378–79.
4. Polybius, *The Histories*, vi.10, 379.
5. Polybius, vi. 4, 373.
6. Thomas Aquinas, "The Summa of Theology," in *St. Thomas Aquinas on Politics and Ethics*, trans. and ed. Paul E. Sigmund (New York: W. W. Norton & Company, 1988), Q. 97.3, 57.
7. Aquinas, *Summa*, Q. 97.3, 57.
8. Aquinas, Q. 90.4, 46.
9. Corey Robin, *The Reactionary Mind: Conservatism from Edmund Burke to Donald Trump,* 2nd ed. (New York: Oxford University Press, 2018), 7–8.
10. Edmund Burke, *Reflections on the Revolution in France*, ed. J. G. A. Pocock (Indianapolis: Hackett Publishing Company, 1987), 66.
11. Burke, *Reflections on the Revolution*, 169.
12. Burke, 170–71 (emphasis mine).
13. Cited in T. A. Jenkins, *Disraeli and Victorian Conservatism* (New York: St. Martin's Press, 1996), 91.
14. Benjamin Disraeli, "Vindication of the English Constitution," in *Whigs and Whiggism: Political Writings of Benjamin Disraeli*, ed. William Hutcheon (London: J. Murray, 1913), 120 (emphasis mine).
15. Disraeli, *Whigs and Whiggism*, 215–18.
16. Disraeli, "Crystal Palace Speech," cited in Leo Paul de Alvarez, "The Romantic Imperialism of Benjamin Disraeli," PhD diss., University of Notre Dame (June 1970), 19. Disraeli makes clear that liberalism's "success" gives rise to socialism's failures ultimately to ground human flourishing on the grounds of bottom-up human association. As political theorist Leo Paul de Alvarez perceptively observed, "Liberalism's failure to establish a true community leads to socialism's 'principle of association,' but socialism does not in fact provide community—it only collectivizes selfishness." In effect, Alvarez summarizes, "liberalism has released the forces of socialism" (Alvarez, 110, 106).
17. Alvarez, "The Romantic Imperialism," 108.
18. Alvarez, 108.
19. Tony Judge, *Tory Socialism in English Culture, Politics, and Society, 1870–1940* (London: Mentor Books, 2019). A more recent expression of "Tory socialism" is captured in the phrase "Blue Labour." See Maurice Glasman, "The Meaning of

Socialism," in *Blue Labour: The Politics of the Common Good* (Cambridge, UK: Polity Press, 2022).

20. Disraeli, *Whigs and Whiggism*, 215.

21. Alexis de Tocqueville, *Democracy in America*, trans. Harvey C. Mansfield and Delba Winthrop (Chicago: University of Chicago Press, 2000), 252.

22. Tocqueville, *Democracy*, 256.

23. Tocqueville, 254 (emphasis mine).

24. Tocqueville, 257, 256.

CHAPTER 6: ARISTOPOPULISM

1. While today the word "dignity" is most often understood to be found equally in all human beings, as Alasdair MacIntyre pointed out in a 2021 lecture at a Notre Dame Center for Ethics and Culture Conference, in its premodern understanding, dignity was a condition that was achieved only by distinctively excellent characters, and could be lost if they no longer exhibited the qualities of a person of dignity. His lecture is available online at https://youtu.be/V727AcOoogQ.

2. *Online Etymology Dictionary*, s.v. "gentle," last modified April 25, 2017, https://www.etymonline.com/word/gentle?ref=etymonline_crossreference.

3. James Madison, Alexander Hamilton, John Jay, *The Federalist Papers,* eds. Isaac Kramnick and Walter F. Pratt (Harmondsworth, UK: Penguin, 1987), no. 10, 126.

4. John Adams, "Thoughts on Government: Applicable to the Present State of the American Colonies," in *The Revolutionary Writings of John Adams*, ed. C. Bradley Thompson (Indianapolis: Liberty Fund, 2001), 292.

5. Michael Lind, *The New Class War: Saving Democracy from the Managerial Elite* (New York: Portfolio/Penguin, 2020), 10–13.

6. Jackie Gu, "The Employees Who Gave Most to Trump and Biden," *Bloomberg*, November 2, 2020, http://www.bloomberg.com/graphics/2020-election-trump-biden-donors/.

7. David Campbell, Geoffrey Layman, and John C. Green, *Secular Surge: A New Fault Line in American Politics* (Cambridge, UK: Cambridge University Press, 2020).

8. Alexis de Tocqueville, *Democracy in America*, trans. Harvey C. Mansfield and Delba Winthrop (Chicago: University of Chicago Press, 2000), 240.

9. Lind, *The New Class War*, ch. 8, 131–45.

10. I have written previously about this insufficiency of Michael Lind's otherwise powerful argument. See my review, "Replace the Elite," *First Things*, March 2020, https://www.firstthings.com/article/2020/03/replace-the-elite.

11. Tyler Cowen, "A New Social Contract?," chap. 12 in *Average Is Over: Powering America Beyond the Age of the Great Stagnation* (New York: Dutton, 2013).

12. Christian Smith, "Rethinking the Secularization of American Public Life," in *The Secular Revolution: Power, Interests, and Conflict in the Secularization of American Public Life,* ed. Christian Smith (Berkeley, CA: University of California Press, 2003), 1–96.

13. Niccolò Machiavelli, "Discourses on Livy," in *Selected Political Writings*, ed. David Wooton (Indianapolis: Hackett Publishing Company, 1994), I.iv, 94.

14. Machiavelli, "Discourses on Livy," I.iv, 94–5.

15. George Will, "Congress Just Isn't Big Enough," *The Washington Post,* January 14, 2001, https://www.washingtonpost.com/archive/opinions/2001/01/14/congress-just -isnt-big-enough/747ccd88-ffdb-4531-8c55-b3adc37d9dd0.

16. Melancton Smith, "Speech of 21 June 1788," in *The Anti-Federalist*, ed. Herbert J. Storing (Chicago: University of Chicago Press, 1985), 340 (emphasis mine).

17. Michael Kazin, *A Godly Hero: The Life of William Jennings Bryan* (New York: Alfred A. Knopf, 2006), 224–25.

18. Ross Douthat, "Break Up the Liberal City," *The New York Times*, March 25, 2017.

19. Charles Murray, *Coming Apart: The State of White America, 1960–2010* (New York: Crown Forum, 2012), 75–99.

20. Pew Research Center Report, "The Military-Civilian Gap: Fewer Family Connections," November 23, 2011, https://www.pewresearch.org/social-trends/2011/11/23 /the-military-civilian-gap-fewer-family-connections/.

21. "Americans are also less personally connected to military service than ever before. According to the Department of Defense, the number of young adults with parents who have served in the military has dropped from 40 percent in 1995 to 15 percent today, and less than 1 percent of the US population currently serves in the armed forces, compared with more than 12 percent during World War II." Kevin M. Schmiegel and Patrick A. Burke, "How to Bridge the Divide between Civilians and the Military, First Responders," *Military Times*, September 10, 2019, https://www .militarytimes.com/opinion/commentary/2019/09/10/how-to-bridge-the-divide -between-civilians-and-the-military-first-responders/.

22. Niccolò Machiavelli, "The Prince," in *Selected Political Writings*, ed. David Wooton (Indianapolis: Hackett Publishing Company, 1994), 39.

23. Brutus, "Essay of 18 October 1787," in *The Anti-Federalist*, ed. Herbert J. Storing (Chicago: University of Chicago Press, 1985), 115.

24. In the lead-up to the war in Iraq, Congressman Charles Rangel of New York introduced legislation that would make universal national military service mandatory. Though the timing was cynical, his reasoning was not: "When you talk about a war, you're talking about ground troops, you're talking about enlisted people, and they don't come from the kids and members of Congress," he said. "I think, if we went home and found out that there were families concerned about their kids going off to war, there would be more cautiousness and more willingness to work with the international community than to say, 'Our way or the highway.'" "Rangel Calls for Mandatory Military Service," CNN Inside Politics, December 30, 2002, https://edition.cnn.com/2002/ALLPOLITICS/12/29/mandatory.military/.

25. Andrew Bacevich, "A Push to Bridge the Gap between Soldiers and Citizens," *Here & Now*, September 2, 2013, https://www.wbur.org/hereandnow/2013/09/02/bacevich -soldiers-citizens.

26. For a conservative version of this argument, see William F. Buckley Jr., *Gratitude: Reflections on What We Owe to Our Country* (New York: Random House, 1990).

27. Peter Turchin, "Blame Rich, Overeducated Elites as Our Society Frays," *Bloomberg*, November 20, 2013, https://www.bloomberg.com/opinion/articles/2013-11-20/blame-rich-overeducated-elites-as-our-society-frays.

28. Matthew Crawford, *Shop Class as Soul Craft: An Inquiry into the Value of Work* (New York: Penguin Press, 2009), 1–10.

29. Alexander Hamilton, "Report on the Subject of Manufactures," in *Writings* (New York: The Library of America, 1979), 647–734. See, for example, pp. 647, 664, 666, 668–69, 688, 698, 705 (encouraging "new inventions and discoveries, at home").

30. I am grateful to the work of Oren Cass, which offers a more fully developed case of the condensed summary I offer here. For a fuller explication, see Oren Cass, *The Once and Future Worker: A Vision for the Renewal of Work in America* (New York: Encounter Books, 2018). Cass explores "government support [for] innovation, infrastructure, and education" on pp. 134–39.

31. Michael Lind, *The New Class War: Saving Democracy from the Managerial Elite* (New York: Portfolio/ Penguin, 2020), 10–13.

32. "Excerpts from Final Report of Commission on Immigration and Refugee Policy," *The New York Times*, February 27, 1981, https://www.nytimes.com/1981/02/27/us/excerpts-from-final-report-of-commission-on-immigration-and-refugee.html.

33. Pascal-Emmanuel Gobry, "A Science-Based Case for Ending the Porn Epidemic," Ethics and Public Policy Center, December 19, 2019, https://eppc.org/publications/a-science-based-case-for-ending-the-porn-epidemic/.

34. Adrian Vermeule, *Common Good Constitutionalism: Recovering the Classical Legal Tradition* (Cambridge, UK: Polity Press, 2022).

35. Timothy P. Carney, *Alienated America: Why Some Places Thrive While Other Places Collapse* (New York: HarperCollins Publishers, 2019), 65–144.

36. Gladdin Pappin and Maria Molla, "Affirming the American Family," *American Affairs* 3, no. 3 (Fall 2019), 67–81.

37. Lyman Stone, "Is Hungary Experiencing a Policy-Induced Baby Boom?," Institute for Family Studies, July 10, 2018, https://ifstudies.org/blog/is-hungary-experiencing-a-policy-induced-baby-boom.

38. Sohrab Ahmari, Gladden Pappin, and Chad Pecknold, "In Defense of Cultural Christianity," *The American Conservative*, November 9, 2021, https://www.theamericanconservative.com/in-defense-of-cultural-christianity/.

CHAPTER 7: TOWARD INTEGRATION

1. Pierre Manent, *A World beyond Politics: A Defense of the Nation-State*, trans. Marc LePain (Princeton: Princeton University Press, 2006), 12.

2. Manent, *Beyond Politics*, 13.

3. Manent, 13.

4. Michael Sandel, *The Tyranny of Merit: What's Become of the Common Good?* (New York: Farrar, Straus and Giroux, 2020), 118.

5. Larry Summers, cited in Sandel, *The Tyranny of Merit*, 79.

6. Sandel, *The Tyranny of Merit*, 186.

7. 1 Corinthians 12:14–16, 18, 20–22, Revised Standard Edition.

8. 1 Corinthians 12:25–26, Revised Standard Edition.

9. John Winthrop, "A Model of Christian Charity," in *The American Puritans: Their Prose and Poetry*, ed. Perry Miller (New York: Anchor Books, 1956), 83.

10. Winthrop, "Christian Charity," 82.

11. Alexis de Tocqueville, *Democracy in America*, trans. Harvey C. Mansfield and Delba Winthrop (Chicago: University of Chicago Press, 2000), I.1.5, 65.

12. Tocqueville, *Democracy*, 57.

13. Tocqueville, 65.

14. Tocqueville, 65.

15. *Grutter v. Bollinger*, 539 US 306 (2003), majority opinion.

16. Robin DiAngelo and Michael Eric Dyson, *White Fragility* (Boston: Beacon Press, 2018); Ibram X. Kendi, *How to Be an Antiracist* (New York: One World, 2019).

17. Michael Lind, *The New Class War: Saving Democracy from the Managerial Elite* (New York: Portfolio/ Penguin, 2020), 12 (emphasis mine).

18. Various studies have provided evidence of the decline of historically black churches, which tracks (even if more slowly) with the decline of religious observance of all religious denominations. According to one recent study, "The share of African Americans who identify as religiously unaffiliated has increased in recent years, mirroring national trends. In 2007, when the first Religious Landscape Study was conducted, only 12 percent of black Americans said they were religiously unaffiliated—that is, atheist, agnostic or "nothing in particular. . . . By the time the 2014 Landscape Study was conducted, that number had grown to 18 percent. As with the general population, younger African American adults are more likely than older African Americans to be unaffiliated. Three in ten (29 percent) African Americans between the ages of eighteen and twenty-nine say they are unaffiliated compared with only 7 percent of black adults sixty-five and older who say this."; David Masci, "Five Facts about the Religious Lives of African Americans," Pew Research Center, February 7, 2018, https://www.pewresearch.org/fact-tank/2018 /02/07/5-facts-about-the-religious-lives-of-african-americans/.

19. Nathan Glazer and Daniel P. Moynihan, *Beyond the Melting Point* (Cambridge, MA: The MIT Press, 1964); Daniel Patrick Moynihan, "The Negro Family: The Case for National Action, Office of Policy Planning and Research United States Department of Labor," March 1965, https://www.dol.gov /general/aboutdol/history/webid-moynihan.

20. Julie Bosman, "Obama Sharply Assails Absent Black Fathers," *The New York Times*, June 16, 2008, https://www.nytimes.com/2008/06/16/us/politics/15cnd-obama .html.

21. Ta-Nehisi Coates, "How the Obama Administration Talks to Black America," *The Atlantic*, May 20, 2013.

22. Gabby Yearwood, "Perspective: On Black Fatherhood, Gender and Family," *Pittwire*, June 19, 2020.

23. Michael Denzel Smith, "The Dangerous Myth of the 'Missing Black Father,'" *The Washington Post*, January 10, 2017, https://www.washingtonpost.com/posteverything /wp/2017/01/10/the-dangerous-myth-of-the-missing-black-father/.

24. A remarkably frank example of this sentiment was previously quoted, but so aptly illustrates this point, it bears repeating. Duke University political scientist James Stimson assessed the condition of the white working class as one of personal moral failing: "I don't see them as once proud workers, now dispossessed, but rather as people of limited ambition who might have sought better opportunity elsewhere and did not. I see their social problems more as explanations of why they didn't seek out opportunity when they might have than as the result of lost employment." Thomas B. Edsall, "The Closing of the Republican Mind," *The New York Times*, July 13, 2017, https://www.nytimes.com/2017/07/13/opinion/republicans-elites-trump.html.

25. "Democratic humanity, Dewey and [Kenneth] Burke might have agreed, has 'more being' than predemocratic humanity." Richard Rorty, *Achieving Our Country: Leftist Thought in Twentieth-Century America* (Cambridge, MA: Harvard University Press, 1998), fn. 12, 143.

26. Discussing Hawthorne's story, May wrote:

    Attachment becomes too quietistic if it slackens into mere acceptance of the child as he is. Love must will the well-being and not merely the being of the other. But attachment lapses into a Gnostic revulsion against the world, if, in the name of well-being, it recoils from the child as it is. Ambitious parents, especially in a meritarian society, tend one-sidedly to emphasize the parental role of transforming love. We fiercely demand performance, accomplishments, and results. Sometimes, we behave like the ancient Gnostics who despised the given world, who wrote off the very birth of the world as a catastrophe. We increasingly define and seize upon our children as products to be perfected, flaws to be overcome. And to that degree, we implicitly define ourselves as flawed manufacturers. Implicit in the rejection of the child is self-rejection. We view ourselves as flawed manufacturers rather than imperfect recipients of a gift. Parents find it difficult to maintain an equilibrium between the two sides of love. Accepting love, without transforming love, slides into indulgence and finally neglect. Transforming love, without accepting love, badgers and finally rejects.

    William F. May, President's Council on Bioethics discussion of "The Birthmark" by Nathaniel Hawthorne, at https://bioethicsarchive.georgetown.edu/pcbe /transcripts/jan02/jansession2intro.html.

27. Christopher Lasch, *The True and Only Heaven: Progress and Its Critics* (New York: W. W. Norton & Company, 1991), 83.

28. Lasch, *The True and Only Heaven*, 81.

29. For Lasch's discussion of "hope without optimism," see *The True and Only Heaven*, 14, 39, 78–81, 390–93, 536. His discussion of "the spiritual discipline against resentment" is found in *The True and Only Heaven*, 329–411, and features largely admiring portraits of Reinhold Niebuhr and Martin Luther King.

30. In a moving personal tribute to her friend "Kit" Lasch, Jean Bethke Elshtain closed with these hope-laden words by Lasch:

> Hope is the rejection of envy and resentment and all that invites them. It's not difficult to see why those would always seem to be compelling moral postures, because we live in a world that doesn't seem arranged for human convenience. It's a world in which human happiness is not the overriding goal, and our plans go awry, and there are terrible limitations on what we can know and understand and control. And in any case our lives are very short. The fact of death is always there, haunting our imagination. All of which seems to justify a renunciation of any belief in the possibility that the world, in spite of these facts, is good, just, beautiful. None of this, of course, implies that this is the best of all possible worlds or that the struggle against injustice ought be suspended on the grounds that whatever is, is right.

Cited by Jean Bethke Elshtain, "The Life and Work of Christopher Lasch: An American Story," *Salmagundi* 106/107 (Spring/Summer 1995), 161.

31. Yoram Hazony, *The Virtue of Nationalism* (New York: Basic Books, 2018); Rich Lowry, *The Case for Nationalism: How It Made Us Powerful, United, and Free* (New York: Broadside Books, 2019); R. R. Reno, *Return of the Strong Gods: Nationalism, Populism, and the Future of the West* (New York: Regnery Gateway, 2021).

32. Brad S. Gregory, "Controlling the Churches," chap. 3 in *The Unintended Reformation: How a Religious Revolution Secularized Society* (Cambridge, MA: Belknap Press, 2012), 129–79.

33. On the intentional (and successful) effort of liberals to achieve this transfer of allegiance, see Stephen Macedo, "Transformative Constitutionalism and the Case of Religion: Defending the Moderate Hegemony of Liberalism," *Political Theory* 26, no. 1 (February 1998), 56–80.

34. Daniel Immerwahr, *How to Hide an Empire: A History of the Greater United States* (New York: Farrar, Straus and Giroux, 2019), 75–76; James M. McPherson, *Battle Cry of Freedom: The Civil War Era* (New York: Oxford University Press, 1988).

35. See my discussion of this subtle teaching of *The Federalist Papers*, particularly no. 17 (Hamilton), 27 (Hamilton), and 46 (Madison), in *Why Liberalism Failed* (New Haven: Yale University Press, 2018), 166–73.

36. Herbert Croly, *The Promise of American Life*, ed. Arthur M. Schlesinger (Cambridge, MA: Belknap Press, 1965), 27–51, 274–77.

37. Croly, *The Promise of American Life*, 280–84, 413–18.

38. Gillis J. Harp, "Herbert Croly: Positivist Progressive," chap. 7 in *Positivist Republic: Auguste Comte and the Reconstruction of American Liberalism, 1865–1920* (University Park, PA: Penn State University Press, 1994), 183–210.

39. The Bellamy salute that accompanied the Pledge, with arm outstretched toward the flag, was later adopted by the Nazis. Its wholly secular devotional was eventually corrected by the insertion of "under God" in 1954, the result of efforts especially by the Catholic group the Knights of Columbus. Bob Greene, "The Peculiar History of the Pledge of Allegiance," CNN, March 23, 2013, https://www.cnn.com/2013/12/22 /opinion/greene-pledge-of-allegiance-salute/index.html.

40. Andrew Delbanco, *The Real American Dream: A Meditation on Hope* (Cambridge, MA: Harvard University Press, 1999); Jean Bethke Elshtain, *Sovereignty: God, State, and Self* (New York: Basic Books, 2008).

41. Pico Iyer, *The Global Soul: Jet Lag, Shopping Malls, and the Search for Home* (New York: Alfred A. Knopf, 2000).

42. Pope Francis, *Fratelli Tutti (On Fraternity and Social Friendship)* (Huntington, IN: Our Sunday Visitor, 2020), 84.

43. Pope Francis, *Fratelli Tutti*, 84–85.

44. Ryan T. Anderson and Robert P. George, "The Baby and the Bathwater," *National Affairs*, Fall 2019, https://www.nationalaffairs.com/publications/detail/the-baby -and-the-bathwater.

45. *Online Etymology Dictionary*, s.v. "common," https://www.etymonline.com/word /common#etymonline_v_17239 (emphasis mine).

46. Jean Daniélou, SJ, *Prayer as a Political Problem* (Providence: Cluny Press, 2020 [1967]), 17.

47. Anne Case and Angus Deaton, *Deaths of Despair and the Future of Capitalism* (Princeton: Princeton University Press, 2020).

48. Philip McCouat, "Millet and the Angelus: How a Painting of Potato Farmers Became the Most Expensive Modern Painting in the World," *Journal of Art in Society*, August 2020, https://www.artinsociety.com/millet-and-the-angelus.html.

49. Daniélou, *Prayer as a Political Problem*, 20.

50. Daniélou, 20–21.

51. Tyler Giles, Daniel Hungerman, and Tamar Oostrom, "Opiates of the Masses?: Deaths of Despair and the Decline of American Religion," https://drive.google.com /file/d/1SOTFylIokbutrHYdD4Le6rGdMZ-rJz1k/view.

52. Daniélou, *Prayer as a Political Problem*, 17.

INDEX